*TERRA A*

MATTHEW FLINDERS is Aust
Born in England in 1774, he entered the navy in 1789 and
embarked on numerous naval explorations of Australia,
documented in *A Voyage to Terra Australis*. He returned to his
wife Ann in England in 1810 and spent three years writing
his magnum opus. He died in 1814 without seeing his book
in print.

TIM FLANNERY is director of the South Australian
Museum. He is author of a number of award-winning
books including *The Future Eaters*, *Throwim Way Leg* and *The
Eternal Frontier*, and has edited and introduced Watkin
Tench's *1788*, *The Explorers* and *The Birth of Sydney*. Tim
Flannery has made contributions of international
significance to the fields of palaeontology, mammalogy
and conservation.

# TERRA AUSTRALIS

Matthew Flinders'
*Great* Adventures
*in the* Circumnavigation
*of* Australia

Edited and Introduced by
# TIM FLANNERY

TEXT PUBLISHING
MELBOURNE AUSTRALIA

## ILLUSTRATION SOURCES

Grateful acknowledgment is made to the following for permission to reproduce the illustrative material in the picture section: plate I, Collection, Powerhouse Museum, Sydney; plates II, III, VIII, IX, X, XI, XII and XIII courtesy of the National Library of Australia; plate IV courtesy of the National Maritime Museum, Greenwich, London; plates V and VI courtesy of the Rare Books Collection, State Library of Victoria; plate VII courtesy of the Mitchell Library, State Library of New South Wales.

Cover: Matthew Flinders, oil painting by Toussaint Antoine De Chazal, Mauritius 1770–1822, courtesy Art Gallery of South Australia, Gift of David Roche in memory of his father, J.D.K. Roche, and the South Australian Government; 'A View of Botany Bay', engraving by Thomas Medland 1755–1822, courtesy State Library of Victoria.

Thanks also to the Petrie family and the Trustees of the National Maritime Museum, Greenwich, for permission to reproduce Flinders' letter from Port Jackson, 25 June 1803 (transcription by Lindsey Shaw) and the excerpt from Isabella Chappelle's papers.

The Text Publishing Company
171 La Trobe Street
Melbourne Victoria 3000
Australia

Copyright introduction © Tim Flannery 2000

*A Voyage to Terra Australis* was first published in 1814
First published by Text Publishing 2000
This edition published 2001, reprinted 2001; 2002

Printed and bound by Griffin Press
Designed by Chong Weng-ho
Typeset in 11.5/14.5 Baskerville MT by Midland Typesetting

National Library of Australia
Cataloguing-in-Publication data:

Flinders, Matthew, 1774–1814.

Terra Australis: Matthew Flinders' great adventures
in the circumnavigation of Australia.

New ed.
ISBN 1 876485 92 2.

1. Australia–Discovery and exploration. 2. Australia–
History–1788–1851. I. Flannery, Timothy Fridtjof. II.
Flinders, Matthew, 1774–1814. Voyage to Terra Australis.
III. Title.

994.02

# [*Contents*]

The Indefatigable Matthew Flinders
by Tim Flannery     vii

*Tom Thumb* and the *Norfolk*
1796 and 1798–99     1

The *Investigator*
January 1801–May 1802     41

The *Investigator*
May–December 1802     115

The *Investigator* 1803     183

The *Porpoise* 1803     227

# CONVERSION TABLE FOR
# WEIGHTS AND MEASURES

*Length*
1 inch = 25.4 mm
1 foot = 30.5 cm
1 yard = 0.914 m
1 mile = 1.61 km

*Mass*
1 ounce = 28.3 g
1 pound = 454 g

*Area*
1 acre = 0.405 ha

*Volume*
1 gallon = 4.55 litres

*Temperature*
$$°C = \tfrac{5}{9} \times (°F - 32)$$

*Depth*
1 fathom = 1.83 metres

# The Indefatigable
# Matthew Flinders

## TIM FLANNERY

Matthew Flinders is the man who gave Australia its name. He was also the first circumnavigator of the continent. Monuments commemorating Flinders' exploits can be found in Sydney, Melbourne and Adelaide, and in many places where he touched the coast. Even his cat Trim—the first feline circumnavigator of Australia—has been graced with a statue, which can be seen perched on a window sill outside the Mitchell Library in Sydney.

Under the acclaim, however, lies a complex individual, one who made his own destiny. Driven, sometimes arrogant and occasionally reckless, Flinders was not always likeable, nor could he always see another's point of view. His early death deprived us of knowing him in the kind of dignified maturity that so enhanced the reputations of James Cook and Joseph Banks. To the reader Flinders is eternally the dashing man of action, his rash youth both an attraction and a cause for lament. Few navigators had a greater share of misfortune than he did.

Flinders was also dogged by a powerful rival in the form of Captain Nicolas Baudin, who was sent by Napoleon to chart the Australian coast in one of the greatest expeditions of the nineteenth century. The French circled the continent in the corvettes *Astrolabe* and *Géographe*, carrying the most capable savants and the best scientific materials of the age. Flinders, in contrast, had to make do with a series of unseaworthy vessels and a limited scientific staff. The French returned to Paris with tens of thousands of specimens, and their reports were illustrated with some of the finest natural history

art ever produced on a voyage of discovery. Flinders, after falling
into the orbit of his nemesis, Governor de Caen of Mauritius,
reached England nearly seven years after departing from Australia
with little more than an incomplete set of his notes and charts. In a
sense he is the archetypal Australian hero—struggling against seemingly impossible odds yet somehow overcoming them—even if
triumph was to prove elusive during his lifetime.

Matthew Flinders was born on 16 March 1774 at Donington,
Lincolnshire. He came from a long line of doctors and in preparation for taking up the family vocation Matthew was sent to grammar
school where he studied Greek and Latin. At fifteen he was
summoned home for 'initiation in the mysteries of physic'. Despite
his father's careful planning, the staid routine of the country surgeon
did not suit young Matthew. Instead he read Daniel Defoe's *Robinson
Crusoe* by stealth, as such material was evidently not approved of in
the Flinders family.

The book gave him his calling. He would go to sea and embark
on a life of adventure and exploration. But how should he begin? He
wrote to a cousin, John Flinders, then in naval service in the West
Indies, who offered the practical advice that he should study 'Euclid
& Robertson's *Elements* & to make himself acquainted with Moore's
*Navigation*'. The adolescent Flinders eagerly pursued this course, and
in 1789 felt he had progressed sufficiently to present himself as a
naval volunteer to Captain Sir Thomas Pasley, then aboard the *Scipio*
at Chatham. Another of Flinders' cousins was working for the
captain and may have provided an introduction.

Flinders was put on the quarter-deck and in August 1791 set sail
in the *Providence* on one of the most celebrated naval expeditions of
the late eighteenth century—Bligh's second voyage to Tahiti in quest
of breadfruit seedlings to carry to the West Indies as food for slaves.
Unlike Bligh's first expedition to Tahiti aboard the *Bounty*, the
voyage of the *Providence* was a spectacular success. Part of the south-
east coast of Tasmania and hundreds of islands, mainly in the Fiji

group, never before seen by Europeans were charted. Bligh saw Flinders' potential, allowing the young midshipman to assist with chart-making and astronomical observations. Towards the end of the voyage Bligh even entrusted Flinders with the care and maintenance of the vessel's all-important time keepers.

Flinders' experiences during the *Providence* expedition were to affect him deeply. It gave him his first sighting of Australia, his first taste of the discovery of unknown lands, and probably his first love. Tahitian women were a temptation that few eighteen-year-old mariners were able to resist and young Matthew it seems was no exception. Ship records show that he purchased dangerously large amounts of mercury from the *Providence*'s surgeon; mercury was, of course, the eighteenth-century cure of choice for a dose of the clap. Gonorrhoea had probably been brought to Tahiti by English vessels a few decades earlier and it spread quickly. By Flinders' time it was a major menace for sailors. Although the mercury appeared to cure him he would never be free of the consequences of the infection.

When the *Providence* returned to England in August 1793 its captain and crew were feted as heroes. Bligh received the Royal Society's gold medal and a prize of 1000 guineas from grateful Jamaican planters. Within a few months and despite the acclaim, Flinders was sailing as aide de camp to his old friend and now commodore, Sir Thomas Pasley, aboard the *Bellerophon*. The French revolutionary wars were in full swing and Flinders played no small part in the celebrated British victory of 1 June 1794. From a memoir of Flinders' life written by his wife Ann shortly after his death, we learn that when Lord Howe broke the French line the *Bellerophon* was the second or third vessel to pass through the gap. Her guns were primed and ready, but no order to fire had been given as the crew was busy managing the sails. Just as the ship was passing under the stern of a French three-decker, Flinders seized a lighted match and fired off as many of the deserted cannon as he could manage. Later, Commodore Pasley reputedly grabbed the young midshipman by the collar, shaking him violently and asking how he dare fire without orders. Flinders is said to have replied he did not know, but 'thought it was a fine chance to have a good shot at 'em'.

Again, despite a homecoming wreathed in glory, Flinders could not remain ashore. Within a month or two he had signed up for service aboard the *Reliance*, with Captain Henry Waterhouse. The vessel was bound for Botany Bay and charged with carrying the colony's second governor, Admiral John Hunter, to the foundling convict settlement. Also aboard was another whose pluck and enthusiasm for discovery matched Flinders. George Bass had signed on as surgeon, and together these young men (Bass was just twenty-four, Flinders twenty-one) would carry out some of the most audacious voyages ever attempted in the history of Australian exploration. While still at Deptford, Bass had begun to equip himself for the venture, purchasing a tiny vessel humorously dubbed the *Tom Thumb*. At 180 centimetres—six feet in the old parlance—Bass was not a small man, a fact accentuated by the vessel he hoped to explore in, which was just 244 centimetres or eight feet long.

The pair stepped ashore at Port Jackson in September 1795 and, as is so typical of Flinders, barely a month elapsed before he was aboard the *Tom Thumb*. The vessel seemed ridiculously over-burdened with its crew of Bass, Flinders and Bass's 'loblolly boy' (general assistant) William Martin, yet in it they intended to pass through Sydney Heads into the Pacific Ocean, then on to Botany Bay to chart the Georges River. 'Projects of this nature,' Flinders wrote, 'when originating in the minds of young men, are usually termed romantic; and so far from any good being anticipated, even prudence and friendship join in discouraging, if not in opposing them.' Granting no transport more suitable than the *Tom Thumb* may have been Governor Hunter's way of discouraging what he saw as a madcap adventure, yet the trio explored twenty miles further up the Georges River than had any European previously.

After a tour of duty to Norfolk Island, Bass, Flinders and Martin again took to sea in a small open boat. This time it was *Tom Thumb* II, a vessel hardly superior to the original, in which they hoped 'to

explore a large river, said to fall into the sea some miles to the south
of Botany Bay'. On 26 March 1796 the trio again passed out
through the heads, but this time sailed directly out to sea 'to be
ready for the sea breeze'. It was a manoeuvre that would have terri-
fied any landsman, but which reveals the almost instinctive ease that
Flinders felt with his second home, the sea.

When the trio again approached land they found that a current
had carried them far south of their intended destination. Not at all
flummoxed by this discovery, they approached the shore at a likely
looking place to replenish their water. As Bass swam ashore with a
cask, the *Tom Thumb* was caught up in a wave that broke further out
to sea than the rest. It dumped the fragile craft on the beach, wetting
supplies, equipment and mariners. Despite the setback they continued their sodden way south in search of water.

The explorers were now in the company of Aborigines (one of
whom was later accused of killing a castaway) who were trying to
lure them into a narrow part of an estuary, later to be named Lake
Illawarra, eighty kilometres south of Sydney. The Aborigines were
cautious in their dealings with the visitors, noting that Bass wore a
red jacket (as did the soldiers at Port Jackson), and among themselves
whispered '*soja*'. Notwithstanding their perilous situation, Flinders
displayed his characteristic sense of humour and as a diversion
offered to trim the Aborigines' beards. He soon had a barber shop
full of customers. 'Some of the more timid,' he recounted, 'were
alarmed at a formidable instrument coming so near their noses, and
would scarcely be persuaded by their shaven friends to allow the
operation to be finished. But when their chins were held up a second
time, their fear of the instrument—the wild stare in their eyes—and
the smile they forced, formed a compound upon the rough savage
countenance, not unworthy the pencil of a Hogarth.'

On their return journey the navigators dropped their stone (the
*Tom Thumb* II apparently did not extend to an anchor) below the
forbidding cliffs of what is now Royal National Park, hopeful of a
night's rest. Nature, however, was disobliging and at around ten in

the evening a tremendous electrical storm broke. It was carried on
a gale from the south and within minutes the explorers were in
grave danger as the sea broke all around their frail craft. They
steered as well as they could by the darkness of the cliff louring
above their heads and the sound of the furious sea breaking against
the rocks. Just when it seemed impossible they could remain afloat
a moment longer, a break in the shadow thrown by the cliff
appeared. Unsure of whether they were facing instant death in a
treacherous cleft in the rocky rampart or were entering a cove, they
turned towards the gap and to their relief soon found themselves
riding a calm sea. They had found shelter in Wattamolla, one of the
jewels in the crown of the future national park, and the only safe
refuge on that section of coast.

After the storm subsided they set off once again, entering and
naming Port Hacking, which they spent two days mapping. In just
seven days they had sailed from Sydney to the Wollongong area and
back, discovering and naming the two principal anchorages on that
coast. It was a perilous and triumphant undertaking, which greatly
boosted Flinders' reputation. About this time, Sir Joseph Banks wrote
to Undersecretary (later Governor) King, recommending his 'fellow
countryman' Flinders for a greater role in exploration. Indeed, Banks
suggested that Flinders might team up with the renowned African
explorer Mungo Park in an attempt to follow rivers into Australia's
inland. Park, however, would never travel to Australia.

In December 1797, while Flinders was occupied supervising
repairs to the *Reliance*, George Bass sailed off yet again, leading six
volunteers on a voyage south to determine whether a strait existed
between Van Diemen's Land and New South Wales. The three-
month voyage was an epic one, undertaken in turbulent seas in a
six-oared whaleboat just under five metres long. They endured enormous difficulties and despite being unable to prove definitively the
existence of the strait, Bass made many vital discoveries, among
them Westernport Bay. The admiration of those who saw the vessel
return was still evident five years later, when the greatest honour

Governor King could bestow on Captain Baudin was a gift of a piece of wood from the boat, encased in a silver box inscribed with the principal findings of the expedition. François Péron, naturalist to the Baudin expedition, recorded that the boat (which strangely seems to have remained unnamed) was long preserved on the fore-shore of Port Jackson where it was treated with a 'kind of religious respect'.

In October 1798 Governor Hunter, realising the value of the service that Bass and Flinders were providing the colony, lent them the *Norfolk* for a three-month voyage of discovery to prove once and for all, by circumnavigating Van Diemen's Land, the existence of a strait. The sloop was an intriguing vessel and the first built on Norfolk Island, constructed from its plentiful pines. At twenty-five tons she was hardly a substantial craft and leaked copiously on her maiden voyage. Nonetheless she was a decided step up from the *Tom Thumb*, or even George Bass's whaleboat.

The *Norfolk* expedition was to be Bass and Flinders' greatest joint venture. In her they were to complete the circumnavigation of Van Diemen's Land and make many important discoveries, including Port Dalrymple, the future site of Launceston. Bass's work (recorded in a separate account of the voyage) was principally dedicated to natural history and to the study of the Tasmanian Aborigines. The wildlife they encountered on the islands of the strait was, in the days before sealing, incredibly abundant. One evening a flight of 100 million mutton birds passed overhead, while at other times they saw islands filled with seals, albatross rookeries and the nesting grounds of myriad other seabirds.

Among his zoological exploits, Bass conducted the first anatomi-cal dissections of the wombat (a creature then almost unknown even at Port Jackson) and described for the first time the nesting habits of the white-capped albatross. While climbing Mount Wellington he had his first and only opportunity to interact with the Tasmanian Aborigines, meeting a man whose countenance was 'more expres-sive of benignity and intelligence than ferocity', and to whom he

gave a swan, shot in the Derwent. After a brief walk these odd
companions parted, without Bass being able to learn the man's
name or anything much of the Tasmanian people or their language.
Four years later it was to fall to the lot of Flinders' great competi-
tor, the Baudin expedition, to leave the world its first comprehensive
account of the culture of these intriguing people.

As they approached Cape Grim, Tasmania's north-western-most
point, they saw a great swell breaking on a reef. Despite the danger
it represented Flinders wrote that 'Mr Bass and myself hailed it with
joy and mutual congratulation'. They had discovered the western
entrance to what Flinders would dub Bass Strait.

The journey's great success again opened the door wide to
opportunities for the young Lieutenant Flinders. In July 1799, after
completing a voyage in the *Reliance* to the Cape of Good Hope for
livestock (during which time Flinders acquired his cat, Trim), the
young explorer was off yet again in the *Norfolk*, this time to chart the
coast of what is now southern Queensland. Bass, whose health was
suffering, had been invalided out of the navy in May, and decided
to leave Port Jackson for Canton. Bass briefly returned to England
where he married, but was back in Port Jackson again by early 1803.
On 5 February that year, while Flinders was trying to cope with
pilfering Aborigines in Caledon Bay in Australia's top end, George
Bass sailed out of Sydney Heads for the last time, in command of
the *Venus* and bound for South America. He was never heard
of again; his disappearance rates as one of the most intriguing
mysteries of maritime exploration history.

On the second *Norfolk* voyage in 1799 Flinders was accompanied
by his younger brother, midshipman Samuel Flinders, and
Bongaree, an Eora man from Port Jackson, 'whose good disposition
and manly conduct' had attracted him. In an essay written in tribute
to Trim, Flinders describes how Bongaree and the cat 'formed an
intimate acquaintance. If he had occasion to drink, he mewed to
Bongaree and leaped up to the water cask; if to eat he called him
down below and went straight to his kid, where there was generally

a remnant of black swan. In short, Bongaree was his great resource, and his kindness was repaid with caresses.'

As was its wont, the *Norfolk* sprang a leak while in Glasshouse (now Moreton) Bay. Flinders' troubles were increased when he was forced to fire on some Aborigines who attacked the party at a place he named Point Skirmish, one of whom was wounded. It was the first time hostility had broken out between the explorer and the Aborigines, but unhappily it would not be the last.

As the *Reliance* was thought to be needed for service in the near future, Governor Hunter had placed a six-week limit on the expedition, and Flinders expressed disappointment that he had found no means of penetrating the interior of the continent during his brief excursion. He was back in Port Jackson by 20 August, just two days after Hunter's deadline for return had expired.

Matthew Flinders' first visit to New South Wales was drawing to an end. In March 1800 he sailed for England aboard the *Reliance*, arriving towards the end of that year. He lost no time in establishing his reputation at home, for he set about publishing the results of his work while simultaneously laying the foundation for the greatest expedition of his life.

By February 1801 it must have seemed as if all of Flinders' dreams had come true. He had been promoted to the rank of commander and been given charge of the *Investigator*, 334 tons and nearly thirty-three metres long, with instructions to explore and chart the hitherto unknown southern coast of the continent, and to fill some of the blanks on the map left by Cook. Despite the frenzy of activity that his new duties entailed, Flinders found time to marry and on 17 April he wed Ann Chappell.

We know from the remarks of Sir Francis Galton that Ann was two years her husband's senior and 150 centimetres or five feet tall, with raven black hair and rich red-brown eyes, one of which had been blinded in a clumsy attempt at lancing for the smallpox when she was twelve years old. She was of a 'sweet, perfect temper. Beloved by all who knew her. Witty. Generous. Nervous.' Flinders,

Galton informs us, had dark hair and eyes. He was 'Firm, just, punctual, clear-headed. Liberal and kind.' Later he was to be nick-named 'Indefatigable'. He also played the flute.

The Flinders' life together was to be bitterly short and unfortu-nate. Within two months of marrying Matthew was to set sail on a voyage of unknown duration, though certainly some years. Understandably he wished to take his wife with him, and indeed such a thing was not entirely unheard of in the Royal Navy, but his patron Sir Joseph Banks was outraged when he took her aboard. Cowed by Banks' wrath, Flinders reluctantly put his love for Ann in second place and set off upon exploration. His patron's reaction was to prove crueller than either Ann or Matthew realised, for almost a decade was to pass before the couple would be reunited, and even then their time together would be brief.

Among the crew of the *Investigator* were (later Sir) John Franklin, who would go on to become governor of Tasmania and a cele-brated polar explorer, and Matthew's brother Samuel. A small team of naturalists and artists also sailed with the *Investigator*, including the botanist Robert Brown and the botanical painter Ferdinand Bauer. William Westall, aged nineteen, was selected to paint more general subjects. The choice was an unfortunate one for Westall was unsuited to a life at sea. By disposition he was, according to Flinders, 'inclined to retirement and seclusion', and he found no inspiration in the dry, flat landscapes of Australia. Westall produced just 140 watercolours and sketches during the voyage, many of which are rudimentary. Compared with the 2000 botanical sketches completed by Bauer, the result was paltry.

Years after Westall's return to England, the Admiralty commis-sioned nine oil paintings based on his works. They were exhibited widely and used to illustrate *A Voyage to Terra Australis*. Westall became involved with the engraving as well as the painting, yet to the modern eye they are disappointing for they are a very loose interpretation of what the artist had seen. Indeed, they could easily mislead one as to the nature of Australia in 1802–1803. John

Crosley, astronomer, Peter Good, gardener, and John Allen, miner, also sailed on the *Investigator* and their contributions in their chosen fields seem to have been equally meagre.

Cape Leeuwin, on the south coast of Western Australia, was sighted on 6 December 1801 and by 28 January of the following year the *Investigator* had reached the limits of the charted region. From there on, Flinders was in a terra incognita. The crew were the first Europeans to see the spectacular Nullarbor cliffs (which Flinders hoped might hide some inland waterway), Spencer Gulf, Gulf St Vincent and Kangaroo Island. On 22 April they made the most surprising discovery to date—the French exploratory vessel *Le Géographe*, captained by Nicolas Baudin, moored in a broad embayment that Flinders dubbed Encounter Bay.

The French had been busy charting their Terre Napoleon along the eastern edge of the same unknown south coast that Flinders had been following. As Louis de Freycinet later quipped to Flinders in Sydney, had the French not been 'kept so long picking up shells and catching butterflies at Van Diemen's Land, you would not have discovered the South Coast before us'. Flinders, of course, was exultant at having beaten the French to the discovery of the majority of the coast, and was barely able to disguise his glee at writing that 'Terre Napoleon is therefore comprised [of] 50 leagues of coast, in which, as Captain Baudin truly observed, there is neither river, inlet, nor place of shelter; nor does even the worst parts of Nuyt's Land exceed it in sterility.'

By the time Flinders came to write those words around 1813, he had suffered terribly at the hands of the French. That bitter experience, however, lay far in the future on the day in 1802 when the two great expeditions crossed paths close to the Murray mouth. If Flinders had only realised it, he would never be closer to the entrance of that great inland waterway that he had dreamed about for so long and hoped would carry him into the heart of the continent. Distracted by the French, however, he sailed off without discovering the mouth of Australia's most extensive river system.

After scouting Port Phillip Bay (which had been discovered but not entered a year or so earlier by Captain Grant in the *Lady Nelson*) Flinders set sail for Port Jackson. At 1 p.m. on Sunday 9 May, he once again passed between the rocky heads of Sydney Harbour, the officers and crew 'in better health than on the day we sailed from Spithead, and not in less good spirits'.

Flinders had orders for Governor King to make the *Lady Nelson* available to accompany the *Investigator* on its circumnavigation. The brig turned out to be more of a liability than an acquisition for she was a poor sailor, and Flinders sent her back to Sydney from the Cumberland Isles in far north Queensland: the *Investigator* would continue on alone.

Flinders also acquired two important crew members in Port Jackson: Nanbaree, who had been rescued from the smallpox epidemic of 1798 by Surgeon-General John White, and Bongaree, who had earlier sailed with Flinders in the *Norfolk*. Nanbaree would return to Port Jackson with the *Lady Nelson*, but Bongaree completed the circumnavigation—the first Aborigine to sail around the massive land where his race had lived for 60,000 years. Bongaree had the most difficult and dangerous job in the ship, for it was he who was expected to make contact with the Aborigines they encountered. None understood the language of Port Jackson, and on more than one occasion Bongaree, stripped and unarmed, had to approach a group of armed and hostile warriors, hoping to gain acceptance for the strangers to land.

In addition to the two Eora men, Flinders was forced to take aboard nine convicts to replace eight officers and men drowned off the southern coast, and one who had been bitten by a seal on Kangaroo Island. Pending a favourable report from Flinders the convicts were to be emancipated upon their return to Port Jackson.

Baudin arrived in Port Jackson on 20 June 1802 while Flinders was still preparing his ships for their journey north, and the young Englishman was appalled to see the condition of the French crew. Scurvy had laid them low, with only twelve of the 170 able to man

their stations. Little did Flinders know that some months later he
too would return to the port in a similarly distressed condition.
Although France and England had been at war, Governor King
provided every comfort to the sick, going as far as slaughtering some
of the precious government stock (which he had refused to do for
Flinders) for the ailing visitors. Flinders had Captain Baudin and
naturalist François Péron to dine aboard the *Investigator*, a kindness
which Péron fails to mention in his official account of the French
voyage. The party toasted the declaration of peace between
England and France, news of which had just arrived at this distant
outpost of empire.

In these two rival expeditions, with their widely differing results,
lies the key to understanding both the greatness and failings of
Matthew Flinders. Flinders was obsessed with his beloved naviga-
tional charts. Geographical discovery in the narrow sense was all
that mattered to him. In pursuit of it he had left Ann behind, risked
death countless times, clashed, perhaps unnecessarily, with the
Aborigines and ultimately was wrongly imprisoned.

The French, in contrast, were pursuing discovery of a broader
kind. Their Terre Napoleon might have consisted of a mere fifty
leagues of coast, but they returned to Europe with a word list of the
now vanished Tasmanian language. They also collected specimens
of the now extinct Tasmanian and King Island emus, a comprehensive suite of Aboriginal artefacts and fauna and thousands of
sketches and drawings of a land and a people that are now forever
altered. Theirs was one of the greatest scientific expeditions of all
time and, by all accounts, they did not lift a gun in fear or anger at
the Aborigines. Nowhere, perhaps, is the difference between the
British Admiralty and Napoleon, nor between Baudin and Flinders,
so apparent.

Flinders' main objective as he travelled up the east coast was to
fill in various blanks in the charts left by James Cook. His principal
difficulty seems to have been caused by the poor sailing of the *Lady
Nelson*, but he was not aided by his younger brother's neglect of duty.

Samuel had been left in charge of the all-important chronometers,
without which longitude could not be accurately measured, and on
22 September 1802 he neglected to wind them up. It was a derelic-
tion of duty young Samuel would repeat on several occasions.

One of Flinders' most useful accomplishments on this leg of the
journey was to find a reasonably direct route through Torres Strait;
the *Investigator* made the crossing in just three days. As it sailed south
down the western shore of Cape York, Flinders was jubilant at
having beaten the north-western monsoon into the Gulf of
Carpentaria. Now, he believed, nothing stood between him and a
careful examination of the entire north coast of Australia.

The region he was passing through appeared dismal. Termite
mounds stood like lonely sentinels among the straggling trees. The
flatness and sterility of the landscape depressed even further the
young artist Westall, but far worse was to come. On 21 November
Flinders ordered that the *Investigator* be caulked. The operation was
to take place in a sheltered spot called Investigator Road, between
Sweer's and Bentinck's islands in the gulf. Once the hull was examined it was evident that something was critically amiss. The
carpenters' report of the state of the boat shocked and depressed
Flinders. A large number of boards were found to be entirely rotten
and it was thought that 'if the ship should get on shore under any
unfavourable circumstances, she would immediately go to
pieces...she could not bear heaving down on any account...in 12
months there will scarcely be a sound timber in her; but that if she
remain in fine weather and happen no accident, she may run six
months longer without much risk.'

Flinders knew that he had to return to Port Jackson but was not
yet ready to cease exploring. After shifting some of the worst of the
rotten planking, the *Investigator* continued its voyage among the
islands.

On Bentinck's Island Flinders found evidence of earlier visitors—a broken earthen jar and the stumps of some trees that had
been felled with an iron axe. Just who these visitors were remained

a mystery until a month later when, on visiting Vanderlin Island, they found rubbish indicating that the visitors were from Asia. The mystery would not be fully resolved for some time, however, and Flinders directed his attention to local productions. Among the most annoying of these were 'common black flies' which 'from their extraordinary numbers and impudence, were scarcely less annoying than mosquitoes; they get into the mouth and nose, and settle upon the face or any other part of the body, with as much unconcern as they would alight on a gum tree; nor are they driven away easily'. Flinders, writing at his best and most observant, found that 'the society of man wrought a change in the manners even of these little animals', for after a few days confined aboard ship with the crew 'they soon became more cautious, went off when a hand was lifted up, and in three or four days after quitting the land, behaved themselves orderly, like other flies'.

A few days later, off Groote Eylandt, Flinders' mind turned to the future. Here he named a small nub of land Nicol's Island 'after His Majesty's book seller', who would eventually publish the navigator's epic work. It was in this area that the most tragic episode of the northern exploration occurred. Flinders had anchored near an island he called Woodah, after its resemblance to the wooden 'sword' used by the Aborigines of Port Jackson. Perhaps Flinders meant it as a tribute to 'my humble friend' Bongaree, whose 'modesty and forbearance' so impressed the captain. Whatever the case, relations with the traditional owners of the island went horribly wrong.

Mr Whitewood, the master's mate, and a party of woodcutters were working on a small island off Woodah when a group of six Aborigines rowed over to meet them. As the Europeans approached, the natives fled. The sailors soon caught up, and Whitewood, who was in the lead, 'put out his hand to receive a spear which he supposed was offered; but the Indian, thinking perhaps that an attempt was made to take his arms, ran the spear into the breast of his supposed enemy'. Three more spears followed. The Europeans

responded but their guns misfired. Whitewood survived but Thomas
Morgan, who had been bareheaded throughout the episode, died
later that night 'in a state of frenzy' from sunstroke.

What followed was truly disgraceful. 'So soon as the master had
learned what had happened,' Flinders wrote, 'he went round in the
whaleboat to the east end of the island, to secure the canoe; and
forgetting the orders I had given him sent Mr Lacy [the master's
mate] with the wooders overland to intercept the natives on that
side.' They encountered a group of Aborigines in a canoe, and 'a
sharp fire was commenced after them; and before they got out of
reach one fell and the others leapt out and dived away. A seaman
who gave himself the credit of having shot the native swam off to
the canoe, and found him lying dead in the bottom, with a straw
hat on his head which he recognised to be his own. Whilst displaying this in triumph, he upset the ticklish vessel, and the body sunk.'

The next morning Flinders sent a boat for the dead body, 'the
painter being desirous of it to make a drawing, and the naturalist
and surgeon for anatomical purposes. The corpse was found lying
at the water's edge, not lengthwise as a body washed up, but with
the head on shore and the feet touching the surf. The arms were
crossed under the head with the face downward, in the posture of
a man who was just able to crawl out of the water and die; and I
very much apprehend this to have been one of the two natives who
had leaped out of the canoe, and were thought to have escaped.'

Although Flinders was an almost painfully honest narrator, it was
perhaps too appalling to mention directly that the man had been
shot in the back while retreating.

Just what the naturalist and surgeon did with the body is unclear,
but William Westall made a compelling sketch of the scene. It shows
a man of middle age, lying prone face up, a strip of material
modestly covering the genitals. In his right hand he holds a twig,
while a bleeding entry hole from a bullet is evident on his chest. At
least some of these details were invented. The genital covering is so
tastefully arranged as to be highly unlikely, and the bullet hole is

incorrectly placed, for Flinders tells us that the bullet entered through his back. He may well have grasped the twig as he lay dying on the beach, but its presence looks contrived. Just what Westall was trying to convey in the picture is not clear. Was he trying to give the man dignity in death? Was the twig meant to be a symbol of peace, and the bullet hole an attempt to obviate the guilt of the English murderers?

The killers of the man from Woodah were never punished. Other captains would perhaps have had Lacy and the sailor who fired the shot flogged or strung up from the yardarm for such a flagrant disregard of orders. Flinders seems simply to have ignored the crime and carried on exploring, even going so far (admittedly years later) as to recommend Lacy for promotion. Later that fateful day, Thomas Morgan, the victim of sunstroke, was 'committed to the deep with the usual ceremony; and the island was named after him'.

Shortly after this episode Flinders had repeated contact with Aborigines in Caledon Bay. They stole a number of articles from the Europeans, and in retaliation Flinders took a hostage, a youth called Woga, whom he released a few days later when the purloined goods did not turn up.

As they continued west past Cape Wilberforce, Flinders solved the mystery of the Asiatic visitors when he encountered, 'in a sort of roadstead...six vessels covered over like hulks, as if laid up for the bad season'. He had met the Macassan fleet on its annual visit to northern Australia to harvest trepang, the Malayan word for the sea cucumber.

The six Malay commanders of the fleet boarded the *Investigator*, and Flinders was able to converse with them via his Malayan cook. One, a man called Pobassoo, informed Flinders that there were sixty vessels on the coast engaged in the operations, carrying a thousand Macassans, and that the trepang was sold to the Chinese at Timorlaoet, an island off Ceram.

Pobassoo also told Flinders that he had made six or seven journeys to Australia over the previous twenty years, and that he was among the first Macassans to make the voyage. Flinders was later able to confirm these details at Timor, placing the Macassan discovery of Australia at around 1780, almost a decade before the arrival of the First Fleet in Port Jackson. In honour of the meeting, Flinders named the place Malay Road, and a nearby island, Pobassoo's Island. After he gave Pobassoo a Union Jack and some iron tools the vessels parted; the Macassans to pursue their fishery in the Gulf of Carpentaria, Flinders to wend his way west.

In early March 1803 the *Investigator* was in Arnhem Bay. The boat was evidently still rotting, but the crew's health was deteriorating even faster. It is here that Flinders finally refers to his own condition, admitting he was 'disabled by scorbutic sores'. Even Trim was suffering, for he 'became almost grey, lost much of weight, and seemed to be threatened with a premature old age'. As Flinders was the only one able to survey and map, and his illness prevented him from carrying out those duties, the entire raison d'etre of the expedition had vanished.

There was nothing to be done except return to Port Jackson, but first Flinders would have to obtain supplies. To this purpose the *Investigator* would touch at Kupang (Coepang) in Dutch Timor on its way home. The voyage from Timor to Port Jackson was an audacious one: down the west coast and across the Great Australian Bight. Flinders chose this route in part because he needed salt, which he had discovered before on islands in the Recherche Archipelago. The route would also allow him to complete his circumnavigation, if not the charting of the continent.

As well as shipping supplies in Kupang, the vessel had taken aboard a severe dysentery which infected most of the crew. Flinders, it seems, had avoided scurvy, but only at the price of inflicting a new scourge upon his ailing sailors. Even now, he could not give up his surveying, for after leaving Timor he sought but did not find the Trial Rocks. By 15 May 1803 the *Investigator* approached the Recherche Archipelago, whose outer margin he intended to skirt as it previously had been mapped imperfectly, and to pick up salt and geese on Middle Island. As they neared their destination boatswain Charles Douglas breathed his last. Flinders 'affixed his name to the two lumps of land' he could see ahead. Barely able to get out of the boat due to scurvy sores, Flinders was mortified to find that rains had fallen and dissolved the salt, while most of the geese had departed on their annual migration. The circumnavigator soon noted that William Hillier, 'one of my best men', died of dysentery and fever and soon after that James Greenhalgh and John Draper were consigned to the deep. Still he kept on charting.

The *Investigator* finally anchored off Garden Island in Port Jackson at noon on 9 June and the sick were placed under the care of the principal surgeon of the colony. It was too late, however, for a further four sailors who succumbed to the fatal flux. Flinders now faced his worst nightmare—an inevitable delay in completing his survey. The *Investigator* was clearly incapable of further work and there was no suitable replacement in port. Ironically, fate dictated that the *Investigator* would, despite her rotten state, reach England before Flinders, for she was repaired somewhat in Sydney and despatched home within a few years.

The navigator was not to know this, however, and faced a dilemma. He could try to continue his explorations in the *Lady Nelson* or an equally unsuitable vessel and risk repetition of the disaster he had just experienced. Alternatively he could wait for the right ship to turn up, or return to England to obtain a sloop in which to continue the survey. And all the time the French were working away, ever ready to snatch the palm of glory from Flinders' hand.

Flinders' greatest fear, delay, loomed large and, as the lesser evil, he chose to travel as a passenger aboard the *Porpoise*, which was then returning to England. The vessel was to sail in convoy with two others, the *Cato* and *Bridgewater*. On the evening of 17 August 1803, while off the Queensland coast, Flinders was engaged in convivial conversation with gentlemen in the ship's gun room. He heard a noise, but being a passenger and supposing the noise to have arisen from the parting of the tiller rope (a minor matter), he remained below. Going up on deck a few minutes later, however, he discovered that the *Porpoise* was about to be carried onto a coral reef. Within a minute she struck, soon followed by the *Cato*. To Flinders' astonishment the *Bridgewater*, which had escaped the trap, sailed blithely into the distance, making no attempt to rescue the stricken.

In the morning a large sandbank was seen inside the reef, and when all had been landed there Flinders, as senior naval officer, took command. It was determined that he should take their cutter, an open boat, on the 1100-kilometre journey to Port Jackson. The shore party was left under the command of Matthew's brother, Samuel. If Flinders did not return within two months, a back-up plan would swing into action: the second, smaller boat available to the castaways was to sail for Port Jackson. Flinders wished to give his brother command of this venture also, but Mr Fowler, captain of the *Porpoise*, claimed it as a post of honour and Matthew acceded. It was an action that deepened the rift between the brothers.

Flinders made the journey to Sydney in less than two weeks and quickly began to organise a rescue mission. It was at this time of stress and hateful delay that the great navigator made his fatal error. 'My anxiety to get back to Wreck Reef and from thence to England with the greatest despatch, induced the Governor to offer me one of the schooners to go through Torres Strait and by the most expeditious passage to Europe, rather than take the long route [in a safer vessel] by China.' In effect, Flinders opted to sail halfway round the world in a clapped-out boat of twenty-nine tons burthen, rather than suffer a delay of a couple of months in China on his way home.

The *Cumberland* was barely seaworthy. Her pumps, which were nearly useless, had to be worked continuously or the cabin floors would be awash. The hold half filled with water before she had passed Port Stephens, but still Flinders continued. When he finally made Wreck Reef, the relief on all sides was almost palpable. Samuel Flinders alone did not seem overjoyed to see his brother: he was 'in his tent calculating some lunar distances, when one of the young gentleman ran to him calling, "Sir, Sir, a ship and two schooners in sight!" After a little consideration, Mr Flinders said he supposed it was his brother come back, and asked if the vessels were near? He was answered, not yet; upon which he...very calmly resumed his calculations.'

In a personal letter to his friend Governor King from aboard the *Cumberland*, Matthew describes the conditions under which he sometimes wrote his journal. 'I am now sitting on the lee locker with my knees up to my chin for a table to write on, and in momentary expectation of a sea coming down the companion and sky light, for they have broken two panes out of the four already...writing here is like writing on horseback in a rainy day, and much worse than in the *Norfolk* sloop.' This sojourn on the locker seems to have been caused by a brief cessation in pumping, during which water washed over the cabin floor.

Despite her small size the *Cumberland* was a vermin-pit. Flinders wrote that 'for bugs, fleas, lice, weevils, mosquitoes, cockroaches (large and small), and mice [this schooner] rises superior to them all. We have almost got the better of the fleas, lice and mosquitoes, but in spite of boiling water and daily destruction amongst them, the bugs still keep their ground. I have never stripped myself before the last two nights, but usually spent upon the lee locker with my clothes on, notwithstanding which I have at least one hundred lumps upon my body and arms; and before this vile bug-like smell will leave me, must, I believe, as well as my clothes, undergo a good boiling in the large kettle. I shall set my old friend Trim to work upon the mice.'

After picking up Trim and his charts and notes from Wreck Reef, Flinders continued his long voyage to England. The *Cumberland*, however, was clearly not up to the task, for as she crossed the Indian Ocean she leaked like a sieve, and only the starboard pump worked. With a fresh wind on the starboard side, the hold would half fill with water before the working pump could touch it. On top of that, even this pump was showing signs of failure. Flinders had no choice. He must touch at the nearest port, and that was French-held Mauritius.

He arrived there on 17 December 1803, the day after the *Géographe* left for France.

The peace celebrated by Baudin and Flinders in Sydney was fragile, and by this time, unbeknownst to Flinders, war had broken out again. He was apprehensive about stopping over, but held a French passport as well as orders from Governor King explaining his command of the vessel.

The *Cumberland* weighed anchor in Port Louis at four in the afternoon. News of the war and the fact that he was aboard the *Cumberland* rather than the *Investigator* (as specified in his French passport) left Flinders uneasy and he decided to go directly to Governor de Caen to explain his situation. Ominously, the governor was unable to see him, and Flinders spent an hour or two in the company of some French officers of the port. They questioned him about the voyage of a certain Monsieur Flinedare, of which Flinders, speaking no French, professed to have no knowledge. Only later did he realise that they were asking about his own explorations, and in a nation at war such misunderstandings could be looked upon with suspicion rather than hilarity. Perhaps Flinders was attempting to travel incognito?

When he was finally admitted to an interview, de Caen demanded without preliminaries to see Flinders' French passport and commission. Flinders held his honour precious, and was clearly incensed by the lack of respect shown by the governor. After a terse conversation de Caen lost his temper, shouting 'You are imposing on me, Sir.' Flinders was led away to what he suspected was the jail, but turned out to be the Café Marengo, on the way proclaiming that 'the Captain General's conduct must alter very much before I should pay him a second visit'. The Café Marengo was dismal. It was full of mosquitoes and bed-bugs, the food was poor, and Flinders and his companions in misfortune, Mr Aken (ship's master) and Trim, were under constant guard.

The following day Governor de Caen's aide de camp, Monsieur Monistrol, paid Flinders a visit and asked for, among other things,

Flinders' orders from Governor King. He also brought an invitation to dine with the governor. Despite being urged to attend by Monistrol, Flinders hotly declined, saying that he would accept only when set at liberty. The aide de camp reluctantly carried the message to the governor, who replied that the next invitation would come only after Flinders' liberation.

This hot-headed refusal would chagrin Flinders for the rest of his life, for he wrote years later that de Caen's offer was probably intended as an honour extended to an enemy and an officer of inferior rank. It was thus possibly a subtle attempt to offer recompense for his initial poor treatment. But Flinders' refusal so injured the governor's pride that what might have been a few days' detention extended to six and a half years.

To keep themselves occupied, Flinders and Aken 'commenced a series of observations for a new error and rate, ready against the day of our departure'. Yet the noose gradually tightened: Flinders' papers were confiscated, his ship's stores landed and his imprisonment extended. Of particular concern was the confiscation of his third logbook which dealt with the *Cumberland* voyage. In time his sword would also be demanded, making him a prisoner of war.

Flinders' indignation, which occasionally bordered on arrogance, was maintained throughout his internment and expressed through letters and via his visitors. De Caen refused to see him and would only correspond through inferiors. On 25 December 1804 he wrote to Flinders demanding that he 'cease all correspondence tending to demonstrate the justice of your cause; since you know so little how to preserve the rules of decorum'. Flinders saw only 'embarrassment sheltering under despotic power' in de Caen's ultimatum.

By April 1805, Flinders had been moved from the awful Café Marengo to the Maison Despeaux, or 'garden prison', a more salubrious accommodation that he shared with other English captives. It was here, shortly after the other British had been released, that Trim disappeared. Worried that the guards had designs on his feline, Flinders had arranged Trim's care to a French woman just prior to

his disappearance. Although he offered a reward of ten Spanish
dollars for the cat's return, Trim was never seen again. Flinders
believed that it was 'but too probable that this excellent unsuspect-
ing animal was stewed and eaten by some hungry black slave'.

In his depression Flinders continued to contrast de Caen's actions
with the treatment of the Baudin expedition by Governor King in
Sydney. Baudin wrote that at the time of their arrival in Port
Jackson a flood had destroyed the harvest but 'Nevertheless we were
made perfectly welcome, and so soon as our present and future
wants were known, the ration given daily to the inhabitants and the
garrison was reduced one half. The Governor and the civil and mili-
tary officers set the example of this generosity, which was
immediately followed by the others. We were not only strangers, but
still at war.' De Caen's refusal to reciprocate continued to be an
enigma to this man of more generous spirit.

In August, after eight months on the island, Flinders was allowed
to leave Port Louis for a villa in the country. In his years there he
was to learn French, examine the natural history of the region,
teach mathematics to his host's children and participate in a local
literary circle, the Society for Emulation, which evidently gave him
pleasure. Although he did not know it, his release had been authorised by the French Minister of Marine in July 1804. It had lain over
until March 1806, when it was approved by Napoleon. Flinders
received a copy in July 1807; yet de Caen, a dangerously vindictive
man, still refused to release his prisoner.

All this time the separation from Ann weighed heavily. In March
1806 Flinders wrote to Sir Joseph Banks indicating that he had
sought permission for Ann to join him, but that he feared for her
health were she to undertake the voyage, adding 'your heart will tell
you the distress and hardships of a separation without end of two
young people so attached to each other as we are'.

To add insult to injury, Flinders learned a year or two later of
the publication of François Péron's *Voyage to the Southern Hemisphere*.
This work presented the achievements of the Baudin expedition,

including the discoveries made on Australia's southern coast. The world now knew all about Terre Napoleon, but nothing of Gulfs Spencer and St Vincent. Of course Péron completely ignored Flinders, who was left to lament that 'No means were spared by the French Government to enhance the merit of this voyage, and all the officers employed in it had received promotion; but the *Investigator*'s voyage seemed to obtain as little public notice in England as in France...'

In late 1809, Flinders' spirits were raised by a visit from the appropriately named Mr Hope, Commissary for Prisoners, who had come to Mauritius to arrange an exchange of captives. After many false starts, Flinders was finally freed in June 1810. 'At length,' he wrote, 'I had the inexpressible pleasure of being out of the reach of General de Caen.'

On 23 October 1810, Matthew Flinders set foot again on English soil after an absence of nine years and three months. He set off for London that very evening and was soon reunited with Ann. He had returned to an England full of change. On their first holiday together the couple visited Hull, where they saw Watt's steam engine, little imagining that its evolution would soon usher out the age of sail. But before Flinders could devote time to contemplating change in his homeland he had duties to perform, the foremost being to obtain the freedom of French prisoners whose relatives had treated him so well in Mauritius.

After these duties were completed, Matthew and Ann embarked on a peripatetic life; finances and changing needs driving them from one home to another—in all they moved six times in four years. All the while Flinders was working on his *Voyage*. This work was to be written and printed at his own cost, with profits (if any) to accrue to the author, yet in the end the profits made from the sales failed to cover the expenses of publication. If only Flinders could know that his *Voyage* is one of the most expensive and sought after books today, selling for tens of thousands of dollars.

Relations with his brother Samuel also remained unsettled.

Samuel had been court-martialled for disobeying orders, and in a rage at his treatment by the navy he resolved to retain the books of Matthew's voyage in which he had made entries, claiming them to be his. The ensuing furore distressed Matthew, and only a threat of severe repercussions for his career convinced Samuel to hand them over.

Since at least 1804 Flinders had suffered attacks of a complaint he referred to as 'the gravelly'. The malady resulted from the development of crystals in the bladder, which can be extremely painful to pass. Such crystals form when the urine becomes concentrated due to the bladder being incompletely emptied. Sufferers from an enlarged prostate are often afflicted, though Matthew was probably too young for this, as are those whose urethra is constricted due to an accident such as falling astride on a spar. Gonorrhoea can also leave the urethra constricted and, judging from his life history, this appears to be what happened to Matthew.

On 1 April 1812, Ann bore Matthew a daughter, christened Ann. She needed a wet nurse and Matthew saw little of her until his illness had become quite serious. By late 1813 his attacks of 'the gravelly' had become more frequent, and by February 1814 the doctor was in attendance every couple of days. In terrible pain, Flinders took calcined magnesia to ease his condition. When the crystals he passed in his urine were examined they were found to have been exacerbated by the magnesia; this compound can indeed crystallise in the urinary system if it is too concentrated. Matthew, it seems, was being slowly martyred by an unholy alliance between a long-ago Tahitian lover and a London quack.

Through March his condition steadily worsened and he needed to urinate more and more frequently—in one twenty-four-hour period he counted fifty-two times. Flinders spared no detail in recording his ordeal. On 26 March he wrote: 'Continue to pass gravel, consisting of oblong small crystals, some bright, others discoloured with blood…these crystals have always been more or less enveloped in mucus forming a pulpy mass…the detached pieces feeling to be too large for the passage. Had more pain today, and the urine more red than lately.'

By now he had completed his magnum opus and was trying to hang on long enough to see it published. It seems likely that the weekend of 16–17 July 1814 saw the staff of G. & W. Nicol hard at work in their Pall Mall premises. The *Voyage* was almost ready, but its author was slipping away. On Monday Mr Nicol rushed the first leather-bound copy to the Flinders' rented premises at 14 London Street. Despite their efforts it was too late. The great explorer was unconscious by the time Ann placed the volumes in his hands.

The following morning, Isabella Tyler, Ann's sister, who had come to assist the family, was wakened by Ann's sobbing. Isabella wrote: 'The sun shone brightly on me as I went down the stairs, all seemed still...I entered the drawing room—his bedroom opened into it, the door was open—I went in—there lay the corpse, the spirit flown, his countenance placid and at rest—Dear Matthew!— I stood at the foot of the bed contemplating the scene for a few moments, then rushed upstairs to my Sister—She was soon in the room of death & pressed his cold lips to hers—it was a heart-breaking effort...'

And so the world lost one of its most intrepid explorers and most celebrated hydrographers. Flinders, the man whose maps gave the great south land its shape, was gone. In his forty years, four months and three days, he had achieved far more than most of his compatriots who served out their allotted threescore and ten. Tellingly, Samuel was not executor of his brother's will.

*The Voyage to Terra Australis* is a monumental work. It documents the exploration undertaken by previous vessels around Australia, reports Flinders' own immense contribution and concludes with a lengthy and detailed account of the author's imprisonment on Mauritius. The book lying open before you is a much-abbreviated version, lacking the historical material and regrettably the account of the imprisonment which is too lengthy to reproduce here. Flinders'

painstaking and detailed notes on navigation have also been edited
out, a decision he would not have approved at all. What remains,
however, is a fascinating account of coastal Australia as it was two
centuries ago. Flinders is an engaging, no-nonsense writer, who
enables us to see through his own clear eyes a continent that had
scarcely changed for thousands of years. His very last words in the
edition concern the third logbook that de Caen had confiscated and
never returned. To the very end, Flinders' gaze was fixed on his
grand obsession.

Where necessary, I have modernised punctuation and spelling,
silently corrected a handful of obvious errors, inserted the occasional explanatory date, and sometimes added a word or two of
clarification in a footnote, marked by a dagger (†). Matthew
Flinders' original footnotes are indicated by an asterisk (*).
Otherwise his work is presented as first printed in 1814, with omis-
sions of text indicated by an ellipsis (…).

REFERENCES

*Australian Dictionary of Biography*, vol. I A–H, Douglas Pike (ed.),
    Melbourne University Press, Carlton, 1983.

*A Biographical Tribute to the Memory of Trim*, Matthew Flinders, Angus
    & Robertson, Sydney, 1997.

Flinders' papers, National Maritime Museum, Greenwich, London.

*Historical Records of New South Wales*, vol. III, F. M. Bladen (ed.), first
    published 1895, facsimile reprint, Lansdown Slattery &
    Company, Mona Vale, 1978; vol. V, first published 1897, facsimile
    reprint 1979.

*Letters to Ann: The Love Story of Matthew Flinders and Ann Chappelle*,
    Catharine Retter and Shirley Sinclair, Angus & Robertson,
    Sydney, 1999.

*Terra Australis*

*[Tom Thumb* and the *Norfolk]*
1796 and 1798–99

The year 1788 will ever be a memorable epoch in the history of Terra Australis. On 18 January, Captain Arthur Phillip arrived in Botany Bay, with His Majesty's brig *Supply;* and was followed by the *Sirius*, Captain John Hunter, six sail of transports, and three store ships. The purpose of this armament was to establish a colony in New South Wales, over which extensive country Captain Phillip was appointed governor and captain-general. Botany Bay proved to be an unfavourable situation for the new colony; it was, therefore, abandoned in favour of Port Jackson, which lies three leagues to the northward, and was found to be one of the finest harbours in the world.

A history of this establishment at the extremity of the globe, in a country where the astonished settler sees nothing, not even the grass under his feet, which is not different to whatever had before met his eye, could not but present objects of great interest to the European reader; and the public curiosity has been gratified by the perusal of various respectable publications, wherein the proceedings of the colonists, the country round Port Jackson, its productions, and native inhabitants, are delineated with accuracy, and often with minuteness.

The subject to be here treated is the progress of maritime geographical discovery, which resulted from the new establishment; and as the different expeditions made for this purpose are in many cases imperfectly, and in some altogether unknown, it has been

judged that a circumstantial account of them would be useful to
seamen, and not without interest to the general reader. These expeditions are, moreover, intimately connected with the *Investigator*'s
voyage, of which they were, in fact, the leading cause...

In Mr George Bass, surgeon of the *Reliance*, I had the happiness
to find a man whose ardour for discovery was not to be repressed
by any obstacles, nor deterred by danger; and with this friend a
determination was formed of completing the examination of the
east coast of New South Wales, by all such opportunities as the
duty of the ship and procurable means could admit.

Projects of this nature, when originating in the minds of young
men, are usually termed romantic; and so far from any good being
anticipated, even prudence and friendship join in discouraging, if
not in opposing them. Thus it was in the present case; so that a
little boat of eight feet long, called *Tom Thumb*, with a crew
composed of ourselves and a boy, was the best equipment to be
procured for the first outset. In the month following the arrival of
the ships, we proceeded round in this boat, to Botany Bay; and
ascending George's River, one of two which falls into the bay,
explored its winding course about twenty miles beyond where
Governor Hunter's survey had been carried...

A voyage to Norfolk Island interrupted our further proceedings,
until March 1796. Mr Bass and myself then went again in *Tom
Thumb*, to explore a large river, said to fall into the sea some miles to
the south of Botany Bay, and of which there was no indication in
Captain Cook's chart.

*25 March 1796* ~ We sailed out of Port Jackson early in the
morning and stood a little off to sea to be ready for the sea breeze.
On coming in with the land in the evening, instead of being near
Cape Solander, we found ourselves under the cliffs near Hat Hill,
six or seven leagues to the southward, whither the boat had been
drifted by a strong current. Not being able to land, and the sea
breeze coming in early next morning from the northward, we
steered for two small islets, six or seven miles further on, in order

to get shelter; but being in want of water, and seeing a place on the way where, though the boat could not land, a cask might be obtained by swimming, the attempt was made, and Mr Bass went on shore. Whilst getting off the cask, a surf arose further out than usual, carried the boat before it to the beach, and left us there with our arms, ammunition, clothes and provisions thoroughly drenched and partly spoiled...

The sea breeze, on the 27th, still opposed our return; and learning from two Indians that no water could be procured at Red Point, we accepted their offer of piloting us to a river which, they said, lay a few miles further southward, and where not only fresh water was abundant, but also fish and wild ducks. These men were natives of Botany Bay, whence it was that we understood a little of their language, whilst that of some others was altogether unintelligible. Their river proved to be nothing more than a small stream, which descended from a lagoon under Hat Hill, and forced a passage for itself through the beach; so that we entered it with difficulty even in *Tom Thumb*. Our two conductors then quitted the boat to walk along the sandy shore abreast, with eight or ten strange natives in company.

After rowing a mile up the stream, and finding it to become more shallow, we began to entertain doubts of securing a retreat from these people, should they be hostilely inclined; and they had the reputation at Port Jackson of being exceedingly ferocious, if not cannibals. Our muskets were not yet freed from rust and sand, and there was a pressing necessity to procure fresh water before attempting to return northward. Under these embarrassments, we agreed upon a plan of action, and went on shore directly to the natives. Mr Bass employed some of them to assist in repairing an oar which had been broken in our disaster, whilst I spread the wet powder out in the sun. This met with no opposition, for they knew not what the powder was; but when we proceeded to clean the muskets, it excited so much alarm that it was necessary to desist. On inquiring of the two friendly natives for water, they pointed upwards to the lagoon; but after many evasions our *barica* was filled at a hole not many yards distant.*

The number of people had increased to near twenty, and others were still coming, so that it was necessary to use all possible expedition in getting out of their reach. But a new employment arose upon our hands: we had clipped the hair and beards of the two Botany Bay natives at Red Point; and they were showing themselves to the others, and persuading them to follow their example. Whilst, therefore, the powder was drying, I began with a large pair of scissors to execute my new office upon the eldest of four or five chins presented to me; and as great nicety was not required, the shearing of a dozen of them did not occupy me long. Some of the more timid were alarmed at a formidable instrument coming so near to their noses, and would scarcely be persuaded by their shaven friends, to allow the operation to be finished. But when their chins were held up a second time, their fear of the instrument— the wild stare of their eyes—and the smile which they forced, formed a compound upon the rough savage countenance, not unworthy the pencil of a Hogarth. I was almost tempted to try what effect a little snip would produce; but our situation was too critical to admit of such experiments.

Everything being prepared for a retreat, the natives became vociferous for the boat to go up to the lagoon; and it was not without stratagem that we succeeded in getting down to the entrance of the stream, where the depth of water placed us out of their reach…

*29 March* ~ By rowing hard we got four leagues nearer home; and at night dropped our stone under another range of cliffs, more regular but less high than those near Hat Hill. At ten o'clock, the wind, which had been unsettled and driving electric clouds in all directions, burst out in a gale at south, and obliged us to get up the anchor immediately, and run before it. In a few minutes the waves began to break; and the extreme danger to which this exposed our

*Barica*: a small cask, containing six or eight gallons.

little bark, was increased by the darkness of the night, and the uncertainty of finding any place of shelter. The shade of the cliffs over our heads, and the noise of the surfs breaking at their feet, were the directions by which our course was steered parallel to the coast.

Mr Bass kept the sheet of the sail in his hand, drawing in a few inches occasionally, when he saw a particularly heavy sea following. I was steering with an oar, and it required the utmost exertion and care to prevent broaching to; a single wrong movement, or a moment's inattention, would have sent us to the bottom. The task of the boy was to bale out the water which, in spite of every care, the sea threw in upon us.

After running near an hour in this critical manner, some high breakers were distinguished ahead; and behind them there appeared no shade of cliffs. It was necessary to determine, on the instant, what was to be done, for our bark could not live ten minutes longer. On coming to what appeared to be the extremity of the breakers, the boat's head was brought to the wind in a favourable moment, the mast and sail taken down, and the oars got out. Pulling then towards the reef during the intervals of the heaviest seas, we found it to terminate in a point; and in three minutes were in smooth water under its lee. A white appearance, further back, kept us a short time in suspense; but a nearer approach showed it to be the beach of a well-sheltered cove, in which we anchored for the rest of the night. So sudden a change, from extreme danger to comparatively perfect safety, excited reflections which kept us some time awake: we thought Providential Cove a well-adapted name for this place; but by the natives, as we afterwards learned, it is called Watta-Mowlee.†

On landing next morning, 30 March, water was found at the back of the beach. The country round the cove is, in general, sandy and barren. No natives were seen, but their traces were recent. The extremity of the reef, which afforded us such signal shelter, bore

† Wattamolla.

SE by E from the centre of the beach, the north head of the cove
ENE; and except at the intermediate five points of the compass,
Watta-Mowlee affords shelter for large boats, with anchorage on a
fine sandy bottom.

Between three and four miles to the northward of this cove, we
found the river, or rather port, which was the original place of our
destination; and it having been a pilot named Hacking, from whom
the first information of it had been received, it was named after
him: by the natives it is called *Deeban*.

*1 April* ~ Was employed in the examination of the port. It is
something more than one mile wide in the entrance; but soon
contracts to half that space, and becomes shallow. Neither have
the three arms, into which it afterwards branches out, any deep
channel into them; although, within the second branch, there are
from 3 to 8 fathoms. Finding there was no part accessible to a ship,
beyond two miles from the entrance, nor any prospect of increasing
our small stock of provisions, Port Hacking was quitted early in the
morning of 2 April.

The shores of the port are mostly rocky, particularly on the north
side; but there is no want of grass or wood; and without doubt there
are many culturable spots on the sides of the streams which
descend, apparently from the inland mountains, into the uppermost
branch. Two natives came down to us in a friendly manner, and
seemed not to be unacquainted with Europeans. Their language
differed somewhat from the Port Jackson dialect; but with the assistance of signs, we were able to make ourselves understood.

After sounding the entrance of Port Hacking in going out, and
finding $3^1/_2$ fathoms water, we steered NE by E for Cape Solander;
and the same evening *Tom Thumb* was secured alongside the *Reliance*
in Port Jackson.

*1798* ~ In September following, His Excellency Governor Hunter
had the goodness to give me the *Norfolk*, a colonial sloop of

twenty-five tons, with authority to penetrate behind Furneaux's Islands; and should a strait be found, to pass through it and return by the south end of Van Diemen's Land; making such examinations and surveys on the way as circumstances might permit. Twelve weeks were allowed for the performance of this service, and provisions for that time were put on board; the rest of the equipment was completed by the friendly care of Captain Waterhouse of the *Reliance*.

I had the happiness to associate my friend Bass in this new expedition, and to form an excellent crew of eight volunteers from the king's ships; but a time keeper, that essential instrument to accuracy in nautical surveys, it was still impossible to obtain...

The wind being fair, we passed Hat Hill at four in the afternoon, and next morning, made Mount Dromedary. I took this opportunity of passing between Montague Isle and the main; but the depth of water being uncertain, the *Nautilus* was desired by signal not to follow. There was no bottom with 13, and afterwards with 20 fathoms, at a mile distance from the island; and the passage seemed perfectly free from danger, and is five or six miles wide. Mount Dromedary, from which the island lies E by N $^1/_2$ N, is the highest land upon this part of the coast; its elevation being, I think, not less than 3000 feet. The top is about three miles long, and the south end is somewhat the most elevated part; it is covered with wood, even there, but still more so down the sides; the shore under it is mostly a white, sandy beach.

At noon the centre of the mountain bore NNW four leagues; but the haziness of the weather prevented an observation being taken for the latitude, as it had before done when passing in the *Francis*. We then hauled further off the coast, with the *Nautilus* in company, and being near the latitude of Cape Howe, at ten o'clock, lay to until daylight, for the purpose of obtaining a good departure; but on the 9th, the wind had veered to south-west, and the weather having a bad appearance, we bore up for Two-fold Bay...

In order to make some profit of this foul wind, Mr Bass landed

early next morning to examine the country, whilst I went with Mr
Simpson to commence a survey of Two-fold Bay. In the way from
Snug Cove, through the wood, to the long northern beach, where
I proposed to measure a base line, our attention was suddenly
called by the screams of three women, who took up their children
and ran off in great consternation. Soon afterward a man made
his appearance. He was of a middle age, unarmed, except with a
*whaddie*, or wooden scimitar, and came up to us seemingly with
careless confidence. We made much of him, and gave him some
biscuit; and he in return presented us with a piece of gristly fat,
probably of whale. This I tasted; but watching an opportunity to
spit it out when he should not be looking, I perceived him doing
precisely the same thing with our biscuit, whose taste was probably no more agreeable to him, than his whale was to me. Walking
onward with us to the long beach, our new acquaintance picked
up from the grass a long wooden spear, pointed with bone; but this
he hid a little further on, making signs that he should take it on his
return. The commencement of our trigonometrical operations was
seen by him with indifference, if not contempt; and he quitted us,
apparently satisfied that, from people who could thus occupy themselves seriously, there was nothing to be apprehended.

We measured 116 chains along the north beach, and having
taken the necessary angles, returned to Snug Cove for the purpose
of observing the latitude; but the thick squalls, which were continually passing over from the south-west, prevented a sight of the sun.
The survey was continued in the afternoon; and on the following
morning, 11 October, the wind being still unfavourable, the west
side of the bay was nearly completed.

I was preparing the artificial horizon for observing the latitude,
when a party of seven or eight natives broke out in exclamation
upon the bank above us, holding up their open hands to show they
were unarmed. We were three in number, and, besides a pocket
pistol, had two muskets. These they made no objection to our
bringing, and we sat down in the midst of the party. It consisted

entirely of young men, who were better made, and cleaner in their persons than the natives of Port Jackson usually are; and their countenances bespoke both good will and curiosity, though mixed with some degree of apprehension. Their curiosity was mostly directed to our persons and dress, and constantly drew off their attention from our little presents, which seemed to give but a momentary pleasure. The approach of the sun to the meridian calling me down to the beach, our visitors returned into the woods, seemingly well satisfied with what they had seen. We could perceive no arms of any kind amongst them; but I knew these people too well not to be assured that their spears were lying ready, and that it was prudent to keep a good lookout upon the woods, to prevent surprise whilst taking the observation...

Besides its latitude, Two-fold Bay may be known by Mount Dromedary, which will be seen, in moderately fine weather, at the distance of fifteen or sixteen leagues to the northward; and also by the land behind the bay lying more in hummocks than elsewhere...

Wood, in abundance, can be procured on every side of the bay; but there are only two places where fresh water was found, and that not very good...The ponds and lagoons, which are to be found at the back of most of the beaches, are frequented by ducks, teal, herons, red-bills, and some small flights of the curlew and plover. The bay seemed to be well stocked with fish; and our success with hook and line made us regret having no seine, for the hauling of which many of the beaches are particularly well adapted. It is not improbable that Two-fold Bay, like some of the open bays on the east coast of Africa, may be frequented by whales at certain seasons: of this I have no decisive proof; but the reef of rocks, called Whale Spit, received its name from the remains of one found there. The natives had taken their share; and the dogs, crows and gulls were carrying away the rest...

At daybreak of the 16th, the sloop was then put on the northern tack. No land was visible in any direction; nor was there any at noon, when the observed latitude was 38° 42'. The wind veered

round by the south until it fixed itself at east; and when the day
broke, on the 17th, the signal was made to the *Nautilus*, and we bore
away SW by W until noon. The course steered at noon was west;
but in half an hour it was altered for high irregular land which
came in sight to the south-westward, and proved to be the largest
of the two clusters which I had discovered when in the *Francis*, and
named Kent's Groups…we came up with the group at four o'clock,
and steered through the channel by which the principal islands are
separated. It is about three miles long, and a full mile in width; is
free from danger, and so deep, that our hand line could not reach
the bottom. There are two sandy coves on the east, and one on the
west side of the channel, where small vessels might find shelter, if
there were any inducement to visit these steep, barren, granitic
masses of rock. Above the cliffs we could occasionally perceive a
brown-looking vegetation of brush wood, and here and there a few
starved gum trees; but there was neither bird nor quadruped to
enliven the dreary scene…we then hauled the wind to the southward, for Furneaux's Islands, that the *Nautilus* might no longer be
detained from her sealing business…

    *19 October* ~ The wind was at north-east; and we bore away to
pass between Mount Chappell and the low islands lying to the
westward. The passage is about two miles wide, and the water
much discoloured; but 10 fathoms of line did not reach the bottom.
A similar appearance in the water had been observed several
leagues to the westward of the low islands, where there was 23 to
25 fathoms, on a bottom of sand and broken shells.

    This small group, to which the name of Chappell Isles is affixed
in the chart, consists of three, or perhaps four islands, for the
mount seemed to stand detached from the land on the east side of
the passage. The basis of the whole is probably of granite, and they
seemed nothing superior in fertility to the worst of Furneaux's
Islands; but in a distant view, a slight covering of small herbage
upon their sloping, even surfaces, gave them a prepossessing
appearance. Mount Chappell is five or six hundred feet above the

water, a very conspicuous object until, by the clearing away of the haze, the high mountains of the great island behind it became visible: their white, towering peaks, bathed in the late showers, reflected the gleaming sunshine with great splendour, and presented a spectacle so magnificent, that the circular, gently sloping Mount Chappell no longer attracted attention.

We joined the *Nautilus* off the south side of the islands and, after passing several rocks in our course eastward, anchored at the east end of Preservation Island about noon. Mr Hamilton had left his house standing, with some fowls and pigeons in it, when we had quitted the island nine months before. The house remained in nearly the same state, but its tenants were not to be found, having probably fallen a prey to the hawks.

*20 October* ~ The wind was at north-west, and blew a gale, accompanied with rain, which continued for several days. This weather very much impeded our progress with the *Nautilus* in Armstrong's Channel, but Captain Bishop at length moored in Kent's Bay, the most secure place to be found within reach of the sealing points. The greater part of Kent's Bay is occupied by shoals; but along the shore of Sloping Point there is a deep channel running northward, which leads into the western head of the bay; and there, behind a reef of dry rocks, several ships may lie in 4 or 5 fathoms, sheltered from all winds. The *Nautilus*'s tents were pitched upon the borders of a run of fresh water, about one mile north of the anchorage; and a garden, which Captain Bishop made there, produced some tolerable vegetables.

We had no prospect of advancing along the north coast of Van Diemen's Land whilst the strong western winds continued to blow; and therefore, whilst Mr Bass explored some of the islands, I occupied myself in sounding different parts of Armstrong's Channel, and in making some other additions to my former survey. At length, on 31 October, the gale moderated to a light breeze, and we stretched over, with the flood tide, towards the Swan Isles...

I landed with Mr Bass; and leaving him to pursue his researches, went round to the north side of the island, to take angles...

One mile from the north-west end, lies a low, rocky islet, and several rocks both above and under water. All these are compre- hended under the general name of the Swan Isles; a name which, on examination, they appeared very little to deserve, for we did not see a single bird of that species, or any of their nests; but there were several of the barnacle geese, and two of them were shot by Mr Bass.[†]

The length of the largest Swan Isle is two and a quarter miles, by a medium breadth of one mile. The stony parts are over-run with thick brush wood, and the sandy are mostly covered with has- socks of wiry grass, to which the sooty petrels resort. In external appearance, this island bears a resemblance to that of Preservation; but its sterility is greater, and it is destitute of the kangaroo. We did not see any fresh water in the valleys, a seal upon the shores, nor any marks of the island having been ever visited by the natives of the opposite coast.

*1 November* ~ ...From the eastern extremity, the coast trends about N62°W six leagues, and terminates in a point, off which lie some small rocky islets. The shore consists of long, sandy beaches, separated by low and stony points, which project very little beyond the coastline. The country for two or three miles behind the shore is low and sandy; but it then ascends in gradations of gently rising hills, and being covered with verdure, interspersed with clumps of wood and single trees of a fair growth, it had a very pleasing appearance. At the back of these hills, the bare and rugged tops of a ridge of distant mountains appeared here and there, and formed a striking contrast with the verdure of the front scene...

Soon after four o'clock, the ebb appeared to be making; and the anchor was dropped in 11 fathoms, sandy bottom, about one mile west of Cape Portland. The shore on this side of the cape trends south, in rocky heads and beaches, and afterwards curves westward,

† Cape Barren geese.

forming an extensive bay, which terminates in a point. To this the name of Point Waterhouse was given, in honour of the commander of the *Reliance*; and an island, whose top is level and moderately high, lying off the point, was named Isle Waterhouse.

The bottom of the large bay is sandy, and the hills of Cape Portland there retiring further back, permitted a view of the inland mountains, of which there was a high and extensive ridge. Mountains like these are usually the parents of rivers; and the direction of the ebb tide, which came from between SW by S and SW by W at the rate of two and a half miles an hour, gave hopes of finding some considerable inlet in the bay, and increased our anxiety for a fair breeze...

*2 November* ~ A light breeze having sprung up from the eastward we steered for the bottom of the bay, and at noon the nearest part of the beach was distant only two miles...

We stood on another mile, and then bore away westward, following the round of the shore, but no inlet could be perceived. At three o'clock, we had passed Point Waterhouse, and seeing a fair channel of about two miles wide between it and the island, steered through, SW by W.

Isle Waterhouse is near four miles in length. Its southern shore consists of beaches and rocky points; but it rises abruptly to a moderate elevation. The level top is mostly covered with wood; and although its appearance did not bespeak fertility, it was superior to any we had seen of Furneaux's Islands. The land at the back of Point Waterhouse is higher than that of the island, and is composed of grassy, woody hills, rising over each other by gentle ascents... The islet was almost covered with sea birds and hair seals; from which circumstance we judged, that the natives of Van Diemen's Land were not able to get across here, any more than to the Swan Isles; and that, consequently, they had no canoes upon this part of the coast...

Resuming our former course along shore, we passed close to Stony Head at ten o'clock, when two sets of distances of the sun

east of the moon, gave its corrected longitude 147° 10' east. The
wind having then veered more to the north, we hauled further off,
and passed a rocky islet (the tenth), upon which a few overgrown
hair seals were sunning themselves...

Stony Head is the extremity of a ridge of hills which branches
out from the inland mountains, and stretches across the low, sandy
land in front, to the sea. On each side of the ridge there were
several smokes, which induced me to suppose the flat lands might
contain lakes of fresh water. The low head, bearing S35°W seemed
to be the termination of another branch from the inland mountains; round it there was some appearance of an opening, and at
two o'clock, this excited so much hope that I ventured to bear away
before the wind. We advanced rapidly with the flood, and at four,
had passed Low Head and were steering SE by S, up an inlet of
more than a mile wide. Some shoals, not quite covered, we left on
the starboard hand; keeping a straight course for the entrance of a
basin or bay, at which the inlet seemed to terminate...

We could not but remark the contrast between the shores of this
inlet, covered with grass and wood down to the water's edge, and
the rocky sterile banks observed in sailing up Port Jackson: it spoke
favourably for the country, and added to the satisfaction we felt in
having made the discovery. There was, however, little time for
meditation: the tide drove the sloop rapidly onward to the basin;
and the evening coming on, I pushed between some dry rocks and
a point on the western side, and anchored in 2 fathoms, on a
bottom of sand and mud.

There appeared to be three arms, or rivers, discharging themselves into this extensive basin. That which came from the
westward, had its *embouchure* close to the sloop; and Mr Bass went
off in the boat to look up it. His attention was, however, soon called
to another pursuit: a number of black swans were swimming before
him, and judging from former experience in Western Port, that
several of them were unable to fly, he gave chase with the boat. On
his return at dusk, he rejoiced us with the sight of four, and with

a promise that we should not be in want of fresh provisions in this port.

*4 November* ~ I landed Mr Bass with two men, to examine the country, and then commenced a survey of the port by an examination of the Western Arm. It is narrow, and has not more in the entrance than 3 fathoms, although, about one mile up, there be 7 near the starboard shore. This arm is not accessible to ships beyond three miles; and even in that distance there is much more shoal than deep water...

Green Island is covered with long, coarse grass and bushes, with a few small trees intermixed. The large, noisy gulls frequent it for the purpose of breeding, as do the swans, several of whose deserted nests were found with the broken egg-shells in them. These were corroborating proofs, that the natives of this part of Van Diemen's Land have not the means of transporting themselves across the water; for Green Island is scarcely two cables length from the shore.

In returning to the sloop, I took off Mr Bass and his party, together with a kangaroo weighing between eighty and ninety pounds, which he had shot out of a considerable flock. Our fresh provisions were still further increased by an addition of six swans, caught this evening with the boat.

*5 November* ~ Was employed in the survey of the Western Arm, and searching, but in vain, for the means of conveniently replenishing our water casks. Next morning we steered across the basin, and sought to anchor under an island which, from its situation at the entrance of the eastern arm, was called Middle Island; but there not being a sufficient depth of water behind it, the course was continued up the eastern arm, in 10 or more fathoms water, for two or three miles; when we anchored upon a five-fathom bank, near a small cove on the northern shore. On landing, a little stream was found descending from the hills into the south-east corner of the cove, and in the middle was a gully with several deep holes in it full of excellent water: this last, though not accessible till half flood, was the most convenient for our purpose.

There were many recent traces of natives on the shore; and
after returning to the sloop, we saw, on the opposite side of the
arm, a man who employed or amused himself by setting fire to the
grass in different places. He did not stay to receive us, and we
rowed down to Middle Island where a smoke was rising. The
natives shunned us there also; for soon after landing, I saw three of
them walk up from the shoal which joins Middle Island to the
opposite low, sandy point. The party appeared to consist of a man,
a woman, and a boy; and the two first had something wrapped
round them which resembled cloaks of skins...

*10 November* ~ Being under the necessity of going down to Brush
Island, to bring the survey up from thence to the position of the
sloop, we did not get under way till near noon. The wind was from
the westward, and I went forward in the boat to Egg Island, so
named from the number of eggs, mostly of the gull and red-bill,
which were there found. It is small and stony; but covered with
grass, and had not been visited by the natives. My next station was
on the opposite side of the river, upon a low sandy point which is
lengthened by a dry shoal. These project out from the general line
of the southern shore, and contract the river to less than half a
mile; whereas its width above and below, is one mile and a half. On
the east, or lee side of this point and shoal was a flock of swans, in
number not less than from three to five hundred; and their cast
quills were so intermixed with the sand, as to form a component
part of the beach. This countless number of quills gave me an
insight into the cause why so many of the swans, though not young
birds, were unable to fly: they moult their wing feathers, probably
at stated periods, though not, I should think, every year. This sandy
projection was named Swan Point.

On steering southward from thence, I found that the bight in
which this great number of birds had assembled, was full of shoals
producing the long aquatic grass which forms the principal part, if
it be not their sole food. We sailed through the flock, and might
have procured a good number, had not the progress of the sloop

obliged us to hasten onward to Shoal Point: one incautious bird was caught by his long neck as we sailed past him.

The change in the direction of the river, from south-east to south, made the extension of a new base necessary...The shoal was dry in the evening, within two cables length of the vessel, and rendered the fresh stream inaccessible to a boat.

The time of our absence from Port Jackson being restricted to the beginning of January, I did not think it advisable to take the sloop any further up the river; but determined, after devoting one day more to an excursion in the boat, to return and proceed along the north coast of Van Diemen's Land, in prosecution of the main object of the voyage...

*22 November* ~ ...So soon as I had satisfied myself that this could be no other than the hilly land lying five leagues to the northward of the Chappell Isles, we bore away before the sea; and by carrying all sail, secured an anchorage in Hamilton's Road before dark.

It was not safe to move on the 23rd, and there being a lunar eclipse announced in the ephemeris to take place in the following night, I landed to observe it with the telescope of the sextant. The times at which the beginning and end happened by the watch, being corrected from altitudes of the stars Rigel and Sirius observed in an artificial horizon, gave $148° 37^1/_2'$ for the uncorrected longitude of Preservation Island; which is 37' more than was deduced from the lunar distances in the *Francis*. The penumbra attending the earth's shadow is usually supposed to render this observation uncertain to two or three minutes of time, or more than half a degree of longitude.

*24 November* ~ The gale had subsided to a moderate breeze, and we tried to beat back to the westward; but finding too much sea, bore away into Armstrong's Channel to speak to the commander of the *Nautilus*; that, through him, Governor Hunter might be informed of our discoveries thus far, and of the delays experienced from the western winds. I was happy to find Captain Bishop proceeding successfully in his sealing business, though slower than he might have done, had the anchorage been nearer to the eastern points.

In the evening it fell calm, and the tide being favourable, we rowed back for Hamilton's Road; but a fair breeze springing up when abreast of it, instead of anchoring we made all sail to the west-south-west for Van Diemen's Land...we had scarcely passed Stony Head, next morning, when another gale sprung up from the north-west. It was a happy circumstance that we were able to reach our new discovered port, and take refuge at the former secure anchorage near the Shag Rocks; for this gale was more violent and of longer continuance than any of the preceding. This long succession of adverse winds caused us almost to despair of accomplishing the principal object of the voyage; for of the twelve weeks, to which our absence from Port Jackson was limited, nearly eight were already expired.

*2 December* ~ The gale moderated, and we made an attempt to continue the voyage, but were driven back. On the 3rd, the attempt was repeated; and the wind being light, we anchored at the entrance of the port, to prevent losing by the flood what had been gained by the ebb tide. In the evening a fair wind sprang up; and at length, to our great satisfaction, we were enabled to proceed in the discovery of the strait.

The harbour, which we entered with so much pleasure on 3 November, and finally quitted with still more on 3 December, was named Port Dalrymple, by His Excellency Governor Hunter, as a mark of respect to Alexander Dalrymple, Esq., the late hydrographer to the Admiralty.†

Port Dalrymple and the River Tamar occupy the bottom of a valley betwixt two irregular chains of hills, which shoot off north-westward, from the great body of inland mountains. In some places, these hills stand wide apart, and the river then opens its banks to a considerable extent; in others, they nearly meet, and contract its bed to narrow limits. The Tamar has, indeed, more the appearance of a chain of lakes, than of a regularly formed river;

† Port Dalrymple: later the site of Launceston.

and such it probably was, until, by long undermining, assisted perhaps by some unusual weight of water, a communicating channel was formed, and a passage forced out to sea. From the shoals in Sea Reach, and more particularly from those at Green Island which turn the whole force of the tides, one is led to suppose, that the period when the passage to sea was forced has not been very remote.

Of the two chains of hills which bound the valley, the eastern one terminates at Low Head; the other comes down to the sea, five or six miles from it, on the west side of the port. The ends of these chains, when seen from directly off the entrance, appear as two clusters of hills having some resemblance to each other; and in fine weather, the distant blue heads of the back mountains will be seen over the tops of both clusters...

Three or four leagues to the westward of the port, the back land is uncommonly high, and the top of the ridge is intersected into uncouth shapes. From the brilliancy of some of these mountains, on the appearance of the sun after rain, I judged them to be of granite, like those of Furneaux's Islands. These mountains, with the direction of the coast and what has been said of the clusters of hills, may serve as marks for Port Dalrymple to ships coming along shore from the westward...

We found Port Dalrymple to be an excellent place for refreshment. Out of the flocks of black swans, from one-fifth to one-tenth of them were unable to fly; and since the same thing has been found to obtain in the months of January and May, as well as in October, it is probably so at all times of the year. These birds are endowed with a considerable portion of sagacity: they cannot dive, but have a method of immersing themselves so deep in the water, as to render their bodies nearly invisible, and thus frequently to avoid detection. In chase, their plan was to gain the wind upon our little boat; and they usually succeeded when the breeze was strong, and sometimes escaped from our shot also.

Kangaroos appeared to be rather numerous in this part of Van

Diemen's Land; but as they were shy, and we had little time or necessity to go after them, one only was procured; it was of the large, forest kind, and the flesh was thought superior to that of the same animal at Port Jackson.

Ducks and teal went by flocks in Port Dalrymple; but they were shy, and we took no trouble after them. The white-bellied shag, and the black and pied red-bills were common in the lower parts of the port, and some pelicans were seen upon the shoals. The large black shag, usually found in rivers, was seen in different parts of the Tamar; and upon another occasion, we found these birds to be tolerable food.

Neither our wants nor leisure were sufficient to induce any attempt to catch fish. Mussels were abundant upon those rocks which are overflowed by the tide; and the natives appeared to get oysters by diving, the shells having been found near their fireplaces...

*3 December* ~ In the evening, the *Norfolk* was lying at anchor off the entrance of the port, when a breeze sprang up from the north-eastward, and enabled us to proceed along the coast...

On the 8th a breeze sprang up from the south-westward, and threatened a gale...Circular Head was still visible, bearing S35°E; and the difference of longitude made from Port Dalrymple was calculated at $1^3/_4°$, subject to future revision.

Mr Bass and myself landed immediately to examine the country and the coast, and to see what food could be procured; for the long detention by foul winds had obliged me to make a reduction in the provisions, lest the object of our voyage and return to Port Jackson should not be accomplished in the twelve weeks for which we were victualled. At dusk, we returned on board, having had little success as to any of the objects proposed; but with the knowledge of a fact, from which an interesting deduction was drawn: the tide had been running from the eastward all the afternoon, and contrary to expectation, we found it to be near low water by the shore; the flood, therefore, came from the west, and not from the eastward, as at Furneaux's Isles. This we considered to be a strong proof, not only of the real existence of a passage betwixt this land and New South Wales, but also that the entrance into the Southern Indian Ocean could not be far distant.

The little time there was for examining the coast, confined my observations to what were necessary for giving it the formation it has in the chart. The country is hilly, and Mr Bass found it impenetrable from the closeness of the tall brush wood, although it had been partially burnt not long before. There was very little soil spread over the rock and sand, and the general aspect was that of sterility. Several deserted fireplaces, strewed round with the shells of the sea ear, were found upon the shore.

The south-west wind died away in the night; and at six next morning, 9 December, we got under way with a light air at southeast. After rounding the north-east point of the three-hummock land, our course westward was pursued along its north side.

A large flock of gannets was observed at daylight, to issue out of the great bight to the southward; and they were followed by such a number of the sooty petrels as we had never seen equalled. There was a stream of from fifty to eighty yards in depth, and of three hundred yards, or more, in breadth; the birds were not scattered, but flying as compactly as a free movement of their wings seemed to allow; and during a full hour and a half, this stream of petrels continued to pass without interruption, at a rate little inferior to the swiftness of the pigeon. On the lowest computation, I think the number could not have been less than a hundred millions; and we were thence led to believe, that there must be, in the large bight, one or more uninhabited islands of considerable size.

From the north-east point of the three-hummock land, the shore trended W1°N three miles; then S39°W four miles, to a rocky point, forming the south-west extremity of what was then ascertained to be Three-hummock Island. The channel which separates it from the land to the west, is, at least, two miles in width, and is deep; so that it was difficult to conjecture how the Indians were

able to get over to the island. It was almost certain that they had
no canoes at Port Dalrymple, nor any means of reaching islands
lying not more than two cables length from the shore; and it therefore seemed improbable that they should possess canoes here. The
small size of Three-hummock Island rendered the idea of fixed
inhabitants inadmissible; and whichever way it was considered, the
presence of men there was a problem difficult to be resolved.*

The coast on the west side of the channel lies nearly south, and
rises in height as it advances towards the cliffy head. The north end
of this land is a sloping, rocky point; and the first projection which
opened round it, was at S32°W, five or six miles. Beyond this there
was nothing like mainland to be seen; indeed, this western land
itself had very little the appearance of being such, either in its
form, or in its poor, starved vegetation. So soon as we had passed
the north sloping point, a long swell was perceived to come from
the south-west, such as we had not been accustomed to for some
time. It broke heavily upon a small reef, lying a mile and a half
from the point, and upon all the western shores; but, although it
was likely to prove troublesome, and perhaps dangerous, Mr Bass
and myself hailed it with joy and mutual congratulation, as
announcing the completion of our long-wished-for discovery of a
passage into the Southern Indian Ocean.

We had a fine breeze at east; and our course was directed for a
small, rocky island which lies W$^1$/$_2$N six miles from the north point
of the barren land. This island appeared to be almost white with
birds; and so much excited our curiosity and hope of procuring a
supply of food, that Mr Bass went on shore in the boat whilst I
stood off and on, waiting his return. No land could be seen to the
northward, and the furthest clearly distinguishable in the opposite

* Future visitants to these islands have seen the Indians passing over in bodies,
by swimming, similar to those whom Dampier saw on the north-west coast of
New Holland. Why the natives of Port Dalrymple should not have had recourse
to the same expedient, where the distance to be traversed is so much less, seems
incomprehensible.

direction was a steep island at the distance of four leagues...

Mr Bass returned at half past two, with a boat-load of seals and albatrosses. He had been obliged to fight his way up the cliffs of the island with the seals, and when arrived at the top, to make a road with his clubs amongst the albatrosses. These birds were sitting upon their nests, and almost covered the surface of the ground, nor did they any otherwise derange themselves for the new visitors, than to peck at their legs as they passed by. This species of albatross is white on the neck and breast, partly brown on the back and wings, and its size is less than many others met with at sea, particularly in the high southern latitudes. The seals were of the usual size, and bore a reddish fur, much inferior in quality to that of the seals at Furneaux's Islands.

Albatross Island, for so it was named, is near two miles in length, and sufficiently high to be seen five or six leagues from a ship's deck: its shores are mostly steep cliffs. The latitude is 40° 25', and longitude made by the running survey, 2° 7' west of Port Dalrymple; but it afterwards appeared from the *Investigator*'s time keepers, to lie in 144° 41' east of Greenwich.

The tide (apparently the ebb) had set so strong to the southwestward, that notwithstanding our efforts to keep up with the island, it was distant five miles when Mr Bass returned and the boat was hoisted in. A black lump of rock was then seen three or four leagues to the south-westward...We kept close to the wind at northeast, in order to fetch Steep-head Island; but were carried so far to leeward by the tide...

Besides these islands and rocks, we passed another cliffy island four or five miles to the south of Steep-head, and to which I gave the name of Trefoil Island, its form appearing to be nearly that of a clover leaf; there were, also, several others of less importance, mostly lying near the barren land. The steep south end of this land was set over the north end of Trefoil at N65°E; and being almost assured of its separation from Van Diemen's Land, I added it, under the name of Barren Island, to the rest of this cluster; and in honour of His Excellency, the Governor of New South Wales, I gave to the whole the title of Hunter's Isles.

The north-west cape of Van Diemen's Land, or island, as it might now be termed, is a steep, black head, which, from its appearance, I call Cape Grim…There are two rocks close to Cape Grim, of the same description with itself. On the north side of the cape, the shore is a low, sandy beach, and trends north-eastward, three or four miles; but whether there be a sufficient depth for ships to pass between it and Barren Island, has not, I believe, been yet ascertained. To the south of the cape, the black cliffs extend seven or eight miles, when the shore falls back, eastward, to a sandy bay, of which little could be perceived…

The nearest part of the coast was between two and three miles distant, and consisted of sandy beaches, separated by points which had many straggling rocks lying off them. At the back of the shore, the land was low for two or three miles, and then rose gently to a ridge of barren, low hills. The inland mount, set at S53°E, appeared to be the north end of a second chain, much higher, and better wooded, than the front ridge: it lies eight miles back from the shore, and is named Mount Norfolk, after my little vessel…

*11 December* ~ …Behind some low cliffs, passed at seven o'clock, was perceived a small opening like a river, whose course seemed to run northward, between the front and back ridges of hills: a smoke, which arose from the inner side of the opening, was the first seen upon this west coast. I steered a short time for the entrance; but seeing rocks in it, and the wind coming more on shore, hauled off south, to increase our distance…

The heavy south-west swell, which had met us at the entrance of the Indian Ocean, still continued to roll in, and set dead upon this coast; and the wind blew fresh at WNW. Under these circumstances, we looked out for some little beach, where, in case of necessity, the sloop might be run on shore with a prospect of safety to our lives; for should the wind come three or four points further forward, there was no probability of clearing the land on either tack. No such beach could, however, be discovered; and we therefore carried all possible sail to get past this dreary coast. A remarkable pyramid came in sight in the evening; at eight o'clock it was distant five miles to the east, and seen to be a rock on the north side of a point, which projects two or three miles from the coastline. This point, named Point Hibbs after the colonial master of the *Norfolk*, is higher than the neck by which it is joined to the back land; and from thence, it appears to have been taken for an island by Tasman...

*14 December* ~ ...The nearest land, at noon, was a steep head bearing N66°E, one mile and a half; and between this, and the head which bore S74°W, the shore forms a sandy bay four miles deep, where it is probable there may be good anchorage, if two clumps of rock, which lie in the entrance, will admit of a passage in. After taking bearings of Maatsuyker's Isles and the different headlands, we bore away eastward, and passed another deep, sandy bight, probably the same in which Mr Cox anchored in 1789...

At this time we were one mile within, or north of the largest of the islands; and saw with some surprise, for it is three miles from the main, that its grassy vegetation had been burnt. From hence we steered for the easternmost isle, lying off a wide open bight in the coast, and afterwards hauled up for the South Cape. The wind died away at six o'clock, when the cape was one mile distant; but thick clouds were gathering in the south and west, and strong gusts with heavy rain presently succeeded. Fortunately, the squalls came from the westward, so that we were enabled to get further from those stupendous cliffs; had they come from the south, the consequences might have been fatal to the *Norfolk*.

The first steep head, to the eastward of the South Cape, opened round it at E7°N (allowing 4° east variation) and a second from the first, at E16°N, their distances asunder being each about five miles. It is the middlemost of these three heads which is called South Cape by Captain Cook, as appears from the relative situations of his Peaked Hill and of Swilly Rock; but he had not the opportunity of seeing the heads opening one from the other, as we had in the

*Norfolk.* Pedra Blanca, or Swilly Rock, became visible at half past seven, when the squalls had mostly blown over...At nine o'clock we hauled up for D'Entrecasteaux's Channel, of which I had the sketch of Mr Hayes, and stood off and on, in the entrance, during the night; the wind blowing hard at west, with dark rainy weather.

*14 December* ~ At four in the morning, our situation was far to leeward; and having no prospect of fetching into the channel, we bore away for Boreel's Isles, which were seen bearing N65°E two leagues. Three of these produce some vegetation, and that of the largest had been partially burnt not long before. The two eastern-most, called the Friars by Captain Furneaux, are bare pyramidal rocks, and, except where they had been made white by the gannets, are of a black, weather-beaten colour: a patch of breakers lies one mile to the north-east from them.

Fluted Cape opened round Tasman's Head at N18°E. We passed these steep projections at a mile distance; and not being able to fetch into Adventure Bay, did the same by Cape Frederick Henry. At noon, this cape bore S13°W eight miles, and Fluted Cape was behind it in the same bearing. I proposed to enter the Derwent River; but on making a stretch towards Betsey's Island, it appeared that the Henshaw's Bay of Hayes, instead of being a shallow bight, was a deep opening; and as the north-west wind blew out of the Derwent, we stretched on, seven miles above the island, and came to an anchor in 10 fathoms, sandy ground. This opening is the North Bay of D'Entrecasteaux; but I was totally ignorant, at that time, of its having ever been entered.

*15 December* ~ The wind being at north-west, we passed a sloping island (Isle St Aignan of D'Entrecasteaux), and steered north-eastward, to explore the inlet...we anchored under a small island, which lies S75°W, one mile and a half, from Point Renard, the uppermost station of the French boats. This small spot received the descriptive name of Isle of Caves, and lies in the passage from North Bay to a large extent of water which appeared to the east-ward, and which the French boats did not explore.

From the Isle of Caves we ran six miles, ESE up the new bay, for
Smooth Island...Smooth Island, behind which we anchored in
4 fathoms, and where I again landed to take bearings, is three-
quarters of a mile long, and covered with grass and a few small
trees. It had been visited by the natives, as had the Isle of Caves; but
from the eggs of gulls found upon both, I judge they do not go
often.

On the 17th, we landed upon the islet, and killed some out of the
many gulls by which it is frequented. A small arm of the bay extending north-eastward, where we hoped to obtain fresh water, was the
object of our examination in the afternoon. There was a little
stream falling in at the head, but rocks prevented it from being
accessible to boats, or to a raft; and a walk of perhaps a mile to the
eastward, afforded nothing but the sight of a stony country, and of
a few miserable huts. Our greyhound started a kangaroo, but it was
lost in the wood; and there were no birds to shoot...

*19 December* ~ In the evening, we had worked back into North
Bay, and come to an anchor under the north-east end of Sloping
Island.

The great eastern bay now quitted had never been entered till
this time; and as it is proved not to be Frederik Hendrik's, I have
named it Norfolk Bay. It is about eight miles long, north and south,
and three to five miles broad from east to west. The largest fleet
may find shelter here, with anchorage on a good bottom of 4 to 9
fathoms deep. We saw but one small stream of fresh water, and that
was of difficult access; but it is scarcely probable that, amongst the
many coves all around the bay, water convenient for ships should
not be found. The country near the shore is rocky; but as the
kangaroo seemed to be abundant, there are probably many grassy
plains further inland. Wood abounds everywhere, except at Green
Head, which is mostly covered with grass. Of the four islands in
the bay, Smooth and Gull islands were found superior in fertility to
the mainland: the first contains about forty acres of tolerable
pasturage.

*21 December* ~ We proceeded round for the Derwent. On clearing North Bay, I went off in the boat to Betsey's Island, leaving Mr
Bass to conduct the sloop. This island is high, and accessible only
towards its north end; its length is one mile, and mean breadth
about half that quantity; the soil is fertile, and nourishes a luxuriant
vegetation of grass and wood; and though the natives visit it occasionally, none of their traces were recent...

On the 23rd, the wind being fair, we ran upwards between
shores which were sometimes steep, but generally of a gradual
ascent, and well clothed with grass and wood. At nine miles from
the entrance lies Sullivan Cove, on the west side, where a settlement has since been established by Colonel Collins; and here the
width of the river is suddenly contracted, from one mile and a half
to less than three-quarters of a mile, but the depth is not diminished. Four miles higher up we found Risdon Cove, and anchored
there in 4 fathoms, with the intention of filling our empty water
casks at the Risdon River of Mr Hayes; but finding it to be a little
creek which even our boat could not enter, I determined to seek a
more convenient watering place higher up the Derwent.

*24 December* ~ The wind being adverse to proceeding upward,
an extensive set of angles was taken from the top of Mount
Direction; and next day, I carried the survey up the river, whilst Mr
Bass ascended the great Mount Table, on the western side. At the
northern foot of this mount lie King George's Plains, a name given
by Mr Hayes to about three hundred acres of pasture land; and in
the front of the plains is his Prince of Wales' Bay, a small shallow
cove. Such names as these led us, at first, into some errors with
respect to the importance of the places sought; but after the above
examples, we were no longer deceived by them.

In the afternoon of the 25th, we got the sloop, with much difficulty, five or six miles further up the river, to an inlet which I
called Herdsman's Cove...

The width of the Derwent abreast of Herdsman's Cove is half
a mile; but except a very narrow channel close to the eastern shore,

it is too shallow even for boats. The intention of proceeding further with the sloop was therefore abandoned; but so soon as the
rainy, blowing weather permitted, which was not until the 28th, I
accompanied Mr Bass in a boat excursion up the river. Three miles
above Herdsman's Cove the banks open out to a mile in width; the
river, from running north-westward, turns to the south-west; and
the deep channel makes a short cut across to the convex bank,
leaving the mud to collect in the opposite elbow. A great deal of
long, aquatic grass growing upon these mud flats, seemed to have
attracted the black swans, for the number collected there was not
estimated at less than five hundred.

The width of the Derwent is contracted in the south-west reach
to little more than a quarter of a mile, and we had not rowed far
up it before the water became perfectly fresh. The land on both
sides rises to hills of moderate elevation, and the rather steep
acclivities being well clothed with verdure, they had an agreeable
appearance. Our attention was suddenly called from contemplating the country, by the sound of a human voice coming from the
hills. There were three people; and as they would not comply with
our signs to come down, we landed and went up to them, taking
with us a black swan. Two women ran off, but a man, who had two
or three spears in his hand, stayed to receive us, and accepted the
swan with rapture. He seemed entirely ignorant of muskets, nor
did anything excite his attention or desire except the swan and the
red kerchiefs about our necks; he knew, however, that we came
from the sloop, and where it was lying. A little knowledge of the
Port Jackson and of the South Sea Island languages was of no use
in making ourselves understood by this man; but the quickness with
which he comprehended our signs spoke in favour of his intelligence. His appearance much resembled that of the inhabitants
of New South Wales; he had also marks raised upon the skin, and
his face was blackened and hair ruddled as is sometimes practised
by them. The hair was either close cropped, or naturally short; but
it had not the appearance of being woolly. He acceded to our

proposition of going to his hut; but finding from his devious route
and frequent stoppages, that he sought to tire our patience, we left
him delighted with the certain possession of his swan, and returned
to the boat. This was the sole opportunity we had of communicating with any of the natives of Van Diemen's Land…The last day
of December and the first of January were occupied in beating
down to the entrance of the river…

   *4 January* ~ …We had squally weather in the afternoon, with the
wind at north-west; and being unable to get near Maria's Island
before the evening, bore away northward, having then a fresh
breeze at WSW. Schouten's Island was passed within two miles at
ten o'clock, and at eleven, a piece of land called Vanderlin's Island
by Tasman, but which has since been found to be the southern
extremity of a peninsula. We then steered north, to keep in with
the coast; but the wind drawing forward in the morning of the 5th,
the sloop was drifted off, by noon, to four or five leagues. The land
then abreast rose in ranges of irregular, well-wooded hills; and
behind them were two peaks and a flat-topped piece of land, seemingly not many leagues from the shore. The southernmost of the
two peaks is the most elevated, and appears to be the high round
mountain seen by Tasman on 4 and 5 December, 1642; I have,
therefore, called it Tasman's Peak. It is the northernmost part seen
by him on this side of Van Diemen's Land, as Mount Heemskerk
was on the west coast: the flat-topped mountain is that which
Colonel Paterson afterwards named Benlomen…It was to me a
subject of regret, that the wind did not allow of keeping close in
with this east coast, since Captain Furneaux's examination was
made at too great a distance to be exact; but my limited time of
absence being expired, and provisions nearly out, nothing more
could be attempted than what might be done in the way to Port
Jackson.

   *6 January* ~ In latitude 40° 45¹/₂' no land was in sight; but on
the 7th, when in 40° 24³/₄', the high land of Cape Barren was
visible through a thick haze, bearing S76°W five or six miles. The

wind being then nearly at east, we steered to pass between Cape
Barren and the great northern island, intending to explore the
west side of the latter in our way. At five o'clock breakers were
seen two miles to the north, though no bottom could be found at
17 fathoms; at six, however, we fell suddenly into 3 fathoms; but
hoping to find a sufficient depth for the sloop round the island
which lies in the opening, stood on till the soundings diminished
to nine feet, and breakers were seen all round ahead, from beam
to beam. It was then near sunset, and the breeze right aft; but
whilst I was considering what could be done for our safety, the
wind shifted suddenly, as if by an act of Providence, to the opposite quarter, and enabled us to steer back, out of this dangerous
place, with all sail. At nine o'clock the wind returned to the south-
eastward, having just lasted long enough to take us out of danger;
at eleven we had 20 fathoms; and in two hours more steered N by
W, for the Babel Isles, with a fresh and fair wind.

*8 January* ~ At six o'clock, Mr Bass went on shore to the small,
south-eastern islet; whence he brought a boat-load of seals and
gannets. Besides these, the islet is inhabited by geese, shags,
penguins, gulls and sooty petrels; each occupying its separate
district, and using its own language. It was the confusion of noises
amongst these various animals which induced me to give the name
of Babel Isles to this small cluster...

*9 January* ~ The wind blew strong at SSE, with thick, hazy
weather. At eight in the morning, high land was distinguished two
points on the weather bow, and sandhills from thence to abaft the
lee beam, not more than six or seven miles distant. We immediately
hauled the wind to the eastward, and carried every sail the sloop
could bear in such a sea as was then running...

To make certain of clearing Cape Howe, the eastern course was
prolonged until daylight of the 10th; we then bore away and at
noon were in latitude 37° 5'. On the 11th, the observation gave 34°
30'; and the gale still continuing, we anchored within the heads of
Port Jackson at ten o'clock the same evening, having exceeded, by

no more than eleven days, the time which had been fixed for our
return.

To the strait which had been the great object of research, and
whose discovery was now completed, Governor Hunter gave, at my
recommendation, the name of Bass' Strait. This was no more than
a just tribute to my worthy friend and companion, for the extreme
dangers and fatigues he had undergone in first entering it in the
whaleboat, and to the correct judgment he had formed from
various indications, of the existence of a wide opening between
Van Diemen's Land and New South Wales...

The success of this expedition favoured my views of further discovery; and the *Reliance* not being immediately wanted for service, His
Excellency accepted a proposition to explore Glass-house and
Hervey's bays, two large openings to the northward, of which the
entrances only were known.† I had some hope of finding a considerable river discharging itself at one of these openings, and of
being able by its means to penetrate further into the interior of the
country than had hitherto been effected.

The sloop *Norfolk* was again allotted to me, with nearly the same
volunteer crew as before; and I was accompanied by Mr S. W.
Flinders, a midshipman of the *Reliance*, and by Bongaree, a native,
whose good disposition and manly conduct had attracted my
esteem. Of the assistance of my able friend Bass I was, however,
deprived, he having quitted the station soon after our last voyage,
to return to England. The time of my absence was limited by the
governor to six weeks, some arrivals being then expected which
might call the *Reliance* into active service.

We sailed out of Port Jackson on 8 July; and next morning came
in with a part of the coast, north of Port Stephens, which Captain
Cook had passed in the night. Off a projection which I called

† Glass-house Bay is now Moreton Bay, near Brisbane.

Sugar-loaf Point, in latitude 32° 29', lie two rocks to the south-
eastward, at the distances of two and four miles. We passed between
these rocks and the point, and kept close in with the shore as far to
the north as the hills called Three Brothers by Captain Cook, of
which the northernmost and highest lies in latitude 31° 43' south.

*10 July* ~ …In latitude 29° 43', we discovered a small opening
like a river, with an islet lying in the entrance; and at sunset,
entered a larger, to which I gave the name of Shoal Bay, an appellation which it but too well merited. On the south side of the
entrance, which is the deepest, there is ten feet at low water; and
within side, the depth is from 2 to 4 fathoms in a channel near the
south shore: the rest of the bay is mostly occupied by shoals, over
which boats can scarcely pass when the tide is out.

*12 July* ~ The morning was employed in examining the bay, and
in looking round the country. The sloop had sprung a bad leak, and
I wished to have laid her on shore; but not finding a convenient
place, nor anything of particular interest to detain me longer, we
sailed at one o'clock, when the tide began to rise…At eight in the
evening, the anchor was dropped in 7 fathoms at the entrance of
Glass-house Bay, Cape Moreton bearing ESE two or three miles.

Little progress was made up the bay on the 15th, owing to the
many shoals in it, and to a foul wind…In the evening, when the
lunar distances were observed, the sloop was at anchor in 11
fathoms on the west side of the entrance, within two miles of a low
projection which an unfortunate occurrence afterwards causes to
be named Point Skirmish.

On the 16th, whilst beating up amongst the shoals, an opening
was perceived round the point; and being much in want of a place
to lay the sloop on shore, on account of the leak, I tried to enter it;
but not finding it accessible from the south, was obliged to make the
examination with the boat, whilst the sloop lay at anchor five miles
off. There was a party of natives on the point, and our communication was at first friendly; but after receiving presents they made an
attack, and one of them was wounded by our fire. Proceeding up

the opening, I found it to be more than a mile in width; and from
the quantities of pumice stone on the borders, it was named
Pumice-stone River. It led towards the remarkable peaks called the
Glass Houses, which were now suspected to be volcanic, and excited
my curiosity.

On board the sloop, the leak had, in the meantime, been found
to arise from a plank having started from the timbers, at three or
four streaks above the keel; and the open space being filled up with
oakum from the inside, very little water came in; I therefore left the
river and the Glass Houses for a future examination, and
proceeded up the bay with the afternoon's flood...

*25 July* ~ The leaky plank being secured, and the sloop re-stowed
and completed with water, we proceeded two miles further up the
river, amongst mangrove islets and muddy flats. Next morning I
landed on the west side, as far above the sloop as the boat could
advance; and with my friend Bongaree and two sailors, steered
north-westward for the Glass-house peaks. After nine miles of labo-
rious walking, mostly through swamps or over a rocky country, we
reached the top of a stony mount, from whence the highest peak
was four miles distant to the north-west. Three or four leagues
beyond it was a ridge of mountain, from which various small
streams descend into Pumice-stone River; the principal place of
their junction seeming to be at a considerable extent of water
which bore N80°E, and was about six miles above the sloop. Early
on the 27th, we reached the foot of the nearest Glass House, a
flat-topped peak, one mile and a half north of the stony mount. It
was impossible to ascend this almost perpendicular rock; and
finding no marks of volcanic eruption, we returned to the boat,
and to the sloop the same evening.

*28 July* ~ We proceeded down the river; but owing to strong
winds and squalls from the south-east, did not clear it before the
31st. Some communications with the natives had been obtained
whilst the sloop was lying on shore; and this detention afforded
opportunities of repeating them. I am happy to say they were all

friendly, which is attributable to their opinion of us having undergone a salutary change from the effect of our firearms at Point
Skirmish.

These people were evidently of the same race as those at Port
Jackson, though speaking a language which Bongaree could not
understand. They fish almost wholly with cast and setting nets, live
more in society than the natives to the southward, and are much
better lodged. Their spears are of solid wood, and used without the
throwing stick. Two or three bark canoes were seen; but from the
number of black swans in the river, of which eighteen were caught
in our little boat, it should seem that these people are not dextrous
in the management either of the canoe or spear...

*6 August* ~ The wind being off the land, we followed the line of
the coast upwards, as close as the shoals would allow; and before
noon entered an opening formed by the western shore on one side,
and an island of moderate height, three or four miles long, on the
other. The opening was not more than two miles wide, and was still
further contracted by a low islet in the middle, surrounded with
shallow banks. There was a large expanse of water above; but we
had not advanced two miles before shoal water obliged us to tack;
and after having tried for a channel in every direction, without
success, I anchored in 3 fathoms, half a mile north-west from the
low islet, and landed.

This rocky, sandy spot lies in latitude 25° 17'. It is much
frequented by aquatic birds, particularly by that species whence it
obtained the name of Curlew Islet; and since a small shield and
three wooden spears were found there, it must also be visited occasionally by men...

The anchor was weighed soon after four o'clock, and several
attempts made to get round the larger island; but being constantly
repulsed by shoals, I was at length forced to relinquish the hope
of penetrating further up Hervey's Bay. We then steered north-
westward, to complete the examination of the west side down to
the coast seen by Captain Cook.

*7 August* ~ At daylight, a sloping hummock, in latitude 24° 50',
bore W16°N, our distance off the shore under it being one mile
and a half, and the depth 7 fathoms. At nine, the water shoaled
suddenly, and obliged us to haul off north-eastward. The coast was
then seen extending to the WNW, and having been laid down by
Captain Cook, the north-eastern course was continued for
Break-sea Spit, and the examination of Hervey's Bay concluded.

This inlet is about fifteen leagues across, from the sloping hummock to the eastern extremity of Sandy Cape, and nearly as much
in depth. The east side is formed by a great sandy peninsula, of
which the cape is the northern extremity; but about halfway up,
there are several white cliffs, and others in the upper bay, which
had the appearance of chalk. The shores at the head and on the
west side are more rocky than sandy. The back land is low for some
miles, and not ill covered with grass and wood; it then rises to hills
of considerable elevation, amongst which Double Mount was most
remarkable. The smokes in different places bespoke the country to
be inhabited in the scanty numbers usual on other parts of the east
coast; but none of the people were seen.

*7 August* ~ At ten in the evening, we passed the end of Break-sea
Spit in 13 fathoms, and hauled up south-east; but the winds were
so unfavourable, that on the 14th our latitude was no more than
29° 19'. I kept the land barely within sight, in order to obtain the
greatest advantage from the southwardly current...Light northern
winds favoured us for two days; but returning to the south-west,
and sometimes blowing strong, it was the 20th in the evening before
the sloop was secured in Port Jackson, although the current had set
us 210 miles on the way.

I must acknowledge myself to have been disappointed in not
being able to penetrate into the interior of New South Wales, by
either of the openings examined in this expedition; but, however
mortifying the conviction might be, it was then an ascertained fact,
that no river of importance intersected the east coast between the
24th and 39th degrees of south latitude...

The account of the discoveries which resulted from the establishment of the colony in New South Wales, closes with this
expedition; and it remains only to point out what was wanted to be
done in these parts of Terra Australis...

Of the persons, manners, and customs of the inhabitants, little
new information could be expected. The skirts of their country had
been examined in the southern parts, and extensive collections in
natural history made there; but to the north of Endeavour River,
the country had been seen only at a distance. The vast interior of
this new continent was wrapped in total obscurity; and excited, perhaps on that very account, full as much curiosity as did the forms
of the shores...

On a general review of the various objects in Terra Australis, to
which investigation might be usefully directed at the commencement of the nineteenth century, and in which natural history,
geography, navigation and commerce were so much interested, the
question, Why it should have been thought necessary to send out
another expedition? will no longer be asked. But rather it will be
allowed that, instead of one, there was ample room for two or three
ships; each to be employed for years, and to be conducted with a
zeal and perseverance not inferior to the examples given by the
first navigators.

On the arrival of His Majesty's ship *Reliance* in England, at the
latter end of 1800, the charts of the new discoveries were
published, and a plan was proposed to the Right Honourable Sir
Joseph Banks for completing the investigation of the coasts of
Terra Australis. The plan was approved by that distinguished
patron of science and useful enterprise; it was laid before Earl
Spencer, then first Lord Commissioner of the Admiralty; and
finally received the sanction of His Majesty, who was graciously
pleased to direct that the voyage should be undertaken; and I had
the honour of being appointed to the command.

[The *Investigator*]
January 1801–May 1802

On 19 January 1801, a commission was signed at the Admiralty appointing me Lieutenant of His Majesty's sloop *Investigator* to which the name of the ship, heretofore known as the *Xenophon*, was changed by this commission...I took the command at Sheerness on the 25th of the same month.

The *Investigator* was a north-country-built ship, of three hundred and thirty-four tons; and, in form, nearly resembled the description of vessel recommended by Captain Cook as best calculated for voyages of discovery. She had been purchased some years before into His Majesty's service; and having been newly coppered and repaired, was considered to be the best vessel which could, at that time, be spared for the projected voyage to Terra Australis.

The ship was in a state of re-equipment; but, on obtaining permission from the Navy Board to fit her out in such manner as I should judge necessary, without reference to the supplies usually allotted to vessels of the same class, all the stores were returned, and others of the best quality demanded, upon a more extensive scale. Such of the officers and crew as were aged, or did not volunteer for this particular service, were discharged; and able young men were received in lieu from His Majesty's ship *Zealand*, on board of which the flag of Vice-admiral Graeme was flying at the Nore.† Upon one

† The Nore: traditionally an anchorage for the English fleet in the seventeenth and eighteenth centuries.

occasion, where eleven volunteers were to be received from the
*Zealand*, a strong instance was given of the spirit of enterprise preva-
lent amongst British seamen. About three hundred disposable men
were called up, and placed on one side of the deck; and after the
nature of the voyage, with the number of men wanted, had been
explained to them, those who volunteered were desired to go over
to the opposite side. The candidates were not less than two hundred
and fifty, most of whom sought with eagerness to be received; and
the eleven who were chosen, proved, with one single exception, to
be worthy of the preference they obtained...

*16 February* ~ I was promoted to the rank of commander. On
the 14th of the following month, the guns, twelve six-pounders,
with their ammunition and a chest of fireworks were received; and
the provisions and stores being all on board on the 27th, and the
ship ready for sea, we dropped out to the Nore. I was anxious to
arrive upon the coasts of Terra Australis in time to have the whole
of the southern summer before me; but various circumstances
retarded our departure, and amongst others, a passport from the
French government, to prevent molestation to the voyage, had not
arrived. I took advantage of this delay to remedy an inconvenience,
under which we were otherwise likely to suffer. The quantity of
provisions necessary to be carried out did not leave room in the
holds for more water than fifty tons; but by removing ten of the
long guns, and substituting a few light carronades which could be
carried on the upper deck, ten tons more of water might be
received, without reducing our efficient strength; for the ship was
too deep to admit of the guns below being used in bad weather,
whereas the carronades would be always serviceable. My application to have this exchange made, was complied with; and on 20
May was effected.

On the 22nd, a set of astronomical and surveying instruments,
for the use of myself and officers, was sent down by direction of
the Navy Board; as also various articles for presents to, and barter
with, the native inhabitants of the countries to be visited, and many

for our own use and convenience. Amongst the latter were most of the books of voyages to the South Seas, which, with our own individual collections, and the Encyclopedia Britannica, presented by the Right Hon. Sir Joseph Banks, formed a library in my cabin for the use of all the officers. Every chart at the Admiralty, which related to Terra Australis and the neighbouring islands, was copied for us under the direction of the late hydrographer, Alexander. Dalrymple, Esq...

So soon as my sailing orders were received, demands were sent on shore for provisions to replace what had been consumed at Spithead; and they came on board next morning, when the ship was unmoored. We were able to stow a proportion of provisions for twelve months, bread excepted, of which only seven months could be taken, including a part in flour. Of salt meat I took for eighteen months, knowing that little reliance could be had upon the colony in New South Wales for that article; and further to guard against any detriment to the voyage from a want of provisions, I left an application to the Admiralty for a general supply for twelve months to be sent after me and lodged in the store houses at Port Jackson for our sole use.

Of the various extra provisions usually furnished as preservatives of health to the crews of His Majesty's ships going upon similar service, our supply was abundant; and the surgeon was as liberally furnished with antiscorbutic medicines.

The complement of the *Xenophon* had been seventy-five men; but on the name and destination of the ship being changed, the following establishment was ordered. The names of the officers are added to the list, and also of the men of science who took part in the expedition, which left the whole number of persons on board to be eighty-eight, at the time of sailing.


*25 November 1801* ~ In passages like this, when fortunately made, it is seldom that any circumstance occurs, of sufficient interest to be

related. Our employments were to clean, dry and air the ship
below; and the seamen's clothes and bedding, with the sails, upon
deck. These, with the exercise of the great guns and small arms,
were our principal employments in fine weather; and when otherwise, we were wet and uncomfortable, and could do little. It was a
great satisfaction that frequent pumping of the ship was not now
required, the greatest quantity of water admitted during this
passage being less than two inches an hour. The antiseptics issued
were sour kraut and vinegar, to the extent of the applications for
them; and at half an hour before noon every day, a pint of strong
wort, made by pouring boiling water upon the essence of malt, was
given to each man. It was drunk upon deck; and with half a biscuit,
made a luncheon for both officers and people. The allowance of
grog was never issued until half an hour after the dinner time.

On 6 December, our latitude was 35° 10', and longitude 114°
19'; which placed us about SW$^1/_2$S twenty-two leagues from
the westernmost isles lying off the south-west cape of New
Holland, according to their position by the French rear-admiral
D'Entrecasteaux; a traced copy of whose general chart of this coast
had been furnished to me from the hydrographical office at the
Admiralty. There were no names applied in this copy; but in the
charts of the French voyage, lately published, these isles are called
Iles St Alouarn.

Notwithstanding the nearness of the land, there were no signs
of such proximity: no discolouring in the water, no seaweed, no
new birds, and but few of the species before seen...

At two in the afternoon, the wind being north-westward, we
hauled up to make the south-western point of Leeuwin's Land, and
bent the cables. At seven, land was seen right ahead, bearing
N14°E, at the supposed distance of ten leagues; and on sounding,
there was 85 fathoms, coral sand. We stood for it until eleven at
night, and then veered to the south-west, in 65 fathoms, same
bottom.

The examination of Nuyts' and of Leeuwin's Lands was not

prescribed in my instructions to be made at this time; but the difference of sailing along the coast at a distance, or in keeping near it
and making a running survey, was likely to be so little, that I judged
it advisable to do all that circumstances would allow whilst the
opportunity offered; and I had the pleasure to find this slight devi-
ation approved at the Admiralty.

*7 December* ~ At two in the morning; we had 80 fathoms, and
veered towards the land. It was seen from the masthead at five;
and the highest part, the same which had been set in the evening,
bore N12°W. This is the largest of the before-mentioned Isles of
St Alouarn; but at half past seven, we saw hills extending from
behind, and, to all appearance, joining it to the mainland. This
supposed isle is, therefore, what I denominate Cape Leeuwin, as
being the south-western, and most projecting part of Leeuwin's
Land. The highest hill lies nearby in latitude 34° 19' south, and
longitude 115° 6' east; it is a sloping piece of land of about six
hundred feet in elevation, and appeared to be rocky, with a slight
covering of trees and shrubs...On the east side of Cape Leeuwin,
the land falls back north-eastward three or four leagues, and afterwards curves to the south-east, forming a large bight which
appeared to be wholly exposed to the southern winds. The coastline, round the upper part of this bight, was not distinguishable;
but the hills at the back showed more of bare sand, than of
vegetable covering...

*8 December* ~ Some parts of the shore between Point D'Entrecasteaux and Cape Chatham were not distinctly seen. That which
is nearest to the cape, lies in the line of N38°W from its outer part,
and presents an intermixture of steep cliffs and small sandy beaches,
with a back land moderately high, and better covered with wood
than that before described. On the east side of Cape Chatham, the
shore falls back to the northward, and makes a bight in which is a
small reef of rocks. It then projects in a cliffy head, which lies S75°E
seven miles from the cape, and is called Point Nuyts in the French
chart; upon the supposition, probably, that this was the first land

seen by Nuyts, in 1627. Beyond this point, the coast trends very nearly east; but forms several projections, some of which are steep and others low; and between them are sandy bights where small vessels might obtain shelter from all northern winds. The hills lying at the back of the shore seemed to be barren, though trees grew thickly on their eastern sides; they are not high, but it was rare to perceive anything of the interior country above them.

At noon, the nearest parts of the coast were a steep, and a more eastern low point, both distant about four miles; and from the bight between them was rising the first smoke seen upon this coast...

The wind blew fresh at this time, and a current of more than one mile an hour ran with us, so that, by carrying all sail, I hoped to get sight of King George's Sound before dark. At seven, we passed close on the south side of the Eclipse Isles; but Bald Head at the entrance of the sound had so different an appearance from what I had been led to expect, being a slope in this point of view, that the steep east end of Break-sea Island was at first taken for it. The error was fortunately perceived in time; and at eight o'clock we hauled up round the head, with the wind at west, and made a stretch into the sound. It was then dark; but the night being fine, I did not hesitate to work up by the guidance of Captain Vancouver's chart; and having reached nearly into a line between Seal Island and the first beach round Bald Head, we anchored at eleven o'clock, in 8 fathoms, sandy bottom.

*9 December* ~ King George's Sound had been chosen as the proper place in which to prepare ourselves for the examination of the south coast of Terra Australis, and I sought to make the best use of the advantages it might furnish. The first essential requisite was a place of secure shelter, where the masts could be stripped, the rigging and sails put into order, and communication had with the shore, without interruption from the elements; but this, from Captain Vancouver's chart and description, I did not expect the outer sound to afford... and in the morning, after we had sounded round the ship and found her so placed as to require no immediate movement, I went in a boat for the purpose, accompanied by the master and landscape painter; the naturalist, and some other gentlemen landing at the same time, to botanise in the vicinity of Bald Head.

Seal Island, where we stopped in passing, is a mass of granite, which is accessible only at its western end...After killing a few seals upon the shore, we ascended the hill to search for the bottle and parchment left by Captain Vancouver in 1791; but could find no vestiges either of it or of the staff or pile of stones; and since there was no appearance of the natives having crossed over from the main, I was led to suspect that a second ship had been here before us.

At Point Possession, on the south side of the entrance to Princess-royal Harbour, we had a good view of that extensive piece of water. Wood seemed not to be abundant near the shores; and therefore a projection two or three miles to the south-west, which was covered with trees, first attracted my notice. The depth of water in going to it was, however, too little for the ship; nor was there any fresh stream in the neighbourhood. Some person, but not Captain Vancouver, had nevertheless been cutting wood there; for several trees had been felled with axe and saw. Not far from thence stood a number of bark sheds, like the huts of the natives who live in the forests behind Port Jackson, and forming what might be called a small village; but it had been long deserted. Going across from the woody point to the north side of the harbour, we there found 3 fathoms within less than half a mile of the shore; and an increasing depth from thence out to the entrance. The soundings in the entrance were from 5 to 7 fathoms; but the channel was too narrow to admit of getting in without a leading wind and much caution.

*10 December* ~ On Thursday morning, the master was sent to examine the north side of the harbour for water and wood, and we got the ship under way to beat up to the entrance; the wind blowing still from the westward. At eleven o'clock, the anchor was dropped in 6 fathoms, half a mile from Point Possession; and as I was doubtful of the master's success, I went in a boat, accompanied by Lieutenant Flinders, to examine Oyster Harbour...

As I proposed to make a new survey of King George's Sound, we landed to take a set of angles upon the small central island; the same which Captain Vancouver describes, as covered with luxuriant grass and other vegetables; and where he planted vine cuttings, water cress, and the seeds of various fruits. There were no remains of these valuable gifts, although nothing indicated the island to have been visited since his time; and, to our disappointment, the vegetation upon it now consisted of tufts of wiry grass and a few stunted shrubs, supported by a thin layer of sandy soil, which was everywhere perforated with rat holes.

From the island, we rowed in various directions, sounding the harbour; but the boat could seldom approach the shore within a cable's length, or the eighth part of a mile. On the south-west side there were two small streams, in one of which the water was fresh, though high coloured. Returning to the entrance, we landed on the east side, and found a spot of ground six or eight feet square, dug up and trimmed like a garden; and upon it was lying a piece of sheet copper, bearing this inscription: 'August 27, 1800. Chr. Dixson—ship Elligood' which solved the difficulty of the felled trees, and the disappearance of Captain Vancouver's bottle. On digging in this place, I found that fresh water of a high colour, but well tasted, might be obtained; wood was abundant, and the depth of the entrance admitted of the ship being made fast to the shore; so that this was a situation adapted to our purpose of refitment, provided the ship could be got over the bar. This point I was desirous to ascertain in my way on board, but the strength of the wind prevented it.

The report of the master from Princess-royal Harbour was that water could be obtained at the north side by digging near the shore, at the foot of the highest hill; but that there was no wood at a convenient distance. I therefore sent him, next morning, to land the naturalists at the entrance of Oyster Harbour, and then to sound the bar; and not being satisfied with his report, that there was not so much as fourteen feet, which the ship drew, when Captain Vancouver had marked seventeen, I went to the nearest head, with a theodolite and signal flags, to direct his movements. No more, however, than thirteen feet could now be found upon the shallowest part of the bar; and, consequently, the idea of refitting in Oyster Harbour was abandoned. The boat which brought off Mr Brown and his party in the evening collected a good quantity of oysters, and of the large fan mussels from the shoals...

*13 December* ~ Our tents, under the guard of a party of marines, were set up this evening; and in the morning, the observatory and instruments were sent on shore, under the care of Lieutenant Flinders, who had undertaken to assist me in performing the office of astronomer.

Marks of the country being inhabited were found everywhere, but as yet there was nothing to indicate the presence of the natives in our neighbourhood...

*14 December* ~ Some smokes being perceived at the head of the harbour, Mr Brown and other gentlemen directed their excursion that way, and met with several of the natives, who were shy but not afraid. One man with whom they had communication, was admired for his manly behaviour, and they gave him a bird which had been shot, and a pocket-handkerchief; but like the generality of people hitherto seen in this country, these men did not seem to be desirous of communication with strangers; and they very early made signs to our gentlemen to return from whence they came. Next morning, however, we were agreeably surprised by the appearance of two Indians, and afterwards of others, upon the side of the hill behind our tents. They approached with much caution, one coming first with poised spear, and making many gestures, accompanied with much vociferous parleying, in which he sometimes seemed to threaten us if we did not be gone, and at others to admit of our stay. On Mr Purdie, the assistant-surgeon, going up to him unarmed, a communication was brought about, and they received some articles of iron and toys, giving in exchange some of their implements; and after a short stay, left us, apparently on very good terms.

On the 17th, one of our former visitors brought two strangers with him; and after this time, they and others came almost every day, and frequently stopped a whole morning at the tents. We always made them presents of such things as seemed to be most agreeable, but they very rarely brought us anything in return; nor was it uncommon to find small mirrors, and other things left about the shore; so that at length our presents were discontinued.

I formed a party on the 23rd, consisting of the officers of the ship, the scientific gentlemen, and others, amounting to thirteen, well armed and provided for two days, in order to visit the lakes behind West Cape Howe. We walked along the shore to the north-western extremity of Princess-royal Harbour, where several small runs of fresh water were found to drain in, from peaty swamps. Striking from thence into the country in a western direction, we had not advanced far when a native was seen running before us; and soon afterward an old man, who had been several times at the tents, came up, unarmed as usual. He was very anxious that we should not go further; and acted with a good deal of resolution in first stopping one, and then another of those who were foremost. He was not able to prevail; but we accommodated him so far, as to make a circuit round the wood, where it seemed probable his family and female friends were placed. The old man followed us, hallooing frequently to give information of our movements; and when a parakeet was shot, he expressed neither fear nor surprise, but received the bird with gladness; and attended with some curiosity to the reloading of the gun.

Our course for the lakes led us through swamps and thick brush woods, in which our new acquaintance followed for some time; but at length, growing tired of people who persevered in keeping a bad road in opposition to his recommendation of a better, which, indeed, had nothing objectionable in it, but that it led directly contrary to where our object lay, he fell behind and left us. We afterwards took to the skirts of the sea-coast hills, and made better progress; but were obliged to recross the swamps and force our way through a thick brush, before reaching the eastern lake.

This piece of water was found to be one mile and a half, east and west, and one mile in breadth; and appeared to receive the drainings from the numerous swamps round about. In coasting round the north side, to reach the south-western lake, we were stopped by a serpentine stream, upon which were two black swans; but they took to flight before we could get near to shoot them. After following the windings of this rivulet, some distance to the north-west, without being able to pass over, we struck inland towards the skirt of some rising hills; and crossed the stream early enough to walk a mile to the south-west before sunset; when the convenience of dry ground, with wood and water at hand, induced us to halt for the night.

*24 December* ~ On Thursday morning, we reached the south-western lake, and found it to be larger than the first. Its water was brackish, which bespoke a communication with the sea; and as there was no certainty that this communication might not be too deep to be passed, it was thought prudent to give up the intention of proceeding to the sea side; and our steps were retraced across the rivulet and round the northern lake. We then struck southward, and ascended the hills to the top of the cliffs facing the sea; from whence I had an opportunity of seeing the bight near Cape Howe, and the form of the lakes; but no water communication was visible between them.

Our course homeward was pursued along the sandy ridge at the back of the cliffs, where the want of water was as great, as the super-abundance had been in the low land going out. Towards sunset, when Princess-royal Harbour was still some miles distant, the natural-history painter became unable to proceed further, being overcome with the labour of the walk, with the excessive heat, and with thirst. To have detained the whole party in a state of sufferance, would have been imprudent; and Mr Brown and two others having volunteered to stay, we left them the scanty remains of our provision, and pushed forward to the tents, which we reached at eight o'clock. At midnight we had the pleasure to see our friends arrive, and the preparation made for sending to their assistance, at daybreak, become unnecessary.

The country through which we passed in this excursion, has but little to recommend it. The stony hills of the sea coast were, indeed, generally covered with shrubs; but there was rarely any depth of vegetable soil, and no wood. The land slopes down gradually behind these hills; and at the bottom, water drains out, and forms a chain of swamps extending from Princess-royal Harbour to the lakes. Here the country is covered with grass and brush wood, and in the parts a little elevated there are forest trees; nevertheless the soil is shallow, and unfit for cultivation.

On the 30th, our wooding, and the watering of the ship were completed, the rigging was refitted, the sails repaired and bent, and the ship unmoored. Our friends, the natives, continued to visit us; and the old man, with several others being at the tents this morning, I ordered the party of marines on shore, to be exercised in their presence. The red coats and white crossed belts were greatly admired, having some resemblance to their own manner of ornamenting themselves; and the drum, but particularly the fife, excited their astonishment; but when they saw these beautiful red-and-white men, with their bright muskets, drawn up in a line, they absolutely screamed with delight; nor were their wild gestures and vociferation to be silenced, but by commencing the exercise, to which they paid the most earnest and silent attention. Several of them moved their hands, involuntarily, according to the motions; and the old man placed himself at the end of the rank, with a short staff in his hand, which he shouldered, presented, grounded, as did the marines their muskets, without, I believe, knowing what he did. Before firing, the Indians were made acquainted with what was going to take place; so that the volleys did not excite much terror.

The tents and observatory were already struck; and everything being sent on board, we took leave of the natives, and embarked with the intention of running into the Sound this evening; but a change

in the wind, to south-by-east, prevented it. This wind veered to east
and north-east, and for a short time blew strong; so that it was
3 January, in the afternoon, before we steered out of Princess-royal
Harbour. It was not my intention to proceed immediately to sea; and
I therefore took the opportunity of standing backward and forward
in the sound, with the dredge and trawl overboard; and a variety of
small fish were brought up. These were of little use, as food; but with
the shells, seaweeds and corals, they furnished amusement and occupation to the naturalist and draughtsman, and a pretty kind of
hippocampus, which was not scarce, was generally admired.

*4 January* ~ On the 4th, a fresh gale blew from the westward,
and prevented me from moving the ship. A bottle, containing a
parchment to inform future visitors of our arrival and intention to
sail on the morrow, was left upon the top of Seal Island; and the
wind having moderated next day, and the weather become finer,
though still squally, we then made sail out of King George's Sound,
to prosecute the further examination of the coast.

*5 January* ~ The refreshments we had procured were fish and
oysters. The seine was frequently hauled upon the different
beaches; but although it was done in the evening, round fires which
had been previously kindled, little success was obtained in this way.
With hook and line we were more fortunate, both alongside and
from boats stationed off the rocky points; and the whole ship's
company had generally a fresh meal once in three or four days. Of
oysters, as many were taken from the shoals in both harbours, as
we chose to spare time for gathering. Our firewood was procured
from the north point of entrance to Princess-royal Harbour, at the
inner end of the long middle beach; but the trees best calculated
for sawing into planks were obtained at the easternmost of the two
woody projections on the south side of the harbour. A good
number of planks and logs were taken on board, for making
garden boxes to contain the most curious plants collected by the
naturalist, and for a variety of other purposes. The fresh water,
procured by digging near the tents, was a little discoloured, but

good; and it was sufficiently abundant for every purpose: its specific gravity was 1003 at the temperature of 69°.

Captain Vancouver has described the country in the neighbourhood of King George's Sound, and therefore a few observations upon it will suffice. The basis stone is granite, which frequently shows itself at the surface, in the form of smooth bare rock; but upon the sea-coast hills, and the shores on the south sides of the sound and Princess-royal Harbour, the granite is generally covered with a crust of calcareous stone; as it is, also, upon Michaelmas Island. Captain Vancouver mentions having found upon the top of Bald Head, branches of coral protruding through the sand, exactly like those seen in the coral beds beneath the surface of the sea; a circumstance which should seem to bespeak this country to have emerged from the ocean at no very distant period of time. This curious fact I was desirous to verify; and his description was proved to be correct. I found, also, two broken columns of stone three or four feet high, formed like stumps of trees and of a thickness superior to the body of a man; but whether they were of coral, or of wood now petrified or whether they might not have been calcareous rocks, worn into that particular form by the weather, I cannot determine. Their elevation above the present level of the sea could not have been less than four hundred feet…

The soil of the hills is very barren, though, except near the sea coast, generally covered with wood; and that of the plains at the head of Princess-royal Harbour, has been described as shallow, and incapable of cultivation. In the neighbourhood of Oyster Harbour the land was said to be better, especially near the rivulet which falls into the northern corner; and on the borders of a small lake, at the back of the long beach between the two harbours, the country was represented to be pleasing to the eye, and tolerably fertile.

The timber trees of the woods consist principally of different species of that extensive class called *gum-tree* by the colonists at Port Jackson, by botanists *eucalyptus*. They do not grow very large here, and the wood is heavy and seldom fit for other than common

purposes. Amongst the plants collected by Mr Brown and his asso-
ciates, was a small one of a novel kind, which we commonly called
the pitcher plant. Around the root leaves are several little vases lined
with spiny hairs, and these were generally found to contain a sweet-
ish water, and also a number of dead ants. It cannot be asserted that
the ants were attracted by the water, and prevented by the spiny
hairs from making their escape; but it seemed not improbable, that
this was a contrivance of nature to obtain the means necessary
either to the nourishment or preservation of the plant.

Amongst the animal productions, the kangaroo and cassowary
hold the first ranks. The kangaroo appeared to be numerous, and
of more than one species; but none were caught. Three of them
seen by me bore a resemblance to the large kind which inhabits the
forests at Port Jackson; and the cassowary showed nothing distinguishable at a distance from the same animal at that place: both
were shy; as were the ducks, swans, and all the birds.

Near Point Possession were found two nests of extraordinary
magnitude. They were built upon the ground, from which they rose
above two feet; and were of vast circumference and great interior
capacity, the branches of trees and other matter, of which each nest
was composed, being enough to fill a small cart. Captain Cook
found one of these enormous nests upon Eagle Island, on the East
Coast; and if the magnitude of the constructor be proportionate
to the size of the nest, Terra Australis must be inhabited by a
species of bird, little inferior to the condor of the Andes†...

Our frequent and amicable communication with the natives of
this country has been mentioned. The women were, however, kept
out of sight with seeming jealousy; and the men appeared to
suspect the same conduct in us, after they had satisfied themselves
that the most beardless of those they saw at the tents were of the
same sex...with the rest. The belief that there must be women in
the ship induced two of them to comply with our persuasion of

† Possibly the nests of sea eagles.

getting into the boat one morning to go on board; but their courage failing, they desired to be relanded; and made signs that the ship must go on shore to them.

It was with some surprise that I saw the natives of the east coast of New South Wales so nearly portrayed in those of the south-western extremity of New Holland. These do not, indeed, extract one of the upper front teeth at the age of puberty, as is generally practised at Port Jackson, nor do they make use of the *womerah*, or throwing stick; but their colour, the texture of the hair and personal appearance are the same; their songs run in the same cadence; the manner of painting themselves is similar; their belts and fillets of hair are made in the same way, and worn in the same manner. The short, skin cloak, which is of kangaroo, and worn over the shoulders, leaving the rest of the body naked, is more in the manner of the wood natives living at the back of Port Jackson, than of those who inhabit the sea coast; and everything we saw confirmed the supposition of Captain Vancouver, that they live more by hunting than fishing. None of the small islands had been visited, no canoes were seen, nor was any tree found in the woods from which the bark had been taken for making one. They were fearful of trusting themselves upon the water; and we could never succeed in making them understand the use of the fish hook, although they were intelligent in comprehending our signs upon other subjects.

The manners of these people are quick and vehement, and their conversation vociferous, like that of most uncivilised people. They seemed to have no idea of any superiority we possessed over them; on the contrary, they left us, after the first interview, with some appearance of contempt for our pusillanimity; which was probably inferred from the desire we showed to be friendly with them. This opinion, however, seemed to be corrected in their future visits.

Notwithstanding the similarity of person and manner to the inhabitants of Port Jackson, the language of these people is very different. We found their pronunciation difficult to be imitated; more so, indeed, than our language was to them. Several English

words they pronounced perfectly; whilst of such where an *f* or an
*s* entered, they could make but little: Finger was pronounced *bing-
gah*, ship, *yip*; and of King George they made *Ken Jag-ger*. In the
difficulty of pronouncing the *f* and *s*, they resemble the Port
Jackson natives; and the word used by them in calling to a distance,
*cau-wah!* (come here) is nearly similar to *cow-ee!* The word also to
express *eye*, is nearly the same. But in the following table, which
contains all the words that, with any certainty, I was able to collect,

| English | K. George's Sound | Port Jackson* | Van Diemen's Land** |
|---|---|---|---|
| Head | Kaāt | Ca-ber-ra | |
| Hair | Kaat-joū | De-war-ra | Pélilogueni |
| Nose | Mo-il | No-gro | Mugui (Muidge, Cook) |
| Cheek, or beard | Ny-a-nūk | Yar-rin | Canguiné |
| Teeth | Yea-al | Da-ra | Pégui or Canan (Kamy, C.) |
| Ear | Du-ong | Go-ray | Vaigui (Koygee, Cook) |
| Lips | Ur-luk | Wil-ling | Mogudé lia |
| Throat | Wurt | Cad-le-an | |
| Nipple | Bpep | Na-bung | |
| Belly | Ko-bul | Bar-rong | Lomangui |
| Posteriors | Wa-la-kah | Boong | Nuné |
| Thigh | Dtou-al | | |
| Knee | Wo-nat | Go-rook | Ronga |
| Leg | Maāt | Dar-ra | Lerai |
| Foot | Jaān | Ma-no-e | Peré |
| The sun | Djaāt | Co-ing | Panuberé |

* From Collins' *Account of the English Colony in New South Wales*, vol. I. p. 610–11.
** *Voyage de D'Entrecasteaux*, par M. de Rossel. tome I. p. 552 *et seq*. These words
are written after the French pronunciation of the letters.

the most essential differences will be found, both from the Port
Jackson language, and from that of the south end of Van Diemen's
Land; and the words collected by Captain Cook at Endeavour
River bear no resemblance to any of them.

In running along that part of the south coast which lies to the
west of King George's Sound, I had endeavoured to keep so close
in with the land that the breaking water on the shore should be
visible from the ship's deck; by which means our supposed distance
would be little subject to error, and no river or opening could
escape being seen. This close proximity could not, however, be
obtained in every part, especially where the coast retreated far
back; but it was always attempted where practicable and unat-
tended with much danger or loss of time; and when it could not be
done, I was commonly at the masthead with a glass. All the bearings were laid down so soon as taken, whilst the land was in sight;
and before retiring to rest, I made it a practice to finish up the
rough chart for the day, as also my journals of astronomical observations, of bearings, and of remarks. When we hauled off from the
coast at night, every precaution was taken to come in with the same
point in the morning, as soon after daylight as practicable; and
when the situation of the ship, relatively to the land of the preceding evening was ascertained, our route along the coast was
resumed. This plan, to see and lay down everything myself,
required constant attention and much labour, but was absolutely
necessary to obtaining that accuracy of which I was desirous; and
now, on recommencing the survey from King George's Sound to
the eastward, I persevered in the same system; and it was adhered
to although not particularly mentioned, in all the succeeding part of
the voyage.

On 5 January, in the morning, we got under way from the
Sound, having a fresh wind from the westward and squally
weather. I steered between Michaelmas Island and the main, in
order to explore better that part of the Sound, and ascertain the
extent of a shoal running off from the north-west end of the island.

It was found to run out not further than half a mile, at which distance we passed in 5 fathoms water; and at noon, when the east end of Break-sea Island bore S30°W, we had 33 fathoms.

Mount Gardner is a high, conic-shaped hill, apparently of granite, very well delineated in Captain Vancouver's atlas. It stands upon a projecting cape, round which the shore falls back to the northward, forming a sandy bight where there appeared to be shelter from western winds; indeed, as the coastline was not distinctly seen round the south-west corner of the bight, it is possible there may be some small inlet in that part.

The south end of an island, called Ile Pelée (Bald Island) by D'Entrecasteaux, opened round the cape of Mount Gardner at N69°E. The French navigator having passed without side of this island, I steered within, through a passage of a short mile wide; and had 17 fathoms for the shoalest water, on a sandy bottom. Bald Island is of moderate elevation, and barren, as its name implies; it is about two and a half miles in length, and the south end lies in 34° 55' south, and 118° 29' east. It lies off a rocky projection of the mainland, at which terminates a ridge of mountain extending three leagues along the shore from the bight behind Mount Gardner. There are a number of small peaks upon the top of this ridge, which induced me to give it the name Mount Manypeak...

*7 January* ~ Our course was directed to the northward, with the wind at south-east-by-south; but seeing the appearance of an opening in the north-west corner of the bay, with smokes rising there, we steered north-west for it. In an hour the low land was seen from the masthead to extend across the supposed opening, and we then hauled up east-by-north, to the wind, at the distance of five or six miles from the high, rocky shore between the Middle and East Mount Barren. At seven in the evening, the eastern mount bore N44°W, three leagues, and the coast, which from thence becomes sandy, was seen as far as N76°E. A small reef, one of two before laid down both by Vancouver and D'Entrecasteaux, was then observed three or four miles to seaward. It was important to get sight of this reef before dark, for we should otherwise have been at great uncertainty during the night, more especially as the surf upon it broke only at times.

The wind being at south-by-east, we tacked and stood westward, nearly in our afternoon's track, until midnight; and the breeze having then veered to south-west, we were able to stretch off south-south-east, to windward of the breakers. At half past five in the morning, East Mount Barren was four leagues distant to the northward, and our course was resumed along the shore. The breakers were passed at the distance of two miles, and the mount was set over them, bearing N38°W at seven o'clock. The second small reef lies nearly east-north-east from the first; and was left three miles to the northward.

*8 January* ~ ...Before sunset, the westernmost isle of D'Entrecasteaux's Archipel de la Recherche was in sight to the eastward, and at half past seven, our distance from it was about six miles. The French admiral had mostly skirted round the archipelago, a sufficient reason for me to attempt passing through the middle, if the weather did not make the experiment too dangerous. It was fine at this time, and the breeze moderate at south-south-west; and I therefore took measures to be in with the western group as early on the following morning as possible, to have the whole day for getting through.

*9 January* ~ At a quarter past five, we bore away for the south end of the westernmost island, passed it within a mile and a half at seven, and steered eastward for the clusters rising ahead and on both bows. At noon, the number of rocks above water, the patches of breakers, and the islands with which we were surrounded, made it necessary to heave to, in order to take the angles of so many objects with some degree of accuracy...

The chart alone can give any adequate idea of this labyrinth of islands and rocks, or of our track amongst them until half past five in the evening. We were then abreast of the Ile du Mondrain, and the view from the masthead was almost as crowded as before; but with this difference, that the islands were smaller, and the low rocks and patches of breakers more numerous. Seeing no probability of reaching a space of clear water in which to stand off and on during the night, and no prospect of shelter under any of the islands, I found myself under the necessity of adopting a hazardous measure; and with the concurrence of the master's opinion, we steered directly before the wind for the main coast, where the appearance of some beaches, behind other islands, gave a hope of finding anchorage. At seven in the evening we entered a small sandy bay; and finding it sheltered everywhere except to the south-westward, in which direction there were many islands and rocks in the offing to break off the sea, the anchor was dropped in 7 fathoms, sandy bottom. The master sounded round the ship, but nothing was found to injure the cables; and except the water being shallow in the north-west corner of the bay, there was no danger to be apprehended, unless from strong south-west winds. The critical circumstance under which this place was discovered, induced me to give it the name of Lucky Bay.

*10 January* ~ I had intended to pursue our route through the archipelago in the morning; but the scientific gentlemen having expressed a desire for the ship to remain two or three days, to give them an opportunity of examining the productions of the country, it was complied with; and they landed soon after daylight. I went on shore also, to make observations upon the rates of the time keepers; and afterwards ascended a hill at the back of the bay, to take angles with a theodolite. A party of the gentlemen were upon the top, eating a fruit not much unlike green walnuts in external appearance, and invited me to partake; but having breakfasted, and not much liking their flavour, I did but taste them. Mr Thistle and some others who had eaten liberally, were taken sick, and remained unwell all the day afterward. The plant which produced these nuts was a species of *zamia*; a class of plants nearly allied to the third kind of palm found by Captain Cook on the east coast, the fruit of which produced the same deleterious effects on board the *Endeavour*.

The weather, unfortunately for my bearings, was so hazy, that unless objects were eminently conspicuous, they could not be distinguished beyond four or five leagues. My list, however, contained forty-five islands and clusters of rocks, independently of many patches of breakers where nothing above water appeared; yet most of those in the western part of the archipelago were invisible, either from their distance, or from being hidden by other lands.

In turning from the view of these complicated dangers to that of the interior country, the prospect was but little improved. Sand and stone, with the slightest covering of vegetation, everywhere presented themselves on the lower lands; and the many shining parts on the sides of the hills, showed them to be still more bare. The vegetation, indeed, consisted of an abundant variety of shrubs and small plants, and yielded a delightful harvest to the botanists; but to the herdsman and cultivator it promised nothing: not a blade of grass, nor a square yard of soil from which the seed delivered to it could be expected back, was perceivable by the eye in its course over these arid plains.

Upon a rock on the side of the hill I found a large nest, very similar to those seen in King George's Sound. There were in it several masses resembling those which contain the hair and bones of mice, and are disgorged by the owls in England after the flesh is digested. These masses were larger, and consisted of the hair of seals and of land animals, of the scaly feathers of penguins, and the bones of birds and small quadrupeds. Possibly the constructor of the nest might be an enormous owl; and if so, the cause of the bird being never seen, whilst the nests were not scarce, would be from its not going out until dark; but from the very open and exposed situations in which the nests were found, I should rather judge it to be of the eagle kind; and that its powers are such as to render it heedless of any attempts from the natives upon its young.

On the following morning, I sent the master to examine a small

bay or cove, lying two miles to the westward of Lucky Bay. He
found it to be capable of receiving one ship, which might be placed
in perfect security in the western corner, with anchors out on the
off bow and quarter, and hawsers on the other side fast to the
shore. She would thus lie in from 3 to 5 fathoms, almost near
enough to lay a stage to the beach. There was wood for fuel; and
at less than a hundred yards from the shore, a lake of fresh water,
one mile in circumference, from which a small stream runs into the
cove; but another stream, descending from the hills nearer into the
western corner, would better suit the purposes of a ship. This
account was from the master, after whom this little, but useful
discovery was named Thistle's Cove. It seems to be much superior
to Lucky Bay, where neither wood nor water can be procured
without much time and trouble, nor is the shelter so complete.

*12 January* ~ Mr Thistle was sent to examine the coast and
islands to the eastward, when he found the archipelago to be fully
as dangerous in that direction, as to the west. He landed upon an
island three leagues distant, and brought me from thence a list of
other islands and rocks further on, whose bearings had been taken.
Several seals were procured on this and the preceding day, and
some fish were caught alongside the ship; but our success was much
impeded by three monstrous sharks, in whose presence no other
fish dared to appear. After some attempts we succeeded in taking
one of them; but to get it on board required as much preparation
as for hoisting in the launch. The length of it, however, was no more
than twelve feet three inches, but the circumference of the body was
eight feet. Amongst the vast quantity of substances contained in the
stomach, was a tolerably large seal, bitten in two, and swallowed
with half of the spear sticking in it with which it had probably been
killed by the natives. The stench of this ravenous monster was great,
even before it was dead; and when the stomach was opened, it
became intolerable.†

† A Great White shark.

On the 13th, the wind blew fresh from the eastward; and as we could not sail with the ship, Lieutenant Fowler and Mr Thistle went over to Mondrain Island, the largest we had yet seen in the archipelago. An observation of the latitude and a set of angles were there taken, and they brought back some seals of a reddish fur, and a few small kangaroos of a species different from any I had before seen. The island was covered with brush wood; but some of the party, either from accident or design, set it on fire; and the wind being fresh, there was a general blaze in the evening, all over the island...

*14 January* ~ ...At six o'clock we had some larger, flat islands to windward, and in the east-south-east was one much higher and of greater extent, which proved to be the I. du Milieu (Middle Island) of D'Entrecasteaux. Betwixt this island and his Cap Aride on the main, there were many small isles and apparently passages; and we therefore bore away in the hope of finding anchorage against the approaching night. Many patches of breakers were passed; and seeing a small bay in the north side of Middle Island, we stood in for it under shortened sail; and came to an anchor in 7 fathoms, sandy bottom, off the first of three small beaches. The island sheltered us from east-north-east, round by the south to west-by-north; and to the northward there was, besides the mainland, a number of reefs and small isles, of which the nearest and largest was a quarter of a mile distant, as Middle Island was on the other side. The master was immediately sent to examine the passage through to the eastward, that we might know whether there were a possibility of escape in case the anchor should not hold; for the wind blew fresh at west-south-west, and threw some swell into the bay: he found 3 fathoms in the shallow part of the opening.

*15 January* ~ The botanists landed in the morning upon Middle Island; for I had determined to stop a day or two, as well for their accommodation as to improve my chart of the archipelago. I went to the northern island, which is one mile long and near half a mile in breadth, and found it to be covered with tufts of wiry grass intermixed with a few shrubs. Some of the little, blue penguins, like those of Bass' Strait, harboured under the bushes; and amongst the grass and upon the shores were a number of the barnacle geese, of which we killed nine, mostly with sticks; and sixteen more were procured in the course of the day.

After taking bearings from the uppermost of the small eleva-tions of Goose Island, as it was now named, I ascended the high north-western hill of Middle Island, which afforded a more exten-sive view. The furthest visible part of the mainland was a projecting cape, with a broad-topped hill upon it bearing N58°E, six or seven leagues. This projection not having been seen by D'Entrecasteaux, was named after the late admiral Sir Thomas Pasley, under whom I had the honour of entering the naval service. The shore betwixt Cape Pasley and Cape Arid is low and sandy, and falls back in a large bight, nearly similar to what is formed on the west side of Cape Arid. Behind that cape was a high bank of sand, which stretched from one bight nearly to the other, and had the appear-ance of having been the seashore not very long since.

The mount upon which I stood is the highest part of a ridge of almost bare granite, extending along, or rather forming the west side of Middle Island. The other parts of the island are low, and thickly covered with brush wood and some trees, where a small species of kangaroo seemed to be numerous, though none were caught. In the north-eastern part was a small lake of a rose colour, the water of which, as I was informed by Mr Thistle who visited it, was so saturated with salt, that sufficient quantities were crys-tallised near the shores to load a ship. The specimen he brought on board was of a good quality, and required no other process than drying to be fit for use. This lake is at the back of the easternmost of three small beaches on the north side of the island, and it might be concluded, that the salt was formed by the evaporation of the water oozing through the bank which separates it from the sea; but as, in the small drainings from the hills, the water was too salt to be drinkable, this may admit of a doubt.

*16 January* ~ On Saturday morning, a part of the people were employed cutting a boat load of firewood, and the master was again sent to sound the passage out to the eastward, and amongst the rocks lying beyond it. The shallowest depth he found was 3 fathoms, after which the water deepened to 7 and 10, past the north-east point and out to sea. He landed upon some of the rocky islets, and brought from thence twenty-seven more geese, some of them alive. The botanical gentlemen employed the day in going round Middle Island, but they found very little to reward their labour. A piece of fir plank, with nails in it, which seemed to have been part of a ship's deck, was picked up on the shore; but no trace of the island having been visited, either by Europeans or the natives of the mainland, was anywhere seen...

Goose-Island Bay may be useful as a place of refreshment, but the geese were not found to be so numerous at a different season of the year: a few hair seals may be procured, probably at all times. The wood is a species of eucalyptus, neither abundant nor large; but two or three ships may be supplied with fuel. Fresh water was not to be obtained upon either of the islands; but upon the opposite Cape Arid, five miles to the north, I judged there might be small streams running down from the hills. The lake of salt will be the greatest inducement for vessels to stop in this bay; they must not, however, come to it in the winter season, as there will be occasion to show hereafter...

*17 January* ~...We had now altogether lost sight of the Archipelago of the Recherche. The chart which I have constructed of this extensive mass of dangers is much more full, and in many parts should be more accurate than that of D'Entrecasteaux; but I dare by no means assert, that the very great number of islands, rocks, and reefs therein contained, are the whole that exist; nor that every individual one is correctly placed, although the greatest care was taken to obtain correctness. All the islands seem to be more or less frequented by seals; but I think not in numbers sufficient to make a speculation from Europe advisable on their account;

certainly not for the China market, the seals being mostly of the hair kind, and the fur of such others as were seen was red and coarse. There is, besides, a risk of being caught in the archipelago with strong south, or western winds, in which case destruction would be almost inevitable, for I know of no place where a ship might take refuge in a gale. The shelter in Thistle's Cove is, indeed, complete, when a vessel is once placed; but the cove is too small to be entered except under favourable circumstances, and the shelter in the western corner could not be attained with winds blowing strong out of it. The archipelago should not, therefore, be entered without the assurance of carrying fine weather to the proposed anchorage...

*19 January* ~ This afternoon we passed a number of pale red medusas, such as I had usually seen on the east coast at the entrances of rivers, and which, on being touched, produce a sensation like the stinging of a nettle. There was also a red scum on the water, and some of it was taken up to be examined by Mr Brown in a microscope. It consisted of minute particles not more than half a line in length, and each appeared to be composed of several cohering fibres which were jointed; the joints being of a uniform thickness, and nearly as broad as long. These fibres were generally of unequal length, and the extremities of the compound particle thence appeared somewhat torn. The particles exhibited no motion when in salt water; and the sole effect produced by immersing them in spirit of wine was the separation of each into its component fibres.

Until daybreak next morning the wind was unfavourable; but it then veered round to the south, and enabled us to pass Point Culver...

Our course along the shore was so favoured by the wind, that at seven in the evening we had passed another projecting part of the cliffs, named Point Dover, distant from Point Culver fifty miles; and the extreme in sight ahead was twenty miles further, and still cliffy. The nearest part was two or three leagues distant; and the wind being still at south, we hauled up to it, and at nine o'clock stood back to the westward.

The elevation of these cliffs appeared to be about five hundred feet, and nothing of the back country was seen above them. In the upper part they are brown, in the lower part nearly white, and the two strata, as also the small layers of which each is composed, are nearly horizontal.[†] They were judged to be calcareous, as was the white, grey and brown sand which the lead brought up when the bottom was not of coral.

A surveyor finds almost no object here whose bearing can be set a second time. Each small projection presents the appearance of a steep cape, as it opens out in sailing along; but before the ship arrives abreast of it, it is lost in the general uniformity of the coast, and the latitude, longitude, and distance of the nearest cliffs, are all the documents that remain for the construction of a chart. Point Culver and Point Dover are exceptions to this general uniformity; but it requires a ship to be near the land before even these are distinguishable. The latter point was somewhat whiter than the cliffs on each side, which probably arose from the front having lately fallen off into the water...

*22 January* ~ At the end of three days beating, our latitude in the evening of the 22nd was 32° 22', and longitude 126° 23'; the depth in that situation was 7 fathoms, at two miles from the land, and the furthest extremes visible through the haze, bore west-half-north and east, the latter being distant four or five miles. The bank which before formed the cliffs, had retired to a little distance from the coast, and left a front screed of low, sandy shore. Several smokes arose from behind the bank, and were the first seen after quitting the archipelago...

*27 January* ~ The length of these cliffs, from their second commencement, is thirty-three leagues; and that of the level bank, from near Cape Pasley where it was first seen from the sea, is no

[†] The Nullarbor cliffs.

less than one hundred and forty-five leagues. The height of this extraordinary bank is nearly the same throughout, being nowhere less, by estimation, than four hundred, nor anywhere more than six hundred feet. In the first twenty leagues the ragged tops of some inland mountains were visible over it; but during the remainder of its long course the bank was the limit of our view.

This equality of elevation for so great an extent, and the evidently calcareous nature of the bank, at least in the upper two hundred feet, would bespeak it to have been the exterior line of a vast coral reef, which is always more elevated than the interior parts, and commonly level with high water mark. From the gradual subsiding of the sea, or perhaps by a sudden convulsion of nature, this bank may have attained its present height above the surface; and however extraordinary such a change may appear, yet, when it is recollected that branches of coral still exist upon Bald Head, at the elevation of four hundred or more feet, this supposition assumes a great degree of probability; and it would further seem, that the subsiding of the waters has not been at a period very remote, since these frail branches have yet neither been all beaten down nor mouldered away by the wind and weather.

If this supposition be well founded, it may, with the fact of no hill or other object having been perceived above the bank in the greater part of its course, assist in forming some conjecture of what may be within it; which cannot, as I judge in such case, be other than flat, sandy plains, or water. The bank may even be a narrow barrier between an interior, and the exterior sea, and much do I regret not having formed an idea of this probability at the time; for notwithstanding the great difficulty and risk, I should certainly have attempted a landing upon some part of the coast, to ascertain a fact of so much importance...

After steering east-north-east, east, and east-south-east, and having seen the beach all round the head of the Great Bight, we hauled up parallel to the new direction of the coast, at the distance of six miles; and at five o'clock were abreast of the furthest part

seen by the French admiral when he quitted the examination. The
coast is a sandy beach in front; but the land rises gradually from
thence, and at three or four miles back is of moderate elevation,
but still sandy and barren...

*28 January* ~ The aspect of the shore to the northward was
nearly the same as that seen the preceding afternoon, but behind
the second reefs it began to assume a more rocky appearance. A
high cliffy cape is formed a little further eastward, answering to the
broad projection marked *A* in the copy I have given of the Dutch
chart; it has a pyramidal rock near it, and the coast there takes a
direction somewhat on the north side of east. This remarkable
projection, being within a few leagues of the furthest part of the
main coast discovered by the Dutch, I have called Cape Nuyts: its
latitude is 32° 2' south, and longitude 132° 18' east.

After clearing Nuyts' Reefs we steered east-north-east, past the
cape, to look for anchorage in two bights; but there were rocks in
both, and they were open to the southward. Beyond them was a
low, cliffy point, lying E3°N seven or eight miles from Cape Nuyts;
and seeing a bay behind it which promised shelter from south-west
and south winds, we hauled round the point at half past five...

The bay in which we anchored on the evening of 28 January, at
the extremity of the before known south coast of Terra Australis,
was named Fowler's Bay, after my first Lieutenant; and the low,
cliffy point which shelters it from southern winds and, not improbably, is the furthest point (marked *B*) in the Dutch chart, was
called Point Fowler. The botanical gentlemen landed early on the
following morning to examine the productions of the country, and
I went on shore to take observations and bearings, and to search
for fresh water.

The cliffs and rocks of Point Fowler are calcareous, and connected with the mainland by a low, sandy isthmus of half a mile
broad. Many traces of inhabitants were found, and amongst others,
some decayed spears; but no huts were seen, nor anything to indicate that men had been here lately. Upon the beach were the

footmarks of dogs, and some of the emu or cassowary. I found in a hole of the low cliffs one of those large nests which have before been mentioned, but it contained nothing, and had been long abandoned.

No fresh water was discovered round the shores of the bay, nor was there any wood large enough for fuel, nearer than the brow of a hill two or three miles off. Two teal were shot on the beach, whence it seemed probable that some lake or pond of fresh water was not far distant; a sea pie and a gull were also shot, and a few small fish caught alongside. These constituted everything like refreshment obtained here, and the botanists found the scantiness of plants equal to that of the other productions; so that there was no inducement to remain longer.

Fowler's Bay, however, may be useful to a ship in want of a place of shelter. It is open only to the three points of the compass between south-east-by-south and east-south-east; and it was evident from plants growing close to the water side, that a swell capable of injuring a vessel at anchor was seldom, if ever thrown into it...

*2 February* ~ At noon of the 2nd, no land was in sight. The weather was still hazy, and the wind at south-east; but in the afternoon it favoured us two points, and we got sight of a higher and larger island than any before seen on this part of the coast. At half past four, being then near a smaller isle and several rocks, we tacked towards the large island which was six or seven miles to the southward; and soon after eight in the evening, got to an anchor in a little sandy bay on its north side. The depth was 6 fathoms in passing the north-west point of the bay, but 10 within side, on a fine sandy bottom, where the anchor was dropped...

*3 February* ~ This island is the central one of a group; for besides the four small isles to the north-east, there are two close to the west end, and two others, something larger, lying off to the southward. I call these the Isles of St Francis; in the persuasion that the central one is that named St Francis by Nuyts...

For several days before anchoring here, we had observed large

flocks of sooty petrels; and I found the surface of the island, where
it was sandy and produced small shrubs, to be full of their burrows.
Penguins, similar to those of Furneaux's Islands, had their burrows
nearer to the water side. A small species of kangaroo was also
found, and at some preceding season the island had been frequented by geese; but at this time, the vegetation being almost
burnt up, they seemed to have quitted it from want of food. The
heat was, indeed, such as to make walking a great fatigue; and this
was augmented by frequently sinking into the bird holes, and falling
upon the sand. The thermometer stood at 98° in the shade, whilst
it was at 78° on board the ship...

A party was sent on shore at dusk to collect petrels, and in less
than two hours returned with sufficient to give four birds to every
man in the ship. Early in the morning, the boats were again sent
upon the same errand, and to haul the seine; but the birds were
gone off to sea for the day, and no fish were caught. A small kangaroo was brought off, as also a yellow snake, which was the second
killed on this island. The great heat deterred the naturalists from
going on shore this morning, for the very little variety in the
vegetable productions presented no inducement to a repetition of
their fatigue. I landed to see what further could be discovered
of the neighbouring islands; and we then prepared to get under
way so soon as the breeze set in from the south-eastward, which it
usually did about noon, after a few hours of calm or of light airs.

The small bay in the Isle St Francis, which I call Petrel Bay,
affords excellent shelter for two or three ships; but no fresh water,
not even to rinse our mouths, could be found at this time; and a
few scattered bushes were the nearest approach to wood upon the
island. Petrels, penguins and a few hair seals may be procured, and
probably some geese in the wet season...

*5 February* ~ The wind was north-east in the morning; and at
half past four o'clock we filled the sails and steered eastward until
eight, when the central island of St Francis bore N71°W, and
Franklin's Isles, for there are two, besides rocks, were distant four

leagues, the small opening between them bearing N28°W. To the
south-eastward of these islands, at the distance of eleven miles, is
a low projection of the mainland, to which the name of Point
Brown was given, in compliment to the naturalist; and four leagues
further, in the same line, was a cliffy head, called Cape Bauer after
the painter of natural history. Between these projections there was
a wide space where no land was visible, and for which we accordingly steered on the wind veering more to the northward. The
atmosphere was still hazy, more especially about the horizon, and
no observations worthy of confidence could be taken for either latitude or longitude...

No land was yet visible ahead; and there being much refuse
from the shore, as well as seaweed floating about, some hopes of
finding a river were entertained. At half past two, however, low,
sandy land was seen from the masthead, nearly all round, the depth
had diminished from 19 to 7 fathoms, and the water was much
discoloured in streaks, at less than a mile from the ship. Smokes
were rising in three different places; but as the wind was unfavourable, and there was no prospect of any opening sufficiently large
to admit the *Investigator*, I gave up the further examination of this
place, and called it Streaky Bay...

*6 February* ~ All sail was made to fetch between Franklin's Isles
and Point Brown, in order to follow the course of the mainland as
close as possible; but finding, after several tacks, the impossibility of
weathering the isles, we bore away; and at noon hauled up
north-north-east, round them. The wind was light at east, and the
weather fine overhead; but there was so dense a haze below, that the
true horizon could not be distinguished from several false ones, and
we had six or seven different latitudes from as many observers: those
taken by me to the north and south, differed 19 minutes. This dense
haze, from its great refractive power, altered the appearance of
objects in a surprising manner: a sandy beach seemed to be a chalky
cliff, and the lowest islands to have steep shores. The thermometer
stood, at this time, at 82°, and the barometer at 29.60 inches.

On the north side of Point Brown the shore formed a large open
bay, into which we hauled up as much as the wind would permit,
passing near to a reef of rocks and breakers, two miles to the
north-north-east of Franklin's Isles. At half past two, the water had
shoaled to 5 fathoms; and not being able to distinguish any inlet,
we then bore away westward along the land. The number of
smokes rising from the shores of this wide, open place, induced me
to give it the name of Smoky Bay.

At four o'clock we passed the small opening which had been
unsuccessfully attempted in the evening of the 4th, and hauled up
northward under the lee of the island forming its western side. The
mainland then came in sight ahead; but between it and the islands
was a space five or six miles wide, which had the appearance of
being the entrance to a river. No land was visible to the north-east;
and besides quantities of grass and branches of trees or bushes
floating in the water, there was a number of long, gauze-winged
insects topping about the surface, such as frequent fresh-water lakes
and swamps. In order to form a judgment of how much fresh was
mixed with the salt water, or whether any, I had some taken up for
the purpose of ascertaining its specific gravity; but before the
experiment could be made, the depth diminished to 3 fathoms, and
low land was distinguished nearly all round. We then veered ship;
and at seven o'clock came to an anchor in 6 fathoms, off a small
beach on the north side of the western and smallest island, being
sheltered at all points except between S58° and N80°W…

*7 February* ~ Great flocks of sooty petrels were observed coming
in from sea to the island, and at the first dawn next morning, a
boat was sent to collect a quantity of them, and to kill seals; but
the birds were already moving off, and no more than four seals, of
the hair kind, were procured. The botanists preferred going on
shore to the more eastern land, which, though low, was much
more extensive than the island nearer to the ship; and in fact, it
was not yet ascertained whether it were not a part of the main. I
went to the higher island with a theodolite to take bearings; and

as the survey had shown that no dependence was to be placed in
any observations taken on board the ship during the last five days,
I took with me the necessary instruments for determining the
latitude and longitude.

Granite was found to compose the rocks of the shore, and
seemed to be the basis of the island; but it was covered with a crust
of calcareous stone, in some places fifty feet thick. The soil at the
top was little better than sand, but was overspread with shrubs,
mostly of one kind, a whitish velvety plant, nearly similar to what is
called at Port Jackson, Botany-Bay greens. Amongst these, the
petrels had everywhere undermined; and from the excessive heat
of the sun, the reflexion from the sand, and frequently stepping up
to the mid-leg in the burrows, my strength was scarcely equal to
reaching the highest hill near the middle of the island. I had no
thermometer, but judged the temperature could scarcely be less
than 120°; and there was not a breath of air stirring. My fatigue
was, however, rewarded by an extensive set of bearings, and I over-
looked the lower and larger island to the eastward, and saw the
water behind it communicating with Smoky Bay. That low land
and the island upon which I stood, being the north-easternmost of
this archipelago, must I conceive, be the Isles of St Peter in Nuyts'
chart; notwithstanding their relatively small distance from those of
St Francis. The bay to the northward, between these islands and
the mainland, I named Denial Bay, as well in allusion to St Peter
as to the deceptive hope we had formed, of penetrating by it some
distance into the interior country...

On returning to the shore to complete my observations, a flock
of teal presented themselves, and four were shot. There were also
pied shags, and gulls of three species; and in the island were seen
many crows, a green parakeet and two smaller birds. A black
snake, of the common size, was killed, but its form did not bespeak
it to be venomous. After observing the sun's altitude at noon, I returned on board with the intention of getting the ship under way,
to examine more closely a bight in the coast near Point Bell; and

then of returning to Petrel Bay in the Isle St Francis, in order to obtain better observations for a base to my chart of this archipelago. At two o'clock, Mr Brown and his party returned from the eastern island, bringing four kangaroos, of a different species to any before seen. Their size was not superior to that of a hare, and they were miserably thin, and infested with insects...

The anchor was weighed on the return of the botanists, and we steered westward past the small island named Lound's, and as far as Purdie's Isles; when, having seen the whole line of the coast behind them, we hauled to the southward at six o'clock, for Petrel Bay; and at one in the morning came to, in 13 fathoms, near our former anchorage.

It was here confirmed by satisfactory observations on shore, that our former latitudes and longitudes taken on board the ship were erroneous; and the consequent necessity of reconstructing my chart of these islands, induced me to remain at anchor the rest of the day. A boat was sent to fish with hook and line, and had some success; and at dusk a sufficient number of sooty petrels were taken from the burrows to give nine to every man; making, with those before caught, more than twelve hundred birds. These were inferior to the teal shot at the western Isle of St Peter, and by most persons would be thought not eatable, on account of their fishy taste; but they made a very acceptable supply to men who had been many months confined to an allowance of salt meat...

*11 February* ~ The press of sail carried in the night had so much stretched the rigging, that it required to be set up, fore and aft. Whilst this was doing on board, the naturalists landed upon the island [part of Waldegrave's Isles]; where I also went to take bearings with a theodolite, and observations for the latitude and longitude...These islands form the southern boundary, as Cape Radstock does the north point of a great open bay, which, from the night we passed in it, obtained the name of Anxious Bay...Crows of a shining, black colour were numerous; and in two which I shot, the bill was surrounded at the base with small feathers, extending

one-fourth of the length towards the extremity. There were no
appearances of the island having been before visited either by
Europeans or Indians, and a single rat was the sole quadruped
seen; but a few hair seals were killed upon the shore. Mr Brown
remarked, that this was the first island where not a single novelty
in natural history had presented itself to his observation...

*13 February* ~ In the morning, we were surprised to see breaking water about one mile from the ship, and as much from the
shore. It was not far from the place where the last tack had been
made in the evening, and the master found no more than six feet
water close to it; so that we were fortunate in having escaped. The
botanical gentlemen landed early; and I followed them to make the
usual observations for the survey...

Another island, about one mile long and of moderate height,
was discovered bearing S72°W, about four leagues. It was
surrounded with high breakers, as was a smaller isle near it; and
the two were called Ward's Isles. These three small clusters, with
Waldegrave's Isles, and this larger island, which was named
Flinders', after the second Lieutenant, form a group distinct from
Nuyts' Archipelago; and I gave it the name of the Investigator's
Group.

The form of Flinders' Island is nearly a square, of which each
side is from three to five miles in length. Bights are formed in the
four sides; but that to the north seems alone to afford good anchorage. In its composition this island is nearly the same as that of
Waldegrave's largest isle...The vegetation differed from that of
other islands before visited, in that the lower lands were covered
with large bushes; and there was very little, either of the white,
velvety shrub (*atriplex*), or of the tufted, wiry grass. A small species
of kangaroo, not bigger than a cat, was rather numerous. I shot
five of them, and some others were killed by the botanists and their
attendants, and found to be in tolerably good condition. We were
now beginning to want a supply of water, and the northern part of
the island was sought over carefully for it; but the nearest approach

to success was in finding dried-up swamps, in which the growing
plants were tinged red, as if the water had been brackish. No other
trees than a few small *casuarinas* at a distance from the anchorage,
were seen upon the island; but wood for fuel might with some difficulty be picked out from the larger bushes growing near the shore.
The beaches were frequented by seals of the hair kind. A family of
them consisting of a male, four or five females, and as many cubs,
was lying asleep at every two or three hundred yards. Their security was such, that I approached several of these families very
closely; and retired without disturbing their domestic tranquillity,
or being perceived by them...

*16 February* ~ At daylight, Point Drummond was seven miles
distant to the north-by-east. The shore, after falling back four or
five miles from it, trended southward; but there was other land
further out, and we steered for the opening between them, passing
a rocky islet five miles from Point Drummond and nearly as much
from the eastern shore. At eight o'clock we found ourselves in a
bay, whose width, from the outer western point of entrance, named
Point Sir Isaac, to the shore on the east side, was near three
leagues...

The basis of the point seemed to be granitic, with an upper
stratum of calcareous rock, much similar to the neighbouring isles
of the Investigator's Group. Its elevation is inconsiderable, and the
surface is sandy and barren, as is all the land near it on the same
side. The large piece of water which it shelters from western winds,
I named Coffin's Bay, in compliment to the present vice-admiral Sir
Isaac Coffin, Bart.; who, when resident commissioner at Sheerness,
had taken so zealous a part in the outfit of the *Investigator*.

Many smokes were seen round Coffin's Bay, and also two parties
of natives, one on each side; these shores were therefore better
inhabited than the more western parts of the south coast; indeed
it has usually been found in this country, that the borders of
shallow bays and lagoons, and at the entrances of rivers, are by far
the most numerously peopled. These natives were black and naked,

differing in nothing that we could perceive from those of King
George's Sound before described.

*20 February* ~ A tide from the north-eastward, apparently the
ebb, ran more than one mile an hour; which was the more remarkable from no set of tide, worthy to be noticed, having hitherto been
observed upon this coast. No land could be seen in the direction
from whence it came; and these circumstances, with the trending
of the coast to the north, did not fail to excite many conjectures.
Large rivers, deep inlets, inland seas, and passages into the Gulf of
Carpentaria, were terms frequently used in our conversations of
this evening; and the prospect of making an interesting discovery
seemed to have infused new life and vigour into every man in
the ship.

*21 February* ~ Early in the morning, I went on shore to the
eastern land, anxious to ascertain its connection with, or separation from the main. There were seals upon the beach and, further
on, numberless traces of the kangaroo. Signs of extinguished fire
existed everywhere; but they bespoke a conflagration of the woods,
of remote date, rather than the habitual presence of men, and
might have arisen from lightning, or from the friction of two trees
in a strong wind. Upon the whole, I satisfied myself of the insu-
larity of this land; and gave to it, shortly after, the name of Thistle's
Island, from the master who accompanied me. In our way up the
hills, to take a commanding station for the survey, a speckled,
yellow snake lay asleep before us. By pressing the butt end of a
musket upon his neck, I kept him down whilst Mr Thistle, with a
sail needle and twine, sewed up his mouth; and he was taken on
board alive, for the naturalist to examine; but two others of the
same species had already been killed, and one of them was seven
feet nine inches in length. We were proceeding onward with our
prize, when a white eagle, with fierce aspect and outspread wing,
was seen bounding towards us; but stopping short, at twenty yards
off, he flew up into a tree. Another bird of the same kind discovered himself by making a motion to pounce down upon us as we

passed underneath; and it seemed evident that they took us for
kangaroos, having probably never before seen an upright animal
in the island, of any other species. These birds sit watching in the
trees, and should a kangaroo come out to feed in the daytime, it is
seized and torn to pieces by these voracious creatures. This
accounted for why so few kangaroos were seen, when traces of
them were met with at every step; and for their keeping so much
under thick bushes that it was impossible to shoot them. Their size
was superior to any of those found upon the more western islands,
but much inferior to the forest kangaroo of the continent...No
water could be found; and as the ship's hold was becoming very
empty, I returned on board, after observing the latitude, with the
intention of running over to the main in search of it. But on
comparing the longitude observed by Lieutenant Flinders with that
resulting from my bearings, a difference was found which made it
necessary to repeat the observation on shore; and as this would
prolong the time too near dusk for moving the ship, Mr Thistle was
sent over with a cutter to the mainland, in search of an anchoring
place where water might be procured...

At dusk in the evening, the cutter was seen under sail; returning from the mainland; but not arriving in half an hour, and
the sight of it having been lost rather suddenly, a light was
shown and Lieutenant Fowler went in a boat, with a lanthorn,
to see what might have happened. Two hours passed without
receiving any tidings. A gun was then fired, and Mr Fowler
returned soon afterward, but alone. Near the situation where
the cutter had been last seen, he met with so strong a rippling
of tide that he himself narrowly escaped being upset; and there
was reason to fear that it had actually happened to Mr Thistle.
Had there been daylight, it is probable that some or all of the
people might have been picked up; but it was too dark to see
anything, and no answer could be heard to the hallooing, or to
the firing of muskets. The tide was setting to the southward and
ran an hour and a half after the missing boat had been last

seen, so that it would be carried to seaward in the first instance; and no more than two out of the eight people being at all expert in swimming, it was much to be feared that most of them would be lost.*

*22 February* ~...A boat was despatched in search of the lost cutter, and presently returned towing in the wreck, bottom upward; it was stove in every part, having to all appearance been dashed against the rocks. One of the oars was afterwards found, but nothing could be seen of our unfortunate shipmates. The boat was again sent away in search; and a midshipman was stationed upon a headland, without-side of the cove, to observe everything which might drift past with the tide. Mr Brown and a party landed to walk along the shore to the northward, whilst I proceeded to the southern extremity of the mainland, which was now named Cape Catastrophe. On landing at the head of the cove, I found several footmarks of our people, made on the preceding afternoon when looking for water; and in my way up the valley I prosecuted the same research, but ineffectually,

* This evening, Mr Fowler told me a circumstance which I thought extraordinary; and it afterwards proved to be more so. Whilst we were lying at Spithead, Mr Thistle was one day waiting on shore, and having nothing else to do he went to a certain old man, named Pine, to have his fortune told. The cunning man informed him that he was going out a long voyage, and that the ship, on arriving at her destination, would be joined by another vessel. That such was intended, he might have learned privately; but he added, that Mr Thistle would be lost before the other vessel joined. As to the manner of his loss the magician refused to give any information. My boat's crew, hearing what Mr Thistle said, went also to consult the wise man; and after the prefatory information of a long voyage, were told that they would be shipwrecked, but not in the ship they were going out in: whether they would escape and return to England, he was not permitted to reveal.

This tale Mr Thistle had often told at the mess table; and I remarked with some pain in a future part of the voyage, that every time my boat's crew went to embark with me in the *Lady Nelson*, there was some degree of apprehension amongst them that the time of the predicted shipwreck was arrived. I make no comment upon this story, but recommend a commander, if possible, to prevent any of his crew from consulting fortune tellers.

although there were many huts and other signs that natives had resided there lately.

From the heights near the extremity of Cape Catastrophe, I examined with a glass the islands lying off, and all the neighbouring shores for any appearance of our people, but in vain; I therefore took a set of angles for the survey, and returned on board; and on comparing notes with the different parties, it appeared that no further information had been obtained of our unfortunate companions.

Next morning I went in a boat ten miles along the shore to the northward, in the double view of continuing the search, and carrying on the survey. All the little sinuosities of the coast were followed, and in one place I picked up a small keg, which had belonged to Mr Thistle, and also some broken pieces of the boat; but these were all that could be discovered...

*24 February* ~ This morning Lieutenant Fowler had been sent to search the southern islands in Thorny Passage for any remains of our people; but he was not able to land, nor in rowing round them, to see any indication of the objects of his pursuit. The recovery of their bodies was now the furthest to which our hopes extended; but the number of sharks seen in the cove and at the last anchorage, rendered even this prospect of melancholy satisfaction extremely doubtful; and our want of water becoming every day more pressing, we prepared to depart for the examination of the new opening to the northward. I caused an inscription to be engraven upon a sheet of copper, and set up on a stout post at the head of the cove, which I named Memory Cove; and further to commemorate our loss, I gave to each of the six islands nearest to Cape Catastrophe the name of one of the seamen. Thistle's and Taylor's Islands have been already mentioned. Mr Westall's view from the ship in Memory Cove, represents Thistle's Island and three of the small isles in front of it.

The reader will pardon me the observation that Mr Thistle was truly a valuable man, as a seaman, an officer, and a good member of society. I had known him, and we had mostly served together, from the year 1794. He had been with Mr Bass in his perilous expedition in the whaleboat, and with me in the voyage round Van Diemen's Land, and in the succeeding expedition, to Glass-house and Hervey's bays. From his merit and prudent conduct, he was promoted from before the mast to be a midshipman, and afterwards a master in His Majesty's service. His zeal for discovery had induced him to join the *Investigator* when at Spithead and ready to sail, although he had returned to England only three weeks before, after an absence of six years. Besides performing assiduously the duties of his situation, Mr Thistle had made himself well acquainted with the practice of nautical astronomy, and began to be very useful in the surveying department. His loss was severely felt by me; and he was lamented by all on board, more especially by his mess-mates, who knew more intimately the goodness and stability of his disposition.

Mr William Taylor, the midshipman of the boat, was a young officer who promised fair to become an ornament to the service, as he was to society by the amiability of his manners and temper. The six seamen had all volunteered for the voyage. They were active and useful young men; and in a small and incomplete ship's company, which had so many duties to perform, this diminution of our force was heavily felt...

*26 February* ~ Three small isles had been seen from Thistle's Island and their bearings set; and the discovery of them was now augmented by several others, forming a cluster to the eastward of Point Bolingbroke. This was called Sir Joseph Banks Group, in compliment to the Right Honourable President of the Royal Society, to whose exertion and favour the voyage was so much indebted...

The port which formed the most interesting part of these discoveries I named Port Lincoln, in honour of my native province; and having gained a general knowledge of it and finished the bearings, we descended the hill and got on board at ten o'clock. The boat had returned from Boston Island, unsuccessful in her search for water; and we therefore proceeded upward, steering different courses to find the greatest depth…

Fresh water being at this time the most pressing of our wants, I set off the same afternoon, with a party, to examine the lake or mere discovered from Stamford Hill…After walking two miles we reached the lake, but to our mortification, the water was brackish, and not drinkable: the distance, besides, from Port Lincoln was too great to roll casks over a stony road. This piece of water was named Sleaford Mere. It is one mile broad, and appeared to be three or four in length. The shore was a whitish, hardened clay, covered at this time with a thin crust, in which salt was a component part. The sun being too near the horizon to admit of going round the mere, our way was bent towards the ship; and finding a moist place within a hundred yards of the head of the port, I caused a hole to be dug there. A stratum of whitish clay was found at three feet below the surface, and on penetrating this, water drained in, which was perfectly sweet, though discoloured; and we had the satisfaction to return on board with the certainty of being able to procure water, although it would probably require some time to fill all our empty casks.

*27 February* ~…Before the evening, the observations for the rates of the time keepers were commenced; and the gunner was installed in the command of a watering party, and furnished with axes to cut wood at such times as the pits might require to be left for replenishing.

The necessary duties being all set forward under the superintendence of proper officers, I employed the following days in surveying and sounding…Having left orders on board the ship to fire three guns at given times, I went to the south-east end of Boston Island, with a pendulum made to swing half seconds. It was a musket ball slung with twine, and measured 9.8 inches, from the fixed end of the twine to the centre of the ball. From the instant that the flash of the first gun was perceived, to the time of hearing

the report, I counted eighty-five vibrations of the pendulum, and
the same with two succeeding guns; whence the length of the base
was deduced to be 8.01 geographic miles...*

Amongst the various excursions made by the scientific gentlemen, one was directed to Sleaford Mere, of which they made the
circuit. The two southern branches were found to terminate within
a hundred yards of the head of Sleaford Bay, with which the mere
had been suspected to have a communication from its water being
not quite fresh; but they are separated by a stony bank too high for
the surf ever to pass over it. At the head of the bay a boat's sail and
yard were seen floating, and no doubt had belonged to our unfortunate cutter: after being set out to sea by the tide, it had been
driven up there by the late south-east winds.

The refitment of the ship being nearly completed on the 3rd of
March, Lieutenant Fowler was sent round to Memory Cove in a
boat, to make a final search along the shores and round the islands
in Thorny Passage, for the bodies of our late shipmates, which the
sea might have thrown up. On the 4th, the last turn of water was
received, and completed our stock up to sixty tons; and the removal
of our establishment from the shore waited only for the observation of a solar eclipse, announced in the nautical ephemeris for this
day. The morning was cloudy, with rain; but towards noon the
weather cleared up, and I had the satisfaction to observe the eclipse
with a refracting telescope of forty-six inches focus, and a power of
about two hundred...

*4 March* ~ Many straggling bark huts, similar to those on other
parts of the coast, were seen upon the shores of Port Lincoln, and
the paths near our tents had been long and deeply trodden; but
neither in my excursions nor in those of the botanists had any of
the natives been discovered. This morning, however, three or four
were heard calling to a boat, as was supposed, which had just

* This length was founded on the supposition that sound travels at the rate of
1142 feet in a second of time, and that 6060 feet make a geographic mile.

landed; but they presently walked away, or perhaps retired into the wood to observe our movements. No attempt was made to follow them, for I had always found the natives of this country to avoid those who seemed anxious for communication; whereas, when left entirely alone, they would usually come down after having watched us for a few days.

Nor does this conduct seem to be unnatural; for what, in such case, would be the conduct of any people, ourselves for instance, were we living in a state of nature, frequently at war with our neighbours, and ignorant of the existence of any other nation? On the arrival of strangers, so different in complexion and appearance to ourselves, having power to transport themselves over, and even living upon an element which to us was impassable; the first sensation would probably be terror, and the first move-ment flight. We should watch these extraordinary people from our retreats in the woods and rocks, and if we found ourselves sought and pursued by them, should conclude their designs to be inimi-cal; but if, on the contrary, we saw them quietly employed in occupations which had no reference to us, curiosity would get the better of fear and, after observing them more closely, we should ourselves seek a communication.

Such seemed to have been the conduct of these Australians; and I am persuaded that their appearance on the morning when the tents were struck, was a prelude to their coming down; and that had we remained a few days longer, a friendly communication would have ensued. The way was, however, prepared for the next ship which may enter this port, as it was to us in King George's Sound by Captain Vancouver and the ship *Elligood*; to whose pre-vious visits and peaceable conduct we were most probably indebted for our early intercourse with the inhabitants of that place. So far as could be perceived with a glass, the natives of this port were the same in personal appearance as those of King George's Sound and Port Jackson. In the hope of conciliating their goodwill to succeed-ing visitors, some hatchets and various other articles were left in their paths, or fastened to stumps of the trees which had been cut down near our watering pits.

In expressing an opinion that these people have no means of passing the water, it must be understood to be a deduction from our having met with no canoe, or the remains of any about the port; nor with any tree in the woods from which a sufficient size of bark had been taken to make one. Upon Boston Island, however, there were abundant marks of fire; but they had the appearance, as at Thistle's Island, of having been caused by some conflagration of the woods several years before, rather than of being the small fireplaces of the natives...

Behind the beach, near our watering pits, the calcareous stone was so imperfectly formed, that small shells and bits of coral might be picked out of it. This fact, with the saltness of Sleaford Mere and of a small lake on the south side of the port, accords with the coral found upon Bald Head and various other indications before mentioned, to show that this part, at least, of Terra Australis cannot have emerged very many centuries from the sea; the salt imbibed by the rocks having not yet been all washed away by the rains. In the mountains behind Port Jackson, on the east coast, at a vastly superior elevation, salt is formed in some places by the exhalation of the water which drips from the grit-stone cliffs.

Port Lincoln is certainly a fine harbour; and it is much to be regretted that it possesses no constant run of fresh water, unless it should be in Spalding Cove, which we did not examine. Our pits at the head of the port will, however, supply ships at all times; and though discoloured by whitish clay, the water has no pernicious quality, nor is it ill tasted. This and wood, which was easily procured, were all that we found of use to ships; and for the establishment of a colony, which the excellence of the port might seem to invite, the little fertility of the soil offers no inducement...

On the 18th in the morning, we fetched to windward of the island-like point, to which I gave the name of Point Pearce, in compliment to Mr Pearce of the Admiralty. Its latitude is 34° 28½'

south, and longitude 137° 21' east…At sunset, the land was seen
as far as south-west-by-south; and the wind favouring us a little, we
made a stretch for it. A fire upon the shore served as a mark to steer
by; and on approaching it at ten o'clock, the anchor was let go in
6 fathoms, upon a bottom of coarse sand and small stones; the
weather being fine, and wind moderate off the land.

The howling of dogs was heard during the night; and at
daylight the shore was found to be distant two or three miles, and
was woody, rising land, but not of much elevation…

*20 March* ~ The tide appeared to set us along the shore to the
southward, although, from what was observed at Thistle's Island,
it should have been the time of flood. With its assistance, and the
wind having become less unfavourable, we were enabled to make
a course for the furthest land. This proved to be a cape, composed
of three cliffy points, near the northern part of which lay a cluster
of black rocks. The southernmost cliff bore at noon E4½°S six or
seven miles, and beyond it there was no main coast visible; but
three small islands, with several rocks and a reef, were seen to lie
as far as five miles to the southward, out from the cape.

Although the continuation of the main coast was not to be
distinguished beyond the cape, yet there was land in sight at the
distance of seven or eight leagues, from about south to S18½°W.
Whether this land were an island, or a part of the continent, and
the wide opening to the eastward a strait, or a new inlet, was uncertain; but in either case, the investigation of the gulf was terminated;
and in honour of the respectable nobleman who presided at the
Board of Admiralty when the voyage was planned and ship put
into commission, I named it Spencer's Gulf. The cliffy-pointed
cape which forms the east side of the entrance, and lies in 35° 18'
south and 136° 55' east, was named Cape Spencer; and the three
isles lying off it, with their rocks, Allthorpe Isles.

A line drawn from the nearest part of Cape Catastrophe to
Cape Spencer will be forty-eight miles long, and so much is the
entrance of the gulf in width. Gambier's Isles lie not far from the

middle of the line; and if we measure upward from them, the gulf will be found, without regard to the small windings, to extend one hundred and eighty-five miles into the interior of the country. For the general exactness of its form in the chart, I can answer with tolerable confidence; having seen all that is laid down, and, as usual, taken every angle which enters into the construction. Throughout the whole extent of the shores the waterline was almost everywhere distinguished; the only exceptions being, small portions at the head of Hardwicke and Louth Bays, of a bight near Point Lowly, and of the low land at the back of the great Eastern Shoal.

*21 March ~* At ten o'clock we were close under the land; and finding the water tolerably smooth, had shortened sail with the intention of anchoring near a small, sandy beach; but the situation proving to be too much exposed, we steered eastward along the shore under two close-reefed top sails and fore sail, the wind blowing strong in squalls from the south-west. The furthest land seen ahead at noon, was a projecting point, lower than the other cliffs; it bore E7°S, four leagues, and lies in 35° 33' south, and 37° 41' east. It was named Point Marsden, in compliment to the second secretary of the Admiralty; and beyond it the coast was found to trend southward into a large bay containing three coves, any one of which promised good shelter from the gale. This was called Nepean Bay, in compliment to the first secretary (now sir Evan Nepean, Bart.), and we hauled up for it; but the strength of the wind was such, that a head land forming the east side of the bay was fetched with difficulty...

Neither smokes, nor other marks of inhabitants had as yet been perceived upon the southern land, although we had passed along seventy miles of its coast. It was too late to go on shore this evening; but every glass in the ship was pointed there, to see what could be discovered. Several black lumps, like rocks, were pretended to have been seen in motion by some of the young gentlemen, which caused the force of their imaginations to be much admired; next

morning, however, on going towards the shore, a number of dark-
brown kangaroos were seen feeding upon a grass plat by the side
of the wood; and our landing gave them no disturbance. I had
with me a double-barrelled gun, fitted with a bayonet, and the
gentlemen my companions had muskets. It would be difficult to
guess how many kangaroos were seen; but I killed ten, and the rest
of the party made up the number to thirty-one, taken on board in
the course of the day; the least of them weighing sixty-nine, and
the largest one hundred and twenty-five pounds. These kangaroos
had much resemblance to the large species found in the forest lands
of New South Wales; except that their colour was darker, and they
were not wholly destitute of fat.

After this butchery, for the poor animals suffered themselves to
be shot in the eyes with small shot, and in some cases to be knocked
on the head with sticks, I scrambled with difficulty through the
brush wood, and over fallen trees, to reach the higher land with the
surveying instruments; but the thickness and height of the wood
prevented anything else from being distinguished. There was little
doubt, however, that this extensive piece of land was separated
from the continent; for the extraordinary tameness of the kangaroos and the presence of seals upon the shore, concurred with the
absence of all traces of men to show that it was not inhabited.

The whole ship's company was employed this afternoon, in
skinning and cleaning the kangaroos; and a delightful regale they
afforded, after four months privation from almost any fresh provisions. Half a hundred weight of heads, fore-quarters, and tails
were stewed down into soup for dinner on this and the succeeding
days; and as much steaks given, moreover, to both officers and men,
as they could consume by day and by night. In gratitude for so
seasonable a supply, I named this southern land Kangaroo Island.

*23 March* ~ Next day was employed in shifting the top masts, on
account of some rents found in the heels. The scientific gentlemen
landed again to examine the natural productions of the island, and
in the evening eleven more kangaroos were brought on board; but

most of these were smaller, and seemed to be of a different species
to those of the preceding day. Some of the party saw several large
running birds, which, according to their description, seemed to
have been the emu or cassowary...

A thick wood covered almost all that part of the island visible
from the ship; but the trees in a vegetating state were not equal in
size to the generality of those lying on the ground, nor to the dead
trees standing upright. Those on the ground were so abundant, that
in ascending the higher land, a considerable part of the walk was
made upon them. They lay in all directions, and were nearly of the
same size and in the same progress towards decay; from whence it
would seem that they had not fallen from age, nor yet been thrown
down in a gale of wind. Some general conflagration, and there
were marks apparently of fire on many of them, is perhaps the sole
cause which can be reasonably assigned; but whence came the
woods on fire? That there were no inhabitants upon the island, and
that the natives of the continent did not visit it, was demonstrated,
if not by the want of all signs of such visit, yet by the tameness of
the kangaroo, an animal which, on the continent, resembles the
wild deer in timidity. Perhaps lightning might have been the cause,
or possibly the friction of two dead trees in a strong wind; but it
would be somewhat extraordinary that the same thing should have
happened at Thistle's Island, Boston Island, and at this place, and
apparently about the same time. Can this part of Terra Australis
have been visited before, unknown to the world? The French navigator, La Pérouse, was ordered to explore it, but there seems little
probability that he ever passed Torres' Strait.

Some judgment may be formed of the epoch when these con-
flagrations happened, from the magnitude of the growing trees; for
they must have sprung up since that period. They were a species of
eucalyptus, and being less than the fallen trees, had most probably
not arrived at maturity; but the wood is hard and solid, and it may
thence be supposed to grow slowly. With these considerations,
I should be inclined to fix the period at not less than ten, nor more

than twenty years before our arrival. This brings us back to La
Pérouse. He was in Botany Bay in the beginning of 1788; and if he
did pass through Torres' Strait, and come round to this coast, as
was his intention, it would probably be about the middle or latter
end of that year, or between thirteen and fourteen years before the
*Investigator*. My opinion is not favourable to this conjecture; but I
have furnished all the data to enable the reader to form his own
judgment upon the cause which might have prostrated the woods
of these islands.

The soil of that part of Kangaroo Island examined by us, was
judged to be much superior to any before seen, either upon the
south coast of the continent, or upon the islands near it; with the
exception of some portions behind the harbours of King George's
Sound. The depth of the soil was not particularly ascertained; but
from the thickness of the wood it cannot be very shallow. Some sand
is mixed with the vegetable earth, but not in any great proportion;
and I thought the soil superior to some of the land cultivated at Port
Jackson, and to much of that in our stony counties in England.

Never perhaps had the dominion possessed here by the kangaroo been invaded before this time. The seal shared with it upon the
shores, but they seemed to dwell amicably together. It not unfrequently happened, that the report of a gun fired at a kangaroo near
the beach, brought out two or three bellowing seals from under
bushes considerably further from the water side. The seal, indeed,
seemed to be much the most discerning animal of the two; for its
actions bespoke a knowledge of our not being kangaroos, whereas
the kangaroo not unfrequently appeared to consider us to be seals.

*24 March* ~ In the morning, we got under way from Kangaroo
Island, in order to take up the examination of the main coast at
Cape Spencer, where it had been quitted in the evening of the
20th, when the late gale commenced.

*27 March* ~...Many tacks were made in these two days, from the
northern land across to Kangaroo Island...Of the two sides, that
of Kangaroo Island is much the deepest; but there is no danger in

any part to prevent a ship passing through the strait with perfect confidence; and the average width is twenty-three miles. It was named Investigator's Strait, after the ship...

No set of tide was observable until three o'clock, when it made gently to the north-east, towards the new inlet; and a breeze springing up at south-east soon afterward, we pursued the same course, and were well within the entrance at eight o'clock. Fires were seen ahead; but the soundings being regular, and increasing, we kept on until midnight; when the land was seen also, and we stood back for two hours. At daylight I recognised Mount Lofty, upon the highest part of the ridge of mountains which, from Cape Jervis, extends northward behind the eastern shore of the inlet. The nearest part of the coast was distant three leagues, mostly low, and composed of sand and rock, with a few small trees scattered over it; but at a few miles inland, where the back mountains rise, the country was well clothed with forest timber, and had a fertile appearance. The fires bespoke this to be a part of the continent...

*30 March* ~ Early in the morning, I went in a boat, accompanied by the naturalist, to examine more closely the head of the gulf. We carried from 4 to 3 fathoms water four miles above the ship, when it shoaled to fifteen and eight feet, which brought us to mud flats, nearly dry; but by means of a small channel amongst them we got within half a mile of the shore, and walked to it upon a bank of mud and sand.

It was then ten o'clock, and the tide was out; so that I judged the time of high water to be about seven hours after the moon's passage, or three hours later than at Kangaroo Island...

We set off in the afternoon for the Hummock Mount, which stands upon a northern prolongation of the hills on the west side of the inlet, and about eight miles from the water; but finding it could not be reached in time to admit of returning on board the same evening, I ascended a nearer part of the range, to inspect the head of the inlet. It was almost wholly occupied by flats, which seemed to be sandy in the eastern part and muddy to the westward.

These flats abounded with rays; and had we been provided with a harpoon, a boat-load might have been caught. One black swan and several shags and gulls were seen...

Between the two ranges is a broad valley, swampy at the bottom; and into it the water runs down from both sides in rainy weather, and is discharged into the gulf, which may be considered as the lower and wider part of the valley.

This eastern ridge is the same which rises at Cape Jervis; from whence it extends northward towards Barn Hill and the ridge of mountains on the east side of Spencer's Gulf. If it joins that ridge, as I strongly suspect, its length, taking it only from Cape Jervis to Mount Arden, will be more than seventy leagues in a straight line. There are some considerable elevations on the southern part; Mount Lofty is one of them, and its height appeared nearly equal to that of Mount Brown to the north, or about three thousand feet. Another lies six or seven miles to the north-by-east of the Hummock Mount, near the head of this inlet; and seems to have been the hill set from Spencer's Gulf, at the anchorage of 14 March, in the evening, when it was distant ten or eleven leagues and appeared above the lower range in front of Barn Hill.

From my station on the western hills of the new inlet, across to Spencer's Gulf, the distance was not more than thirty miles; but as I did not ascend the highest part of the range, the water to the westward could not be seen. Had the Hummock Mount been within my reach, its elevation of near fifteen hundred feet would probably have afforded an extensive view, both across the penin-sula, and of the country to the northward.

In honour of the noble admiral who presided at the Board of Admiralty when I sailed from England, and had continued to the voyage that countenance and protection of which Earl Spencer had set the example, I named this new inlet, the Gulf of St Vincent. To the peninsula which separates it from Spencer's Gulf, I have affixed the name of Yorke's Peninsula, in honour of the Right Honourable Charles Philip Yorke, who followed the steps of his above mentioned predecessors at the Admiralty...

*1 April* ~ Our examination of the Gulf of St Vincent was now finished; and the country round it had appeared to be generally superior to that on the borders of Spencer's Gulf. Yorke's Peninsula between them, is singular in its form, bearing some resemblance to a very ill-shaped leg and foot...

Having now made myself acquainted with the shores of the continent up to Cape Jervis, it remained to pursue the discovery further eastward; but I wished to ascertain previously, whether any error had crept into the time keepers' rates since leaving Kangaroo Island, and also to procure there a few more fresh meals for my ship's company. Our course was in consequence directed for the island, which was visible from aloft; but the winds being very feeble, we did not pass Kangaroo Head until eleven at night. I purposed to have run up into the eastern cove of Nepean Bay; but finding the water to shoal from 12 to 7 fathoms, did not think it safe to go further in the dark; and therefore dropped the anchor about three-quarters of a mile from the shore, and two miles to the south-west-by-west of our former anchorage.

Early on the following morning a party was sent to shoot kangaroos, another to cut wood, and the naturalists went to pursue their researches. The observations taken by Lieutenant Flinders, compared with those of 24 March, showed the time keepers to have erred 2'10" of longitude to the west, in the nine days we had been absent... The kangaroos were found to be less numerous than at the first anchoring place, and they had become shy; so that very few were killed. Those few being brought off, with a boat-load of wood, we got under way at daylight next morning, to prosecute the examination of the coast beyond Cape Jervis; but the time keepers had stopped, from having been neglected to be wound up on the preceding day. We therefore came to an anchor again; and as some time would be required to fix new rates, the ship was moored so soon as the flood tide made. I landed immediately, to commence the necessary observations, and a party was established on shore,

abreast of the ship, to cut more wood for the holds. Lieutenant
Fowler was sent in the launch to the eastward, with a shooting
party and such of the scientific gentlemen as chose to accompany
him; and there being skins wanted for the service of the rigging, he
was directed to kill some seals.

On the 4th, I was accompanied by the naturalist in a boat
expedition to the head of the large eastern cove of Nepean Bay;
intending if possible to ascend a sandy eminence behind it, from
which alone there was any hope of obtaining a view into the
interior of the island, all the other hills being thickly covered
with wood.

The entrance of the piece of water at the head of Nepean Bay
is less than half a mile in width, and mostly shallow; but there is a
channel sufficiently deep for all boats near the western shore. After
turning two low islets near the east point, the water opens out,
becomes deeper, and divides into two branches, each of two or
three miles long. Boats can go to the head of the southern branch
only at high water; the east branch appeared to be accessible at all
times; but as a lead and line were neglected to be put into the boat,
I had no opportunity of sounding. There are four small islands in
the eastern branch; one of them is moderately high and woody, the
others are grassy and lower; and upon two of these we found many
young pelicans, unable to fly. Flocks of the old birds were sitting
upon the beaches of the lagoon, and it appeared that the islands
were their breeding places; not only so, but from the number of
skeletons and bones there scattered, it should seem that they had
for ages been selected for the closing scene of their existence.
Certainly none more likely to be free from disturbance of every
kind could have been chosen, than these islets in a hidden lagoon
of an uninhabited island, situate upon an unknown coast near the
antipodes of Europe; nor can anything be more consonant to the
feelings, if pelicans have any, than quietly to resign their breath,
whilst surrounded by their progeny, and in the same spot where
they first drew it. Alas, for the pelicans! Their golden age is past;

but it has much exceeded in duration that of man.

I named this piece of water Pelican Lagoon. It is also frequented by flocks of the pied shag, and by some ducks and gulls; and the shoals supplied us with a few oysters...

*5 April* ~ Not being able to return on board the same night, we slept near the entrance of the lagoon. It was high water by the shore, on the morning of the 5th, at six o'clock; but on comparing this with the swinging of the ship, it appeared that the tide had then been running more than an hour from the westward. The rise in the lagoon seemed to be from four to eight feet.

A few kangaroos had been obtained during my absence, as also some seal-skins; but one of the sailors having attacked a large seal incautiously, received a very severe bite in the leg, and was laid up. After all the researches now made in the island, it appeared that the kangaroos were much more numerous at our first landing place, near Kangaroo Head, than elsewhere in the neighbourhood. That part of the island was clearer of wood than most others; and there were some small grass plats which seemed to be particularly attractive, and were kept very bare. Not less than thirty emus or cassowaries were seen at different times; but it so happened that they were fired at only once, and that ineffectually...

*6 April* ~ The approach of the winter season, and an apprehension that the discovery of the remaining unknown part of the south coast might not be completed before a want of provisions would make it necessary to run for Port Jackson, prevented me from stopping a day longer at Kangaroo Island than was necessary...When, therefore, the rising of a breeze made it advisable to get under way from Kangaroo Head, which was not until two in the afternoon, we proceeded for the eastern outlet of the Investigator's Strait...

*8 April* ~ Before two in the afternoon we stretched eastward again; and at four, a white rock was reported from aloft to be seen ahead. On approaching nearer, it proved to be a ship standing towards us; and we cleared for action, in case of being attacked.

The stranger was a heavy-looking ship, without any top-gallant masts up; and our colours being hoisted, she showed a French ensign, and afterwards an English Jack forward, as we did a white flag. At half past five, the land being then five miles distant to the north-eastward, I hove to; and learned, as the stranger passed to leeward with a free wind, that it was the French national ship *Le Géographe*, under the command of Captain Nicolas Baudin. We veered round as *Le Géographe* was passing, so as to keep our broadside to her, lest the flag of truce should be a deception; and having come to the wind on the other tack, a boat was hoisted out, and I went on board the French ship, which had also hove to.

As I did not understand French, Mr Brown, the naturalist, went with me in the boat. We were received by an officer who pointed out the commander, and by him were conducted into the cabin. I requested Captain Baudin to show me his passport from the Admiralty; and when it was found and I had perused it, offered mine from the French marine minister, but he put it back without inspection. He then informed me that he had spent some time in examining the south and east parts of Van Diemen's Land, where his geographical engineer, with the largest boat and a boat's crew, had been left, and probably lost. In Bass' Strait Captain Baudin had encountered a heavy gale, the same we had experienced in a less degree on 21 March, in the Investigator's Strait. He was then separated from his consort, *Le Naturaliste*; but having since had fair winds and fine weather, he had explored the south coast from Western Port to the place of our meeting, without finding any river, inlet, or other shelter which afforded anchorage. I inquired concerning a large island, said to lie in the western entrance of Bass' Strait; but he had not seen it, and seemed to doubt much of its existence.

Captain Baudin was communicative of his discoveries about Van Diemen's Land; as also of his criticisms upon an English chart of Bass' Strait, published in 1800. He found great fault with the north side of the strait, but commended the form given to the south side and to the islands near it. On my pointing out a note upon the chart, explaining that the north side of the strait was seen only in an open boat by Mr Bass, who had no good means of fixing either latitude or longitude, he appeared surprised, not having before paid attention to it. I told him that some other, and more particular charts of the strait and its neighbourhood had been since published; and that if he would keep company until next morning, I would bring him a copy, with a small memoir belonging to them. This was agreed to, and I returned with Mr Brown to the *Investigator*.

It somewhat surprised me, that Captain Baudin made no inquiries concerning my business upon this unknown coast, but as he seemed more desirous of communicating information, I was happy to receive it; next morning, however, he had become inquis-itive, some of his officers having learned from my boat's crew that our object was also discovery. I then told him, generally, what our operations had been, particularly in the two gulfs, and the latitude to which I had ascended in the largest; explained the situation of Port Lincoln, where fresh water might be procured; showed him Cape Jervis, which was still in sight; and as a proof of the refresh-ments to be obtained at the large island opposite to it, pointed out the kangaroo-skin caps worn by my boat's crew; and told him the name I had affixed to the island in consequence. At parting, the captain requested me to take care of his boat and people, in case of meeting with them; and to say to *Le Naturaliste*, that he should go to Port Jackson so soon as the bad weather set in. On my asking the name of the captain of *Le Naturaliste*, he bethought himself to ask mine; and finding it to be the same as the author of the chart which he had been criticising, expressed not a little surprise; but had the politeness to congratulate himself on meeting me.

*9 April* ~ The situation of the *Investigator*, when I hove to for the purpose of speaking with Captain Baudin, was 35° 40' south, and 138° 58' east. No person was present at our conversations except Mr Brown; and they were mostly carried on in English, which the captain spoke so as to be understood. He gave me, besides what is related above, some information of his losses in men, separations from his consort, and of the improper season at which he was directed to explore this coast; as also a memorandum of some rocks he had met with, lying two leagues from the shore, in latitude 37° 1', and he spoke of them as being very dangerous.

I have been the more particular in detailing all that passed at this interview, from a circumstance which it seems proper to explain and discuss in this place.

At the above situation of 35° 40' south, and 138° 58' east, the discoveries made by Captain Baudin upon the south coast have their termination to the west; as mine in the *Investigator* have to the eastward. Yet Mons. Peron, naturalist in the French expedition, has laid a claim for his nation to the discovery of all the parts between Western Port in Bass' Strait, and Nuyts' Archipelago; and this part of New South Wales is called Terre Napoléon. My Kangaroo Island, a name which they openly adopted in the expedition, has been converted at Paris into L'Isle Decrés; Spencer's Gulf is named Golfe Bonaparte; the Gulf of St Vincent, Golfe Joséphine; and so on, along the whole coast to Cape Nuyts, not even the smallest island being left without some similar stamp of French discovery...

It is said by M. Peron, and upon my authority too, that the *Investigator* had not been able to penetrate behind the Isles of St Peter and St Francis; and though he doth not say directly, that no part of the before unknown coast was discovered by me, yet the whole tenor of his chap. XV induces the reader to believe that I had done nothing which could interfere with the prior claim of the French.

Yet M. Peron was present afterwards at Port Jackson, when I showed one of my charts of this coast to Captain Baudin, and pointed out the limits of his discovery; and so far from any prior title being set up at that time to Kangaroo Island and the parts westward, the officers of the *Géographe* always spoke of them as belonging to the *Investigator*. The first Lieutenant, Mons. Freycinet, even made use of the following odd expression, addressing himself to me in the house of Governor King, and in the presence of one of his companions, I think Mons. Bonnefoy, 'Captain, if we had not been kept so long picking up shells and catching butterflies at Van Diemen's Land, you would not have discovered the south coast before us.'

The English officers and respectable inhabitants then at Port Jackson, can say if the prior discovery of these parts were not generally acknowledged; nay, I appeal to the French officers themselves, generally and individually, if such were not the case. How then came M. Peron to advance what was so contrary to truth? Was he a man destitute of all principle? My answer is, that I believe his candour to have been equal to his acknowledged abilities; and that what he wrote was from over-ruling authority, and smote him to the heart: he did not live to finish the second volume.

The motive for this aggression I do not pretend to explain. It may have originated in the desire to rival the British nation in the honour of completing the discovery of the globe; or be intended as the forerunner of a claim to the possession of the countries so said to have been first discovered by French navigators. Whatever may have been the object in view, the question, so far as I am concerned, must be left to the judgment of the world; and if succeeding French writers can see and admit the claims of other navigators, as clearly and readily as a late most able man of that nation has pointed out their own in some other instances, I shall not fear to leave it even to their decision.*

*9 April* ~ I returned with Mr Brown on board the *Investigator* at half past eight in the morning, and we then separated from *Le Géographe*; Captain Baudin's course being directed to the north-west, and ours to the southward...

At the place where we tacked from the shore on the morning of the 8th, the high land of Cape Jervis had retreated from the water

* M. De Fleurieu.

side, the coast was become low and sandy, and its trending was north-east; but after running four or five leagues in that direction, it curved round to the south-eastward, and thus formed a large bight or bay. The head of this bay was probably seen by Captain Baudin in the afternoon; and in consequence of our meeting here, I distinguish it by the name of Encounter Bay. The succeeding part of the coast having been first discovered by the French navigator, I shall make use of the names in describing it which he, or his countrymen have thought proper to apply...

*17 April* ~ On arriving at Port Jackson, I learned, and so did Captain Baudin, that this coast had been before visited. Lieutenant (now Captain) James Grant, commander of His Majesty's brig *Lady Nelson*, saw the above projection, which he named Cape Banks, on 3 December 1800; and followed the coast from thence, through Bass' Strait. The same principle upon which I had adopted the names applied by the French navigators to the parts discovered by them, will now guide me in making use of the appellations bestowed by Captain Grant.

The termination to the west, of that part of the south coast discovered by Captain Baudin in *Le Géographe*, has been pointed out; and it seems proper to specify its commencement to the east, that the extent of his Terre Napoléon may be properly defined...between the latitudes 37° 36' and 35° 40' south, and the longitudes 140° 10' and 138° 58' east of Greenwich; making with the windings, about fifty leagues of coast, in which, as Captain Baudin truly observed, there is neither river, inlet, nor place of shelter; nor does even the worst parts of Nuyts' Land exceed it in sterility...

*22 April* ~ We were now entered into Bass' Strait; and the subsiding of the sea made me suspect that the large island, concerning which I had made inquiry of Captain Baudin, was to windward. The south part of this island was discovered by Mr Reid, in a sealing expedition from Port Jackson; and before quitting New South Wales in 1799, I had received an account of its lying to the north-west of Hunter's Isles. It afterwards appeared, that the northern part was seen in January 1801, by Mr John Black, commander of the brig *Harbinger*, who gave to it the name of King's Island. Of this I was ignorant at the time; but since it was so very dangerous to explore the main coast with the present south-west wind, I was desirous of ascertaining the position of this island before going to Port Jackson, more especially as it had escaped the observation of Captain Baudin.

*22 April* ~...We tacked to the south-south-east at three o'clock, working up for King's Island, which was distant about five or six leagues, directly to windward. In the night we lay up south, parallel with the east side of the island; but the soundings having diminished to 16 fathoms, I feared we might be approaching a reef of rocks lying off the south-east end, of which Mr Reid had spoken. We therefore tacked to the northward at eleven o'clock; and after beating until three in the following afternoon, got to an anchor in 9 fathoms, fine sand, under the north-east end of King's Island.

A boat was immediately hoisted out, and I landed with the botanical gentlemen. On stepping out of the boat, I shot one of those little bear-like quadrupeds, called *Womat*; and another was afterwards killed. A seal, of a species different to any yet seen by us, was also procured; its flippers behind were double, when compared to the common kinds of seal, and those forward were smaller, and placed nearer to the head; the hair was much shorter, and of a blueish, grey colour; the nose flat and broad; and the fat upon the animal was at least treble the usual quantity. I never saw the sea elephant, and possibly this might have been a young female; but there was no appearance of any trunk. A top-mast studding-sail boom, not much injured, was lying near the landing place; and as I afterwards learned that the wreck of a vessel had been found upon the west side of the island, this boom had probably drifted from thence.

The north-east part of King's Island extends south-east-by-east, three or four leagues. The shore is mostly of sand, and behind the beach it was washed or blown up in great ridges, but partly overspread with a kind of dog grass which kept the sand together...

We returned on board at dusk, with our womats, the seal, and a kangaroo; the last being of a middle size between the small species of the lesser islands, and the large kind found at Kangaroo Island and on the continent. It appeared indeed, all along the south coast, that the size of the kangaroo bore some proportion to the extent of land which it inhabited.

*24 April* ~ In the morning, the wind blew fresh from the southward. A boat was sent on shore with Mr Brown and his party; and at eleven o'clock, when they returned, we got under way…Two more womats were killed this morning; and a skull was picked up, which was thought to be of a small dog; but more probably was that of an opossum…

The time was fast approaching when it would be necessary to proceed to Port Jackson; both on account of the winter season, and from the want of some kinds of provisions. Before this took place, I wished to finish as much of the south coast as possible, and would have recommenced at Cape Bridgewater had the wind been favourable; but it still blew fresh from the southward, and all that part remained a lee shore. I determined, however, to run over to the high land we had seen on the north side of Bass' Strait; and to trace as much of the coast from thence eastward, as the state of the weather and our remaining provisions could possibly allow…

At three in the afternoon the northern land was in sight, and the highest hills of King's Island were sinking below the horizon, as seen from the deck. Their distance was twenty-five miles; and consequently the elevation of them is between four and five hundred feet above the level of the sea. At five o'clock, a bluff head, the most projecting part of the northern land, was distant three or four leagues; it was Captain Grant's Cape Otway…

*25 April* ~ The whole of this land is high, the elevation of the uppermost parts being not less than two thousand feet. The rising hills were covered with wood of a deep green foliage, and without any vacant spaces of rock or sand; so that I judged this part of the coast to exceed in fertility all that had yet fallen under observation…

*26 April* ~ In the morning we kept close to an east-south-east
wind, steering for the land to the north-eastward; and at nine
o'clock Captain Grant's Cape Schanck, the extreme of the preceding evening, was five leagues distant to the N88°E, and a rocky
point towards the head of the bight, bore N12°E. On coming
within five miles of the shore at eleven o'clock, we found it to be
low, and mostly sandy; and that the bluff head which had been
taken for the north-end of an island, was part of a ridge of hills
rising at Cape Schanck...

On the west side of the rocky point there was a small opening,
with breaking water across it; however, on advancing a little more
westward the opening assumed a more interesting aspect, and I
bore away to have a nearer view. A large extent of water presently
became visible within side; and although the entrance seemed to
be very narrow, and there were in it strong ripplings like breakers,
I was induced to steer in at half past one; the ship being close upon
a wind and every man ready for tacking at a moment's
warning...In making the last stretch from the shoal, the depth
diminished from 10 fathoms quickly to 3; and before the ship could
come round, the flood tide set her upon a mud bank, and she stuck
fast. A boat was lowered down to sound; and finding the deep
water lie to the north-west, a kedge anchor was carried out; and
having got the ship's head in that direction, the sails were filled and
she drew off into 6 and 10 fathoms; and it being then dark, we
came to an anchor.

The extensive harbour we had thus unexpectedly found I
supposed must be Western Port, although the narrowness of the
entrance did by no means correspond with the width given to it by
Mr Bass. It was the information of Captain Baudin, who had
coasted along from thence with fine weather, and had found no
inlet of any kind, which induced this supposition; and the very
great extent of the place, agreeing with that of Western Port, was
in confirmation of it. This, however, was not Western Port, as we
found next morning; and I congratulated myself on having made

a new and useful discovery; but here again I was in error. This
place, as I afterwards learned at Port Jackson, had been discovered
ten weeks before by Lieutenant John Murray, who had succeeded
Captain Grant in the command of the *Lady Nelson*. He had given
it the name of Port Phillip, and to the rocky point on the east side
of the entrance, that of Point Nepean.

*27 April* ~...The mud bank where the ship had grounded, is
distinct from the middle shoal; but I am not certain that it is so
from the south shore, from which it is one mile distant. The Bluff
Mount (named Arthur's Seat by Mr Murray, from a supposed
resemblance to the hill of that name near Edinburgh) bore S76°E;
but from thence the shore trended northward so far, that the land
at the head of the port could not be seen, even from aloft. Before
proceeding any higher with the ship, I wished to gain some knowledge of the form and extent of this great piece of water; and
Arthur's Seat being more than a thousand feet high and near the
water side, presented a favourable station for that purpose.

After breakfast I went away in a boat, accompanied by Mr
Brown and some other gentlemen, for the Seat. Having observed
the latitude there from an artificial horizon, I ascended the hill; and
to my surprise found the port so extensive, that even at this elevation its boundary to the northward could not be distinguished. The
western shore extended from the entrance ten or eleven miles in a
northern direction, to the extremity of what, from its appearance,
I called Indented Head; beyond it was a wide branch of the port
leading to the westward, and I suspected might have a communication with the sea; for it was almost incredible, that such a vast
piece of water should not have a larger outlet than that through
which we had come...

Arthur's Seat and the hills and valleys in its neighbourhood,
were generally well covered with wood; and the soil was superior
to any upon the borders of the salt water, which I have had an
opportunity of examining in Terra Australis. There were many
marks of natives, such as deserted fireplaces and heaps of oyster

shells; and upon the peninsula which forms the south side of the
port, a smoke was rising, but we did not see any of the people.
Quantities of fine oysters were lying upon the beaches, between
high and low water marks, and appeared to have been washed up
by the surf; a circumstance which I do not recollect to have
observed in any other part of this country.

*28 April* ~ We returned on board at dusk in the evening; and at
daylight the anchor was weighed with the intention of coasting
round the port with the ship…Having left orders with Mr Fowler,
the first lieutenant, to take the ship back to the entrance, I went in
a boat early next morning with provisions for three days; in order
to explore as much of the port as could be done in that time…

*30 April* ~ In the morning, a fire was perceived two hundred
yards from the tent; and the Indians appeared to have decamped
from thence on our landing. Whilst I was taking angles from a low
point at the north-easternmost part of Indented Head, a party of
the inhabitants showed themselves about a mile from us; and on
landing there we found a hut with a fire in it, but the people had
disappeared, and carried off their effects. I left some strips of cloth,
of their favourite red colour, hanging about the hut; and proceeded
westward along the shore, to examine the arm of the port running
in that direction.

Three natives having made their appearance abreast of the
boat, we again landed. They came to us without hesitation,
received a shag and some trifling presents with pleasure, and parted
with such of their arms as we wished to possess, without reluctance.
They afterwards followed us along the shore; and when I shot
another bird, which hovered over the boat, and held it up to them,
they ran down to the water side and received it without expressing
either surprise or distrust. Their knowledge of the effect of firearms
I then attributed to their having seen me shoot birds when unconscious of being observed; but it had probably been learned from
Mr Murray.

At noon, I landed to take an observation of the sun, which gave

38° 7' 6" for the latitude; my position being nearly at the northern
extremity of Indented Head. Some bearings were taken from the
brow of a hill a little way back; and after a dinner of which the
natives partook, we left them on friendly terms, to proceed westward in our examination. The water became very shallow abreast
of a sandy point, whence the shore trends nearly south-west; and
there being no appearance of an opening to the sea this way, I
steered across the western arm, as well to ascertain its depth as with
the intention of ascending the hills lying behind the northern
shore...

*1 May* ~ At dawn I set off with three of the boat's crew, for the
highest part of the back hills called Station Peak. Our way was over
a low plain, where the water appeared frequently to lodge; it was
covered with small-bladed grass, but almost destitute of wood, and
the soil was clayey and shallow. One or two miles before arriving
at the feet of the hills, we entered a wood where an emu and a
kangaroo were seen at a distance; and the top of the peak was
reached at ten o'clock...

Towards the interior there was a mountain bearing N11°E,
eleven leagues distant; and so far the country was low, grassy, and
very slightly covered with wood, presenting great facility to a trav-
eller desirous of penetrating inland.

I left the ship's name on a scroll of paper, deposited in a small
pile of stones upon the top of the peak; and at three in the afternoon reached the tent, much fatigued, having walked more than
twenty miles without finding a drop of water.

In the evening we rowed back to Indented Head, and landed
there soon after dark. Fires had been seen moving along the
shore, but the people seemed to have fled; though we found two
newly erected huts with fires in them, and utensils which must
have belonged to some of the people before seen, since there was
boiled rice in one of the baskets. We took up our quarters here
for the night, keeping a good watch; but nothing was seen of the
Indians till we pushed off from the shore in the morning, when

seven showed themselves upon a hill behind the huts. They ran down to examine their habitations, and finding everything as they had left it, a little water excepted of which we were in want, they seemed satisfied; and for a short time three of them followed the boat...

I find it very difficult to speak in general terms of Port Phillip. On the one hand it is capable of receiving and sheltering a larger fleet of ships than ever yet went to sea; whilst on the other, the entrance, in its whole width, is scarcely two miles, and nearly half of it is occupied by the rocks lying off Point Nepean, and by shoals on the opposite side. The depth in the remaining part varies from 6 to 12 fathoms; and this irregularity causes the strong tides, especially when running against the wind, to make breakers, in which small vessels should be careful of engaging themselves...

The country surrounding Port Phillip has a pleasing, and in many parts a fertile appearance; and the sides of some of the hills and several of the valleys, are fit for agricultural purposes. It is in great measure a grassy country, and capable of supporting much cattle, though better calculated for sheep. To this general description there are probably several exceptions; and the southern peninsula, which is terminated by Point Nepean, forms one, the surface there being mostly sandy, and the vegetation in many places, little better than brush wood. Indented Head, at the northern part of the western peninsula, had an appearance particularly agreeable; the grass had been burned not long before, and had sprung up green and tender; the wood was so thinly scattered that one might see to a considerable distance; and the hills rose one over the other to a moderate elevation, but so gently, that a plough might everywhere be used...

Were a settlement to be made at Port Phillip, as doubtless there will be some time hereafter, the entrance could be easily defended; and it would not be difficult to establish a friendly intercourse with the natives, for they are acquainted with the effect of firearms, and desirous of possessing many of our conveniences. I thought them

more muscular than the men of King George's Sound; but, generally speaking, they differ in no essential particular from the other
inhabitants of the south and east coasts, except in language, which
is dissimilar, if not altogether different to that of Port Jackson, and
seemingly of King George's Sound also. I am not certain whether
they have canoes, but none were seen.

In the woods are the kangaroo, the emu or cassowary, parakeets,
and a variety of small birds; the mudbanks are frequented by ducks
and some black swans, and the shores by the usual sea fowl
common in New South Wales. The range of the thermometer was
between 61° and 67°; and the climate appeared to be as good and
as agreeable as could well be desired in the month answering to
November. In 1803, Colonel Collins of the marines was sent out
from England to make a new settlement in this country; but he
quitted Port Phillip for the south end of Van Diemen's Land, probably from not finding fresh water for a colony sufficiently near to
the entrance...

On 3 May at daylight, the anchor was weighed to go out of Port
Phillip with the last half of the ebb; and the wind being from the
westward, we backed, filled, and tacked occasionally, dropping out
with the tide...Cape Schanck is a cliffy head, with three rocks lying
off, the outermost of which appears at a distance like a ship under
sail: the latitude is 38° 29' or 30' south, and longitude 144° 53' east.
It will always be desirable for vessels to get sight of this cape, before
they run far into the great bight for Port Phillip; and if the wind
blow strong from the southward, it will be unsafe to run without
having seen it.

Cape Schanck is also an excellent mark for ships desiring to go
into Western Port, of which it forms the west side of the principal
entrance; but as there are many breakers and shoals on that side,
which extend almost to mid-channel, it will be necessary to give the
cape a wide berth, by keeping over to Phillip Island on the starboard hand...

We then steered eastward along the south side of Phillip Island,

and passed a needle-like rock, lying under the shore. Cape Wollamai is the east end of the island, and forms one side of the small,
eastern entrance to the port...*Wollamai* is the native name for a fish
at Port Jackson, called sometimes by the settlers, light-horseman,
from the bones of the head having some resemblance to a helmet;
and the form of this cape bearing a likeness to the head of the fish,
induced Mr Bass to give it the name of Wollamai...

*4 May* ~...Wilson's Promontory was no longer visible; but from
the best bearings I had been able to obtain in such blowing
weather, its south-eastern extremity lies in latitude 39° 11½' south,
and longitude 146° 24' east.

Not seeing any more islands to the southward from the masthead we bore away east soon after noon, to make Kent's Groups;
and before three o'clock they both came in sight, as did an island
to the northward, which seems to have been one of the small
cluster discovered by Mr John Black, and named Hogan's Group...

At five in the evening, I thought myself fortunate to get a sight
of Furneaux's great island through the haze; and also of a small,
craggy isle which had been before fixed relatively to the inner
Sister...

At daylight of the 5th, the course was altered more northward;
and at noon, land was seen from the masthead to the north-
north-west, probably some of the hills at the back of the Long
Beach, and distant not less than twenty leagues: our latitude was
38° 32' south, and longitude 149° 35' east. The wind had then
moderated, and having shifted to north-west, we kept close up to
make Cape Howe...

*7 May* ~ After a squally night, the wind fixed at west-by-north;
and at daybreak of the 7th, the land was visible from west to
north-west, and our course was parallel to it. At noon, the latitude
was 36° 24' south, and longitude 151° 16' east; Mount Dromedary
was in sight bearing N85°W, and by the difference of longitude,
was distant fifty-two miles: I estimate its highest southern part to
lie in 36° 19' south, and 150° 11' east. The wind returned to the

north-west in the afternoon, and we lost sight of the land; but becoming fairer afterwards, and the southern current not having much strength, by four next day the heads of Port Jackson were in sight. At dusk the flagstaff upon the South Head bore west-south-west, and our distance from the shore was seven or eight miles.

I tried to beat up for the port in the night, being sufficiently well acquainted to have run up in the dark, had the wind permitted; but we were still to leeward in the morning, and Mr Westall made a good sketch of the entrance. At one o'clock we gained the heads, a pilot came on board, and soon after three the *Investigator* was anchored in Sydney Cove.

[The *Investigator*]
May–December 1802

*Sunday 9 May 1802* ~ There was not a single individual on board who was not upon deck working the ship into harbour; and it may be averred, that the officers and crew were, generally speaking, in better health than on the day we sailed from Spithead, and not in less good spirits. I have said nothing of the regulations observed after we made Cape Leeuwin; they were little different from those adopted in the commencement of the voyage, and of which a strict attention to cleanliness, and a free circulation of air in the messing and sleeping places formed the most essential parts. Several of the inhabitants of Port Jackson expressed themselves never to have been so strongly reminded of England, as by the fresh colour of many amongst the *Investigator*'s ship's company.

So soon as the anchor was dropped, I went on shore to wait upon His Excellency Philip Gidley King, Esq., Governor of New South Wales, and senior naval officer upon the station; to whom I communicated a general account of our discoveries and examinations upon the south coast, and delivered the orders from the Admiralty and Secretary of State. These orders directed the governor to place the brig *Lady Nelson* under my command, and not to employ the *Investigator* on other service than that which was the object of the voyage; and His Excellency was pleased to assure me, that every assistance in the power of the colony to render, should be given to forward a service so interesting to his government, and to himself. The *Lady Nelson* was then lying in Sydney Cove; but her commander,

Lieutenant Grant, had requested permission to return to England, and had sailed six months before.

Besides the *Lady Nelson*, there were in the port His Majesty's armed vessel *Porpoise*, the *Speedy*, south-whaler, and the *Margaret* privateer; also the French national ship *Le Naturaliste*, commanded by Captain Hamelin, to whom I communicated Captain Baudin's intention of coming to Port Jackson so soon as the bad weather should set in. *Le Géographe*'s boat had been picked up in Bass' Strait by Mr Campbell of the brig *Harrington*, and the officers and crew were at this time on board *Le Naturaliste*...

To supply the place of the cutter we had lost at the entrance of Spencer's Gulf, I contracted for a boat to be built after the model of that in which Mr Bass made his long and adventurous expedition to the strait. It was twenty-eight feet seven inches in length over all, rather flat floored, head and stern alike, a keel somewhat curved, and the cut-water and stern post nearly upright; it was fitted to row eight oars when requisite, but intended for six in common cases. The timbers were cut from the largest kind of banksia, which had been found more durable than mangrove; and the planking was of cedar...

Whilst these branches of our refitment were going on, a thorough examination was made and survey taken of all the ship's stores; as well for the purpose of sending away those unserviceable and replacing them with others so far as they could be obtained, as with a view to enable the warrant officers to pass their accounts and obtain their pay up to this time; a precaution which the nature of our voyage rendered more peculiarly necessary. After the surveys were ended, the seamen were employed in stripping and re-rigging the masts, and preparing the hold to receive a fresh stock of provisions and water; the naturalist and his assistants, as also the two painters, made excursions into the interior of the country; and my time was mostly occupied in constructing the fair charts of our discoveries and examinations upon the south coast, for the purpose of their being transmitted to the secretary of the Admiralty.

*June* ~ Captain Baudin arrived in *Le Géographe* on the 20th, and
a boat was sent from the *Investigator* to assist in towing the ship up
to the cove. It was grievous to see the miserable condition to which
both officers and crew were reduced by scurvy; there being not
more out of one hundred and seventy, according to the commander's account, than twelve men capable of doing their duty. The
sick were received into the colonial hospital; and both French ships
furnished with everything in the power of the colony to supply.
Before their arrival, the necessity of augmenting the number of
cattle in the country had prevented the governor from allowing us
any fresh meat; but some oxen belonging to government were now
killed for the distressed strangers; and by returning an equal quantity of salt meat, which was exceedingly scarce at this time, I
obtained a quarter of beef for my people. The distress of the
French navigators had indeed been great; but every means were
used by the governor and the principal inhabitants of the colony,
to make them forget both their sufferings and the war which existed
between the two nations.

His Excellency, Governor King, had done me the honour to visit
the *Investigator*, and to accept of a dinner on board; on which occasion he had been received with the marks of respect due to his rank
of captain-general; and shortly afterward, the Captains Baudin
and Hamelin, with Monsieur Peron and some other French officers, as also Colonel Paterson, the lieutenant-governor, did me the
same favour; when they were received under a salute of eleven
guns. The intelligence of peace, which had just been received,
contributed to enliven the party, and rendered our meeting more
particularly agreeable. I showed to Captain Baudin one of my
charts of the south coast, containing the part first explored by him,
and distinctly marked as his discovery. He made no objection to the
justice of the limits therein pointed out; but found his portion to
be smaller than he had supposed, not having before been aware of
the extent of the discoveries previously made by Captain Grant.
After examining the chart, he said, apparently as a reason for not

producing any of his own, that his charts were not constructed on board the ship; but that he transmitted to Paris all his bearings and observations, with a regular series of views of the land, and from them the charts were to be made at a future time. This mode appeared to me extraordinary, and not to be worthy of imitation; conceiving that a rough chart, at least, should be made whilst the land is in sight, when any error in bearing or observation can be corrected; a plan which was adopted in the commencement, and followed throughout the course of my voyage...

In consequence of the directions given by His Majesty's principal Secretary of State for the Colonies, the *Lady Nelson*, a brig of sixty tons, commanded by Acting-Lieutenant John Murray, was placed under my orders, as a tender to the *Investigator*. This vessel was fitted with three sliding keels; and built after the plan of that ingenious officer commissioner (now vice-admiral) Schanck. When the sliding keels were up, the *Lady Nelson* drew no more than six feet water; and was therefore peculiarly adapted for going up rivers, or other shallow places which it might be dangerous, or impossible for the ship to enter. Mr Murray's crew was mostly composed of convicts; and having no officer in whom he could place entire confidence, I lent to him Mr Denis Lacy, one of my young gentlemen acquainted with the management of a time keeper, to act as his chief mate.

The price of fresh meat at Port Jackson was so exorbitant, that it was impossible to think of purchasing it on the public account. I obtained one quarter of beef for the ship's company, in exchange for salt meat, and the governor furnished us with some baskets of vegetables from his garden; and in lieu of the daily pound of biscuit, each man received a pound and a quarter of soft bread, without any expense to government. But with these exceptions, I was obliged to leave the refreshment of the people to their own individual exertions; assisting them with the payment due for savings of bread since leaving the Cape of Good Hope, and the different artificers with the money earned by their extra services in refitting the ship. Fish are usually plentiful at Port Jackson in the summer, but not in the winter time; and our duties were too numerous and indispensable to admit of sending people away with the seine, when there was little prospect of success; a few were, however, occasionally bought alongside, from boats which fished along the coast.

In purchasing a sea stock for the cabin, I paid £3 a head for sheep, weighing from thirty to forty pounds when dressed. Pigs were bought at 9d per pound, weighed alive, geese at 10s each, and fowls at 3s and Indian corn for the stock cost 5s a bushel.

To complete the ship's provisions, I entered into a contract for 30,000 pounds of biscuit, 8000 pounds of flour, and 156 bushels of kiln-dried wheat; but in the meantime, the ship *Coromandel* brought out the greater part of the twelve months' provisions, for which I had applied on sailing from Spithead; and the contractor was prevailed upon to annul that part of the agreement relating to flour and wheat. The biscuit cost 33s per hundred pounds; and considering that the colony was at short allowance, and that the French ships were to be supplied, it was a favourable price. From two American vessels which arrived, I purchased 1483 gallons of rum at 6s 6d per gallon; which, with what remained of our former stock was a proportion for twelve months. In other respects our provisions were completed from the quantity sent out from England; and the remaining part was lodged in the public stores, in charge of the commissary, until our return.

In addition to the melancholy loss of eight officers and men, at the entrance of Spencer's Gulf, and the previous deficiency of four in the complement, I found it necessary to discharge the man who had been bitten by a seal at Kangaroo Island, as also a marine, who was invalided; so that fourteen men were required to complete my small ship's company. Mr John Aken, chief mate of the ship *Hercules*, was engaged to fill the situation of master, and five men, mostly seamen, were entered, but finding it impossible to fill up the complement with free people, I applied to the governor for his permission to enter such convicts as should present themselves, and could bring respectable recommendations. This request, as every other I had occasion to make to His Excellency, was complied with; and when the requisite number was selected, he gave me an official document, containing clauses relative to these men, well calculated to ensure their good conduct. As this document may be thought curious by many readers, it is here inserted; premising, that the men therein mentioned, with the exception of two, were convicts for life.

> Whereas Captain Matthew Flinders, commander of His Majesty's ship *Investigator*, has requested permission to receive on board that ship the undermentioned convicts as seamen, to make up the number he is deficient. I do hereby grant

> Thomas Toney        Thomas Martin      Joseph Marlow
> Thomas Shirley      Joseph Tuzo        Richard Stephenson
> Thomas Smith        Francis Smith      Charles Brown

> permission to ship themselves on board His Majesty's ship *Investigator*; and on the return of that ship to this port, according to Captain Flinders' recommendation of them, severally and individually, they will receive conditional emancipations or absolute pardons, as that officer may request...

Several of these men were seamen, and all were able and healthy; so that I considered them a great acquisition to our strength. With respect to themselves, the situation to which they were admitted was most desirable; since they had thereby a prospect of returning to their country, and that society from which they had been banished; and judging from the number of candidates for the vacancies, such was the light in which a reception on board the *Investigator* was considered in the colony. When the master was entered, one of the men, being over the complement, was sent to the *Lady Nelson*, with a reserve of the privilege above granted.

I had before experienced much advantage from the presence of a native of Port Jackson, in bringing about a friendly intercourse with the inhabitants of other parts of the coast; and on representing this to the governor, he authorised me to receive two on board. Bongaree, the worthy and brave fellow who had sailed with me in the *Norfolk*, now volunteered again; the other was Nanbaree, a good-natured lad, of whom Colonel Collins has made mention in his *Account of New South Wales*.

My instructions directed me to consult with Governor King upon the best means of proceeding in the execution of the voyage; they also pointed out my return to the south coast, as the first step after refitting the ship at Port Jackson; but His Excellency was of opinion, as well as myself, that it would be unsafe to do this in the middle of the winter season; and that to remain six months in port waiting for the fine weather would be a sad waste of time; I had, besides, left very little of importance to be examined upon the south coast, a circumstance which the instructions had not contemplated. Upon all these considerations, it was decided to proceed to the northward—examine Torres' Strait and the east side of the Gulf of Carpentaria before the north-west monsoon should set in—proceed as I might be able during its continuance—and afterwards explore the north and north-west coasts; returning to Port Jackson when, and by such route as might be found most advisable, and conducive to the general purposes of the voyage.

It was probable that the north-west monsoon would not set in before the beginning of November; I therefore intended to examine such parts of the east coast of New South Wales in my way to the northward, as had been passed by Captain Cook in the night, and were not seen in my expedition with the *Norfolk* sloop in 1799. The openings of Keppel and Shoal-water Bays, and the still larger of Broad Sound, I was also anxious to explore; in the hope of finding a river falling into some one of them, capable of admitting the *Lady Nelson* into the interior of the country. These desirable objects I expected to accomplish before the approach of the monsoon would call me into the Gulf of Carpentaria.

The French ships were in no forwardness for sailing; and it was understood that Captain Baudin intended sending back *Le Naturaliste* to France, by the way of Bass' Strait, so soon as the season should be favourable. He had purchased a small vessel of between thirty and forty tons at Sydney, to serve him as a tender; and he told me that we should probably meet in the Gulf of Carpentaria in December or January. I understood that he meant to return to the south coast, and after completing its examination, to proceed northward, and enter the Gulf with the north-west monsoon; but it appeared to me very probable, that the western winds on the south coast would detain him too long to admit of reaching the Gulf of Carpentaria at the time specified, or at any time before the south-east monsoon would set in against him...

*22 July 1802* ~ Lieutenant John Murray, commander of the brig *Lady Nelson*, having received orders to put himself under my command, I gave him a small code of signals and directed him, in case of separation, to repair to Hervey's Bay; which he was to enter by a passage said to have been found by the south-sea whalers, between Sandy Cape and Break-sea Spit. In the morning of 22 July, we sailed out of Port Jackson together; and the breeze being fair and fresh, ran rapidly to the northward, keeping at a little distance from the coast...

*25 July* ~ The sun was near setting at the time Cape Byron bore west, three or four miles; and the coast from thence to Point Look-out having been seen by Captain Cook, we steered off in order to avoid falling in with the reefs of Point Danger in the night...

A strange vessel seen to the southward, had induced me to carry little sail all the morning; it was now perceived not to be the *Lady Nelson*, but probably one of the two whalers known to be fishing off the coast; we therefore made sail for Cape Moreton, and came up with it at four o'clock. I was much surprised to see a small, but dangerous reef lying between four and five miles off this cape to

the north-east, which had not been noticed in the *Norfolk*; in entering Glass-house Bay I had then hauled close round Cape Moreton
at dusk in the evening, and in coming out had passed too far westward to observe it...

*27 July* ~ After passing the dangerous reef, we steered northward until three in the morning; and then hove to until daylight,
for the purpose of examining the land about Double-island Point
and Wide Bay, which did not appear to have been well distinguished by Captain Cook...On the north side of the point the
coast falls back to the westward, and presents a steep shore of white
sand; but in curving round Wide Bay the sandy land becomes very
low, and a small opening was seen in it, leading to a piece of water
like a lagoon; but the shoals which lie off the entrance render it
difficult of access, if indeed there be a passage for anything larger
than boats. Had the *Lady Nelson* been with me, I should have
attempted to get her into the lagoon, having previously entertained
a conjecture that the head of Hervey's Bay might communicate
with Wide Bay; but the apprehension that Lieutenant Murray
would arrive at the first rendezvous, and proceed to the next before
we could join him, deterred me from attempting it with the
*Investigator* or with boats.

Upon the north side of the opening there was a number of
Indians, fifty as reported, looking at the ship, and near Double-
island Point ten others had been seen, implying a more numerous
population than is usual to the southward. I inferred from hence,
that the piece of water at the head of Wide Bay was extensive and
shallow; for in such places the natives draw much subsistence from
the fish which there abound and are more easily caught than in
deep water. So far as could be seen from the masthead at three or
four miles off, the water extended about five miles westward, to the
feet of some hills covered with small wood. Its extent north and
south could not be distinguished, and it seemed probable that one,
and perhaps two streams fall into it; for there were many large
medusas floating at the entrance, such as are usually found near

the mouths of rivers in this country…Nothing however can well
be imagined more barren than this peninsula; but the smokes
which arose from many parts, corroborated the remark made upon
the population about Wide Bay; and bespoke that fresh water was
not scarce in this sandy country.

Our course at night was directed by the fires on the shore, and
the wind being moderate from the south-westward, it was continued until ten o'clock; after which we stood off and on till daylight,
and then had Indian Head bearing S54°W one mile and a half.
This head was so named by Captain Cook, from the great number
of Indians assembled there in 1770.

*30 July* ~ The first rendezvous appointed for Lieutenant
Murray, was the anchorage near Sandy Cape; but the wind being
unfavourable, we did not reach it till four on the following afternoon…A vessel was seen on the outside of the Spit, which proved
to be the *Lady Nelson*; and the master being sent with a boat to assist
her through the passage, she anchored near us at sunset, and
Lieutenant Murray came on board. The account he gave of his
separation, and the delay in arriving at the rendezvous, convinced
me both of the *Lady Nelson* being an indifferent vessel, and of the
truth of an observation before made upon the currents: that they
run much stronger to the southward at the distance of six, and
from that to twenty leagues off the coast, than they do close in with
the shore. Mr Murray not being much accustomed to make free
with the land, had kept it barely within sight, and had been much
retarded.

In order to give the botanists an opportunity of examining the
productions of Sandy Cape, I determined to remain here a day;
and some natives being seen upon the beach, a boat was sent to
commence an acquaintance with them; they however retired, and
suffered Mr Brown to botanise without disturbance. Next morning
the brig anchored within a quarter of a mile of the shore, to cover
our landing parties; and the armed boats being moored at grapnels, out of the reach of the natives, we separated into three

divisions. The naturalist's party, consisting of six persons, walked along the shore towards the upper part of the bay; Mr Murray and his people went to cut wood for fuel; and the party with me, also of six persons, including my native friend Bongaree, went towards the extremity of Sandy Cape. Several Indians with branches of trees in their hands were there collected and, whilst they retreated themselves, were waving to us to go back. Bongaree stripped off his clothes and laid aside his spear as inducements for them to wait for him; but finding they did not understand his language, the poor fellow, in the simplicity of his heart, addressed them in broken English, hoping to succeed better. At length they suffered him to come up, and by degrees our whole party joined; and after receiving some presents, twenty of them returned with us to the boats, and feasted upon the blubber of two porpoises, which had been brought on shore purposely for them. At two o'clock the naturalists returned, bringing some of the scoop nets used by the natives in catching fish; and we then quitted our new friends, after presenting them with hatchets and other testimonials of our satisfaction.

These people go entirely naked, and otherwise much resemble the inhabitants of Port Jackson in personal appearance; but they were more fleshy, perhaps from being able to obtain a better supply of food with the scoop nets, which are not known on the southern parts of the coast. I noticed in most of them a hard tumour on the outer knuckle of the wrist, which, if we understood them aright, was caused by the stretcher of the scoop coming in contact with this part in the act of throwing the net. Our native did not understand a word of their language, nor did they seem to know the use of his *womerah* or throwing stick; for one of them being invited to imitate Bongaree, who lanced a spear with it very dexterously and to a great distance, he, in the most awkward manner, threw both womerah and spear together. Nothing like a canoe was seen amongst these people; but they must have some means of passing over the water to short distances, since I found, in 1799, that Curlew Islet, near the head of this bay, had been visited...

*9 August* ~ In following the low and rather sandy shore, north-ward to Cape Capricorn, we passed within a rocky islet and another composed of rock and sand, four miles south-east of the cape, the soundings being there from 8 to 9 fathoms; and at ten o'clock hauled round for Cape Keppel, which lies from Cape Capricorn N80°W, ten miles. The shore is low, with some small inlets in it, and sandbanks with shoal water run off more than two miles; at six miles out there is a hummocky island and four rocks, one of which was at first taken for a ship...

My object in stopping at this bay was to explore two openings marked in it by Captain Cook, which it was possible might be the entrances of rivers leading into the interior. So soon as the ship was secured, a boat was sent to haul the seine, and I landed with a party of the gentlemen to inspect the bay from an eminence called Sea Hill...and early next morning I embarked in the *Lady Nelson*, intending to employ her and my whaleboat in exploring the bay and inlets, whilst the botanists made their excursions in the neighbourhood of the ship...

*11 August* ~ The numerous shoals in Keppel Bay rendering the services of the *Lady Nelson* in a great measure useless to the examination, I directed Lieutenant Murray to run out to the hummocky island lying to the north-east from Cape Keppel, and endeavour to take us some turtle; for there were no signs of inhabitants upon it, and turtle seemed to be plentiful in this neighbourhood. He was also to ascend the hills, and take bearings of any island or other object visible in the offing; and after making such remarks as circumstances might allow, to return not later than the third evening.

Next afternoon, I went, accompanied by the naturalist, to examine the eastern arm of the bay, which is divided into two branches. Pursuing the easternmost and largest, with soundings from 6 to 3 fathoms, we came to several mangrove islands, about four miles up, where the stream changed its direction from SSE to ESE, and the deepest water was 2 fathoms. A little further on we landed for the night, cutting a path through the mangroves to a higher part of the northern shore; but the swarms of mosquitoes and sandflies made sleeping impossible to all except one of the boat's crew, who was so enviably constituted, that these insects either did not attack him, or could not penetrate his skin…

*13 August* ~ The *Lady Nelson* had returned from the hummocky island, without taking any turtle. No good anchorage was found, nor was there either wood or water upon the island, worth the attention of a ship. Mr Murray ascended the highest of the hummocks with a compass, but did not see any lands in the offing further out than the Keppel Isles.

I left the ship again in the morning, and went up the southern arm to a little hill on its western shore; hoping to gain from thence a better knowledge of the various streams which intersect the low land on the south side of the bay…Our attempts to reach the top were fruitless. It would perhaps have been easier to climb up the trees, and scramble from one to another upon the vines, than to have penetrated through the intricate network in the darkness underneath.

Disappointed in my principal object, and unable to do anything in the boat, which could not then approach the shore within two hundred yards, I sought to walk upwards, and ascertain the communication between the south and south-west arms; but after much fatigue amongst the mangroves and muddy swamps, very little more information could be gained. The small fish which leaps on land upon two strong breast fins, and was first seen by Captain Cook on the shores of Thirsty Sound, was very common in the swamps round the South Hill. There were also numbers of a small kind of red crab, having one of its claws uncommonly large, being, indeed, nearly as big as the body; and this it keeps erected and open, so long as there is any expectation of disturbance. It was curious to see a file of these pugnacious little animals raise their claws at our approach, and open their pincers ready for an attack; and afterwards, finding there was no molestation, shoulder their arms and march on.

*15 August* ~ At nine in the evening, the tide brought the boat under the hill, and allowed us to return to the ship. All the examination of Keppel Bay which our time could allow, was now done; but a day being required for laying down the plan of the different arms, I offered a boat on Sunday morning to the botanists, to visit the South Hill, which afforded a variety of plants; but they found little that had not before fallen under their observation. A part of the ship's company was allowed to go on shore abreast of the ship, for no Indians had hitherto been seen there; but towards the evening, about twenty were observed in company with a party of the sailors. They had been met with near Cape Keppel, and at first menaced our people with their spears; but finding them inclined to be friendly, laid aside their arms, and accompanied the sailors to the ship in a good-natured manner. A master's mate and a seaman were, however, missing, and nothing was heard of them all night.

At daylight, two guns were fired and an officer was sent up the small inlet under Sea Hill; whilst I took a boat round to Cape Keppel, in the double view of searching for the absentees and obtaining a set of bearings from the top of the cape…

On my return to the ship, the master's mate and seaman were on board. The officer had very incautiously strayed away from his party, after natives had been seen; and at sunset, when he should have been at the beach, he and the man he had taken with him were entangled in a muddy swamp amongst mangroves, several miles distant; in which uncomfortable situation, and persecuted by clouds of mosquitoes, they passed the night. Next morning they got out of the swamp; but fell in with about twenty-five Indians, who surrounded and took them to a fireplace. A couple of ducks were broiled; and after the wanderers had satisfied their hunger and undergone a personal examination, they were conducted back to the ship in safety. Some of the gentlemen went to meet the natives with presents, and an interview took place, highly satisfactory to both parties; the Indians then returned to the woods, and our people were brought on board…

Wherever we landed there had been Indians; but it was near the ship only, that any of them made their appearance. They were described by the gentlemen who saw them, as stout, muscular men, who seemed to understand bartering better than most, or perhaps any people we had hitherto seen in this country. Upon the outer bone of the wrist they had the same hard tumour as the people of Hervey's Bay, and the cause of it was attempted, ineffectually, to be explained to one of the gentlemen; but as cast nets were seen in the neighbourhood, there seems little doubt that the manner of throwing them produces the tumours. These people were not devoid of curiosity; but several things which might have been supposed most likely to excite it, passed without notice. Of their dispositions we had every reason to speak highly, from their conduct to our sailors; but particularly to the master's mate and seaman who had lost themselves, and were absolutely in their power.

On the morning we quitted the bay, a large party was again seen, coming down to the usual place; which seemed to imply that our conduct and presents had conciliated their goodwill, and that they would be glad to have communication with another vessel.

It is scarcely necessary to say, that these people are almost black, and go entirely naked, since none of any other colour, or regularly wearing clothes, have been seen in any part of Terra Australis. About their fireplaces were usually scattered the shells of large crabs, the bones of turtle, and the remains of a parsnip-like root, apparently of fern; and once the bones of a porpoise were found; besides these, they doubtless procure fish, and wild ducks were seen in their possession...

The rocks and islands lying off Keppel Bay to the northward, are numerous and scattered without order; two of them are of greater magnitude than the rest, and Captain Cook had attempted to pass between these and the mainland, from which they are distant about five miles; but shoal water obliged him to desist. When we got under way in the morning of the 18th, our course was directed for the outside of these two islands, and we passed within a mile of them in 9, and from that to 13 fathoms water. They are five miles asunder, and the southernmost and largest is near twelve in circumference; its rocky hills are partly covered with grass and wood, and the gullies down the sides, as also the natives seen upon the island, implied that fresh water was to be had there...

At seven next morning, having then a light air from the land with foggy weather, we steered northward along the coast; and at noon were in latitude 22° 47½', and two rocks near the shore bore S54°W two or three miles. From that time until evening, we worked to windward against a breeze from the north-east, which afterwards veered to NNW; and at nine o'clock, a small anchor was dropped in 14 fathoms, two miles from the shore. The *Lady Nelson* had fallen to leeward; and made no answer to our signals during the night.

At daylight, supposing the brig had passed us by means of a shift of wind to WNW, we proceeded along the coast to the island lying off Cape Manifold...From Cape Manifold the coast falls back to a sandy beach, six miles long, and near it are some scattered rocks. The land is there very low; but at the north end of the beach is a hilly projection, from which we tacked at one o'clock, in 12 fathoms; being then within a mile of two rocks, and two miles from the main land. The brig was seen to the south-eastward, and we made a long stretch off, to give her an opportunity of joining, and at two in the morning lay by for her; but the wind veering to south-west at five, we stretched in for the land, and approached some rocky islets...At half past nine, when we tacked from Harvey's Isles, I was surprised to see trees upon them resembling the pines of Norfolk Island; none such having been before noticed upon this coast, nor to my knowledge, upon any coast of Terra Australis. Pines were also distinguished upon a more southern islet, four miles off, the same which had been the northern extreme at the preceding noon; and behind it was a deep bight in the land where there seemed to be shelter. The breeze had then shifted to south, and the *Lady Nelson* being to windward, the signal was made for her to look for anchorage; but the brig being very leewardly, we passed her and stood into the bight by an opening between the islets of one mile wide and from 10 to 7 fathoms in depth. On the soundings decreasing to 5, we tacked and came to an anchor near the pine island...Instead of a bight in the coast, we found this to be a port of some extent; which had not only escaped the observation of Captain Cook, but from the shift of wind, was very near being missed by us also. I named it Port Bowen, in compliment to Captain James Bowen of the navy...

A boat was despatched with the scientific gentlemen to the north side, where the hills rise abruptly and have a romantic appearance; another went to the same place to haul the seine at a small beach in front of a gully between the hills, where there was a prospect of obtaining fresh water; and a third boat was sent to Entrance Island with the carpenters to cut pine logs for various purposes, but, principally to make a main sliding keel for the *Lady Nelson*. Our little consort sailed indifferently at the best; but since the main keel had been carried away at Facing Island, it was unsafe to trust her on a lee shore, even in moderate weather...

*22 August* ~ A fresh wind from the south-eastward had blown all day, and raised so much surf on the north side of the port, that our watering there was much impeded; a midshipman and party of men remained on shore with casks all night, and it was not until next evening that the holds were completed and pine logs got on board. The water was very good; it drained down the gully to a little beach between two projecting heads which have rocky islets lying off them...

There were pine trees in the watering gully and on the neighbouring hills; but the best, and also the most convenient, were those upon Entrance Island, some of them being fit to make topmasts for ships. The branches are very brittle; but the carpenter thought the trunks to be tough, and superior to the Norway pine, both for spars and planks: turpentine exudes from between the wood and the bark, in considerable quantities. For a ship wanting to take in water and pine logs, the most convenient place is under Entrance Island, where we lay in the *Investigator*; indeed fresh water was not found in any other place...

Of the country round Port Bowen not much can be said in praise; it is in general either sandy or stony, and unfit for cultivation; nevertheless, besides pines, there are trees, principally eucalyptus, of moderate size, and the valleys of Cape Clinton are overspread with a tolerably good grass. No inhabitants were seen, but in every part where I landed, fires had been made, and the woods of Cape Clinton were then burning; the natives had also been upon Entrance Island, which implied them to have canoes, although none were seen. There are kangaroos in the woods; hawks, and the bald-headed mocking bird of Port Jackson are common; and ducks, sea-pies, and gulls frequent the shoals at low water. Fish were more abundant here than in any port before visited; those taken in the seine at the watering beach were principally mullet, but sharks and flying fish were numerous...

*24 August* ~ At daylight we steered out of Port Bowen by the northern passage, as we had gone in. The wind was from the westward; but so light, that when the ebb tide made from the north-west at ten o'clock, it was necessary to drop the kedge anchor for a time. In the evening we came to, in 10 fathoms fine grey sand, one mile and a half from the main; being sheltered between NE by E and E by S by the same cluster of small isles upon which the pine trees had been first seen...

*25 August* ~ A boat was lowered down, and I landed with the botanical gentlemen on the middle islet; where we found grass and a few shrubs, and also ants, grasshoppers and lizards. Upon the rocks were oysters of the small, crumbly kind, which seemed to indicate that the sea here is not violently agitated; and in the water we saw several large turtle, but were not able to harpoon any of them. Several of the Northumberland Isles were in sight from the top of the islet...When the tide slacked in the afternoon we stretched over towards Island Head, and saw a canoe with two

Indians, who made for the shore near a place where the woods were on fire. At dusk we anchored in 18 fathoms, soft mud, in a bight between Island Head and Cape Townshend, at the bottom of which was an opening one mile wide, where Captain Cook had suspected an entrance into Shoalwater Bay.

*26 August* ~ The *Lady Nelson* had fallen to leeward, as usual; and not being come up in the morning, the master was sent ahead of the ship in a boat, and we steered for the opening with a strong flood tide in our favour. From 22 fathoms, the water shoaled to 12, and suddenly to 3, on a rocky bottom, just as we reached the entrance. A kedge anchor was dropped immediately; but seeing that the opening went through, and that the master had deep water further in, it was weighed again, and we backed and filled the sails, drifting up with the tide so long as it continued to run. At nine o'clock the anchor was let go in 6 fathoms, sand and shells, one mile within the entrance, the points of which bore N84° and S89°E; but the extent of deep water was barely sufficient for the ship to swing at a whole cable.

Lieutenant Flinders landed on the north side of the entrance, and observed the latitude 22° 37' 53" from an artificial horizon; and a boat was sent to haul the seine upon a beach on the eastern shore, where fish to give half the ship's company a meal was procured. We had no prospect of advancing up the passage until the turn of tide, at three in the afternoon; and I therefore landed with a party of the gentlemen, and ascended the highest of the hills on the eastern side. From the top of it we could see over the land into Port Bowen; and some water was visible further distant at the back of it, which seemed to communicate with Shoal-water Bay. Of the passage where the ship was lying, there was an excellent view; and I saw not only that Cape Townshend was on a distinct island, but also that it was separated from a piece of land to the west, which Captain Cook's chart had left doubtful...Out at sea there were more of the Northumberland Islands, further westward than those before seen, the largest being not less distant than fifteen leagues; Pier Head, on the west side of Thirsty Sound, was also visible; and in the opposite direction was the highest of the two peaks behind Cape Manifold, the bearing of which connected this station with Port Curtis and Keppel Bay. The view was, indeed, most extensive from this hill; and in compliment to the landscape painter, who made a drawing from thence of Shoal-water Bay and the islands, I named it Mount Westall...

At dusk in the evening, when we returned on board, I found the *Lady Nelson* at anchor near us, and two boats absent from the ship. In hauling them up to be hoisted in, the cutter had been upset from the rapidity of the tides, which ran above four knots, the man in her was thrown out, and the boat went adrift. The man was taken up by the *Lady Nelson*; but the boatswain, who with two men in a small gig had gone after the cutter, was not heard of till next morning, when he returned without any intelligence of his object, having been bewildered in the dark by the rapid tides in a strange place, and in danger of losing himself...

*1 September* ~ During my absence, the naturalist and other gentlemen had gone over in the launch to the west side of the bay, where they had an interview with sixteen natives; their appearance was described as being much inferior to the inhabitants of Keppel and Hervey's Bays, but they were peaceable, and seemed to be very hungry. They had bark canoes which, though not so well formed, were better secured at the ends than those of Port Jackson; and in them were spears neatly pointed with pieces of quartz, for striking turtle. The number of bones lying about their fireplaces bespoke turtle to be their principal food; and with the addition of shellfish, and perhaps fern roots, it is probably their sole support...

*3 September* ~ At every port or bay we entered, more especially after passing Cape Capricorn, my first object on landing was to examine the refuse thrown up by the sea. The French navigator, La Pérouse, whose unfortunate situation, if in existence, was always present to my mind, had been wrecked, as it was thought, some-where in the neighbourhood of New Caledonia; and if so, the

remnants of his ships were likely to be brought upon this coast by
the trade winds, and might indicate the situation of the reef or
island which had proved fatal to him. With such an indication, I
was led to believe in the possibility of finding the place; and though
the hope of restoring La Pérouse or any of his companions to their
country and friends could not, after so many years, be rationally
entertained, yet to gain some certain knowledge of their fate would
do away the pain of suspense; and it might not be too late to
retrieve some documents of their discoveries.

Upon the south-east side of Aken's Island, there was thrown up
a confused mass of different substances; including a quantity of
pumice stone, several kinds of coral, five or six species of shells,
skeletons of fish and sea snakes, the fruit of the pandanus, and a
piece of cocoa-nut shell without barnacles or anything to indicate
that it had been long in the water; but there were no marks of shipwreck. A seine was hauled upon the small beaches at the south end
of the island, and brought on shore a good quantity of mullet, and
of a fish resembling a cavally; also a kind of horse mackerel, small
fish of the herring kind, and once a swordfish of between four and
five feet long. The projection of the snout, or sword of this animal,
a foot and a half in length, was fringed with strong, sharp teeth;
and he threw it from side to side in such a furious way, that it was
difficult to manage him even on shore...

*4 September* ~ At noon when the botanical gentlemen returned
from their excursion to Pine Mount, we made sail out of
Shoal-water Bay with a breeze from the eastward. In steering
north-west amongst the small islands, the soundings were between
9 and 14 fathoms; and nearly the same afterwards, in keeping at
three or four miles from the coast. I intended to go into Thirsty
Sound; but not reaching it before dark, the anchor was dropped in
8 fathoms, sandy bottom, when the top of Pier Head bore west,
three miles. In the morning we ran into the Sound, and anchored
in 6 fathoms, with the points of entrance bearing N16° and S67°E,
one mile. The carpenters had for some time been employed in

making a sliding keel for the *Lady Nelson*, from the pine logs cut in Port Bowen; and being now finished, it was sent on board...

*7 September* ~ In the morning I ascended the highest hill on the seventh island, and took bearings; but the hazy weather which had come on with a strong wind at ESE, confined them within a circle of three leagues. This island is somewhat more than a mile in length, and was covered with grass, but almost destitute of wood; the rock is a greenish, speckled stone, with veins of quartz finely inserted, and is something between granite and porphyry...

I looked anxiously, but in vain, for Lieutenant Fowler to come out of Thirsty Sound; for the wind blew so strong that it was uncertain whether the boat could fetch over, or that it was even safe to attempt it; our provisions, besides, were nearly exhausted, and nothing more substantial than oysters could be procured. Pressed by necessity, we set off under close-reefed sails; and the boat performing admirably, fetched the low neck to leeward of Pier Head, whence another boat took us to the ship; and at high water in the evening, the whaleboat floated over the neck and followed...

*15 September* ~ Towards Double Mount and Shoal-water Bay, the country consisted of gently rising hills and extensive plains, well covered with wood and apparently fertile. The stream at the head of Broad Sound could not be traced from hence more than three or four miles above the tent; but it may possibly run up much further to the south-eastward, though too small to be distinguished in the wood, or to be navigable for boats. To the south and westward there was a ridge of high land, which appeared to be a prolongation of the same whence the upper branches of Port Bowen and Shoal-water Bay take their rise, and by which the low land and small arms on the west side of Broad Sound are bounded. A similar ridge ran behind Port Curtis and Keppel Bay, and it is not improbable that the two are connected, and of the same substance; for at Port Curtis the basis stone of the country was a granite, and this small hill was the same. It has been more than once observed, that granite is amongst the substances which exert an influence upon the magnetic needle; and it is to the attraction of the ridge of mountains to the south and westward, that I attribute the great variation found in the bearings at this station.

We returned to the tent at sunset; and there passed a disagreeable night amongst mosquitoes, sandflies and ants. At four in the morning the ebb had made, and we embarked in the boat; but the depth of water was so little that we could not proceed, and were obliged to re-land and wait for the following tide; not without apprehension of being left till the next springs came on. At two in the afternoon the flood came up rapidly, and in half an hour it was high water; we set off immediately, and after some trouble from the shoals, reached the brig at five o'clock.

*17 September* ~ Mr Murray got under way at three the next morning to beat down to Upper Head, the wind being from the northward; but the *Lady Nelson* getting aground, I went off with Mr Brown in my boat, and reached the ship at seven o'clock, and in the evening, the brig arrived.

Lieutenant Fowler had gone through the most essential duties, and the ship was nearly ready for sea; but on landing at the tents I found that the time keepers had been let down, and the business of finding new rates for them was to be recommenced. This accident would require a week to be repaired; and being unwilling to remain so long inactive, I determined to leave Mr Flinders at Upper Head, and take the ship over to the inner end of Thirsty Sound, where it appeared there was something to correct in Captain Cook's chart.

*18 September* ~ The *Lady Nelson* had lost two sheets of copper, and the trunks of the sliding keels required some reparation; I therefore desired Lieutenant Murray to lay his vessel on shore and get these matters arranged, to cut wood for himself, and be ready to sail in a week for Torres' Strait; and his stock of water was completed out of the *Investigator*...

*21 September* ~ The botanical gentlemen went over in the launch to the east side of Thirsty Sound, the mainland having been always found more productive in the objects of their pursuit, than any island however large. I went to examine along the west side of Long Island; but had not proceeded two miles before an opening presented itself amongst the mangroves. It led to the eastward, and then separated into two branches; and in following that which trended north-east I came into Thirsty Sound, and landed five miles above the inner entrance, at an islet in mid-channel, which had been set from Pier Head and is laid down by Captain Cook.

No less than five different pieces of land were found to be cut off from the south end of Long Island, by winding channels amongst the mangroves; and I now saw the prospect of a passage through the middle, leading out at the bight between the north point and Pier Head...

Not a single Indian was seen during this excursion round Long Island; nor from the length of the grass and appearance of their fireplaces, do I think they had been there for some months.

*23 September* ~ I made a further examination of the winding channels at the south end of Long Island; and also went to an inlet on the east side of Broad Sound, the entrance of which is so much obstructed by shoals, that it was difficult to find a sufficient depth, even for the boat. I landed with the naturalist at a low, cliffy head on the north side of the entrance; but not without wading a quarter of a mile in the mud. We saw from thence, that this inlet, though presenting the appearance of a respectable river when the tide was in, had no perceptible breadth at five miles within the land, that it was almost wholly dry at low water, and that the shores were covered with mangroves to a great extent; even the cliffy head where we stood, was surrounded with mangroves, and appeared to be insulated at spring tides.

*24 September* ~ In the morning we got under way to return to Upper Head; and having the same difficulties to encounter amongst the shoals as before, did not reach our former anchorage until next day. On landing at the tents, I found, to my no less surprise than regret, that the time keepers had again been let down;

and no more than one day's rates had been since obtained. Twenty-five sets of distances of the sun and moon had been taken to correspond with an equal number on the opposite side; and it appeared that Lieutenant Flinders being intent upon these, had forgotten to wind up the time keepers on the 22nd at noon.

This fresh difficulty was very embarrassing. To go away for Torres' Strait and the Gulf of Carpentaria without good rates, was to cripple the accuracy of all our longitudes; and on the other hand, the expected approach of the contrary monsoon on the north coast admitted of no longer delay in Broad Sound. On comparing the last day's rates with those of the four days previously obtained, the letting down did not appear to have produced any material alteration; and I therefore determined to combine the whole together, and to sail immediately...

*28 September* ~ On quitting Broad Sound, we steered for the north-easternmost of the Northumberland Islands, which I intended to visit in the way to Torres' Strait. These are no otherwise marked by Captain Cook, than as a single piece of land seen indistinctly, of three leagues in extent; but I had already descried from Mount Westall and Pier Head a cluster of islands, forming a distinct portion of this archipelago; and in honour of the noble house to which Northumberland gives the title of Duke, I named them Percy Isles...

*29 September* ~ We got under way again in the morning; but the wind being light and unfavourable, and the tide adverse, I went off in the whaleboat, accompanied by Messrs Brown and Westall, to examine the passage between the rocky islets and No. 2 [the largest of the Percy Isles], directing Lieutenant Fowler to follow with the ship when the signal should be made. We first landed at the islets, where the same kind of pine as seen at Port Bowen and other places, was abundant; and leaving the two gentlemen there, I sounded the passage, which was a mile and a half wide, with a sandy bottom of 8 to 13 fathoms deep, and sheltered from all eastern winds. The signal was then made to the ship; and so soon as she was brought to anchor, I went to examine a little cove, or basin, into which the height of the surrounding hills gave expectation of finding a run of fresh water. The entrance is little more than wide enough for the oars of a rowing boat, the basin, within side, is mostly dry at low water, and the borders are over-run with the tiresome mangrove; but when the tide is in, it is one of the prettiest little places imaginable. In searching round the skirts, between the mangroves and feet of the hills, a torrent-worn gully was found with several holes of water; and one in particular, near the edge of the mangroves, where, by cutting a rolling way for the casks, the holds of the two vessels might be filled; and at a beach without side of the entrance to the basin, several hauls of the seine were made with good success.

Early next morning, Lieutenant Fowler landed with a party of men prepared to cut through the mangroves; but fresh water was discovered to ooze out from amongst them, much below high-water mark; and by digging in the sand at half ebb, our casks might be filled more easily, and with better water than in the gully. Whilst this duty was going on, the carpenters were sent to cut firewood and pine logs upon the rocky islets, the botanical gentlemen followed their pursuits where it best pleased them, and my time was occupied in surveying...

*3 October* ~ ...No inhabitants were seen upon any of the islands, but there were deserted fireplaces upon all. The Indians probably come over from the mainland at certain times, to take turtle, in which they must be much more dexterous than we were; for although many turtle were seen in the water, and we watched the beaches at night, not one was caught. There are no kangaroos upon the Percy Isles; nor did we see any useful birds. The large bats or vampires, common to this country, and called flying-foxes at Port Jackson, were often found hanging by the claws, with their heads downward, under the shady tops of the palm trees; and one solitary eel of a good size was caught on clearing out the hole where our water casks had been first intended to be filled. Pines, fresh water, and fish will be some inducement to visit the Percy Isles; as perhaps may be the hump-backed whales, of which a considerable number was seen in the vicinity...

Early in the morning of the 4th, we got under way, with the *Lady Nelson* in company, to proceed on our voyage to Torres' Strait and the Gulf of Carpentaria...

During the night we tacked every two hours, working to the eastward, in from 30 to 36 fathoms; and at daylight, my station on the eastern isle No. 4 bore N89°W, four leagues. Nothing was seen in the offing, but in stretching to the NNE, reefs were discovered from the masthead a little before noon; and after the observation for the latitude was taken, I set one bearing east to E by S, two leagues, and another N14°W to 29°E, four or five miles. Our situation was in 21° 15²/₃' south, and longitude from the bearing of the Pine Peak, 150° 34' east.

These reefs were not exactly those seen by Mr Campbell; but they are probably not more than five or six leagues to the north-westward of them, and form part of the same barrier to the coast. In standing on between the two reefs above set, others, or parts of the same, came in sight ahead; upon which I shortened sail to the three top sails, desired the *Lady Nelson* to take the lead, and bore away north-westward along the inner side of the northern reef. In an hour we had passed its west end; but another reef came in sight, and for a time obliged us to steer W by S. At four o'clock we ran northward again, following the direction of the reef on its lee side...The reefs were not dry in any part, with the exception of some small black lumps, which at a distance resembled the round heads of negroes; the sea broke upon the edges, but within side the water was smooth, and of a light green colour...

*5 October* ~ Until midnight, five hours after the moon had passed the meridian, a tide came from S by E, half a mile per hour. The ship then tended to the NE by E; and this tide, whose rate was one mile, appearing to be the flood, led me to suppose there might be an open sea in that direction. In the morning, I sent a boat to

Lieutenant Murray with instructions for his guidance in case of
separation; and appointed him Murray's Islands in Torres' Strait,
discovered by Captain Edwards in 1791, for the first rendezvous;
cautioning him to be strictly on his guard against the treachery of
the natives...

*8 October* ~ At seven, when the flood had done running, the two
vessels were lying up ENE, with a light breeze from the northward;
but a rippling which extended a mile from the reef, caused us to
tack until a boat was sent to sound upon it; for the *Lady Nelson* was
so leewardly, that much time was lost in waiting for her. At ten we
passed through the rippling, in from 14 to 34 fathoms; and at noon
were in latitude 20° 55', and longitude 150° 55' by time keeper. We
seemed at this time to be surrounded with reefs; but it was ascertained by the whaleboat, that many of these appearances were
caused by the shadows of clouds and the ripplings and eddies of
tide, and that the true coral banks were those only which had either
green water or negro heads upon them. Of these, however, there
was a formidable mass, all round ahead, with but one small
channel through them; and this I was resolved to attempt, in the
hope of its carrying us out to windward of the high breakers.

At two o'clock, the eastern reef, which was a mile distant to
leeward and nearly dry, was seen to terminate, whilst the northern
reefs extended out of sight to the north-east; the opening between
them was a mile and a half wide, and full of ripplings; but having the
whaleboat ahead, we bore away ESE, to go through the least agitated
part. Having little wind and a flood tide making against us, the boat
was called back to tow, and the brig directed to take its station by
means of her sweeps. At sunset, the stream anchor was dropped on
a bottom of coral sand and shells; the reefs then in sight extending
from about ESE, round by the north to NW, where was the great
northern bank. Whether there were any passage through them, could
not be discerned; but the breakers on many of the outer parts proved
the open sea to be not far distant, and that the waves ran high; whilst
within side, the water was as tranquil as in harbour...

*9 October* ~ In the morning we steered ENE, with a light air from the southward; the brig was ahead, and at half past nine, made the signal for immediate danger; upon which the stream anchor was dropped in 16 fathoms. The tide ran one mile and a half to the ENE, and this leading me to expect some opening in that direction, I sent the master to sound past the brig; and on his finding deeper water we followed, drifting with the tide. At eleven he made the signal for being on a shoal, and we came to, in 35 fathoms, broken coral and sand; being surrounded by reefs, except to the westward from whence we had come. On the outside were high breakers, not more than three or four miles distant; these terminated at E by S, and between them and other reefs further on, there seemed a possibility of finding an outlet; but no access to it could be had, except by a winding circuit amongst the great mass of banks to the southward, which it was not advisable to make upon such an uncertainty. I therefore determined to remain at the present anchorage till low water when the reefs would be dry, and the channels between them, if any such there were, would be visible; and should nothing better then present itself, to steer north-westward, as close within the line of the high breakers as possible, until an opening should be found.

The latitude observed to the north and south, at this fifth anchorage amongst the reefs, was 20° 53' 15"; longitude by time keeper, 151° 5' east. In the afternoon, I went upon the reef with a party of the gentlemen; and the water being very clear round the edges, a new creation, as it was to us, but imitative of the old, was there presented to our view. We had wheat sheaves, mushrooms, stags horns, cabbage leaves, and a variety of other forms, glowing under water with vivid tints of every shade betwixt green, purple, brown, and white; equalling in beauty and excelling in grandeur the most favourite *parterre* of the curious florist. These were different species of coral and fungus, growing, as it were, out of the solid rock, and each had its peculiar form and shade of colouring; but whilst contemplating the richness of the scene, we could not long forget with what destruction it was pregnant.

Different corals in a dead state, concreted into a solid mass of a dull-white colour, composed the stone of the reef. The negro heads were lumps which stood higher than the rest; and being generally dry, were blackened by the weather; but even in these, the forms of the different corals, and some shells were distinguishable. The edges of the reef, but particularly on the outside where the sea broke, were the highest parts; within, there were pools and holes containing live corals, sponges, and sea eggs and cucumbers; and many enormous cockles (*chama gigas*) were scattered upon different parts of the reef. At low water, this cockle seems most commonly to lie half-open; but frequently closes with much noise; and the water within the shells then spouts up in a stream, three or four feet high: it was from this noise and the spouting of the water, that we discovered them, for in other respects they were scarcely to be distinguished from the coral rock. A number of these cockles were taken on board the ship, and stewed in the coppers; but they were too rank to be agreeable food, and were eaten by few. One of them weighed 47½ lbs as taken up, and contained 3 lbs 2 oz of meat; but this size is much inferior to what was found by captains Cook and Bligh, upon the reefs of the coast further northward, or to several in the British Museum; and I have since seen single shells more than four times the weight of the above shells and fish taken together.

There were various small channels amongst the reefs, some of which led to the outer breakers, and through these the tide was rushing in when we returned to the ship; but I could not anywhere see an opening sufficiently wide for the vessels...

*10 October* ~ At daylight we steered NNW; but reefs were presently seen all round in that direction, and the course was altered for the small passage through which we had come on the 8th. Such, however, was the change in the appearance of the reefs, that no passage could then be discovered; and fearing to be mistaken, I dared not venture through, but took a more southern channel, where before no passage had appeared to exist.

The *Investigator*, with Flinders' often used whale-boat in the foreground. This model was made by Roland Michel Laroche in 1980.

'Firm, just, punctual, clear-headed. Nicknamed "Indefatigable". Liberal and kind.' Portrait of Matthew Flinders, painted in Mauritius around 1806 by Toussaint Antoine de Chazel.

The great map which Matthew Flinders risked so much to create.
His life's work is encapsulated in its detail.

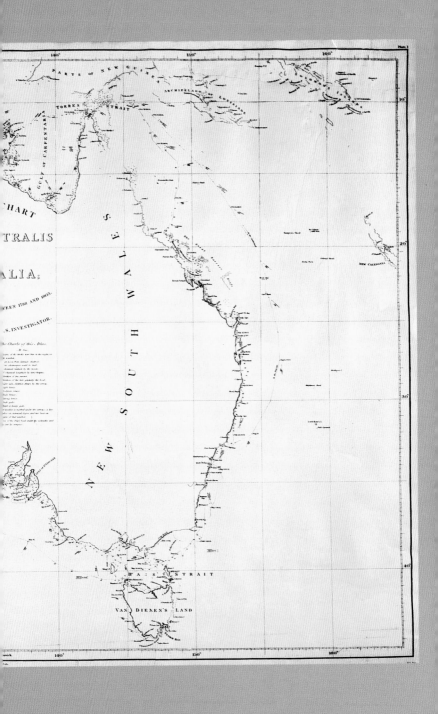

King George's Sound, Western Australia. This was the first port of call for William Westall, who painted this oil many years later.

This peaceful view of Kangaroo Island stands in stark contrast to Flinders' account while on the island. This 1814 William Woolnoth engraving is based on an original Westall drawing.

Opposite: Ferdinand Bauer's *Banksia coccinea*, a species restricted to the south-west of Western Australia. Bauer was a prolific botanical artist.

*Banksia coccinea.*

Brown. prod. fl. nov. holl. p. 394. n. 17.

Ferd. Bauer

Above: Bongaree (Bungaree) accompanied Flinders on two of his voyages and was the first Aboriginal circumnavigator of Australia.

Top right: Pobassoo, the captain of the Macassan fleet Flinders encountered off Arnhem Land in 1803. Pobassoo first visited Australia some ten years before the arrival of the First Fleet.

Right: A rough sketch of Woga (Woogah), one of the Caledon Bay natives who proved so troublesome to Flinders.

This watercolour of the Murray Isles is a composite of a number of Westall's drawings depicting the natives greeting Flinders' ship and keen to barter.

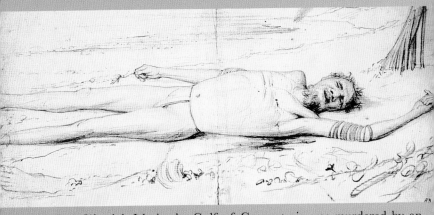

A man from Woodah Isle in the Gulf of Carpentaria was murdered by an *Investigator* crew member on 20 January 1803. In making this sketch William Westall was careful to omit incriminating details.

The *Porpoise* cast upon what was to be known as Wreck Reef. In the foreground crew members are plucked from the water.

Wreck Reef with the *Porpoise* and *Cato* encampment. William Westall's painting shows a fanciful coral reef exposed in an unlikely manner.

Next morning, the brig and whaleboat went ahead, and we steered north, after them; the eastern opening was choked up with small reefs, and we had scarcely entered that to the west when Mr Murray made the signal for danger, and hauled the wind to the southward. We did the same, round two inner shoals; and finding the bottom irregular, and more shallow than usual, dropped the stream anchor in 27 fathoms. The *Lady Nelson* was carried rapidly to the south-west, seemingly without being sensible of it, and I therefore made the signal of recall; but although favoured by a fresh breeze, she did not get up against the tide till past nine o'clock. We rode a great strain on the stream cable, and the ship taking a sudden sheer, it parted at the clinch and we lost the anchor; a bower was immediately let go; but the bottom being rocky, I feared to remain during the lee tide, and in a short time ordered it to be weighed. Mr Murray had lost a kedge anchor, and was then riding by a bower; and when the signal was made to weigh, he answered it by that of inability. The tide was, indeed, running past the brig at a fearful rate, and I feared it would pass over her bows; for she lay in one of the narrow streams which came gushing through the small openings in the outer reef. So soon as our anchor was purchased, a boat's crew was sent to her assistance; and just before noon she got under sail.

We beat up till one o'clock, towards the anchorage of the preceding evening; but the reefs being deeply covered, they could not be distinguished one from the other; and having found a good bottom, in 35 fathoms, we came to, and made signal for the brig to do the same. Lieutenant Murray informed me that his anchor had come up with a palm broken off; and having only one bower left, he applied to me for another. Our anchor had swivelled in the stock; and the work required to it, with getting the last stream anchor out of the hold, and sending Mr Murray two grapnels, which were all that our own losses could allow of being spared, occupied us till the evening...

The loss of anchors we had this day sustained, deterred me

from any more attempting the small passages through the Barrier
Reef; in these, the tide runs with extraordinary violence, and the
bottom is coral rock; and whether with, or without wind, no situation can be more dangerous. My anxious desire to get out to sea,
and reach the north coast before the unfavourable monsoon should
set in, had led me to persevere amongst these intricate passages
beyond what prudence could approve; for had the wind come to
blow strong, no anchors, in such deep water and upon loose sand,
could have held the ship; a rocky bottom cut the cables; and to
have been under sail in the night was certain destruction. I therefore formed the determination, in our future search for a passage
out, to avoid all narrow channels, and run along, within side the
larger reefs, until a good and safe opening should present itself...

*17 October* ~ At daylight the breeze was moderate at E by N,
with fine weather; and in steering northward, close to the wind, we
passed three miles to leeward of a dry bank of rocks and sand.
Several of the Cumberland Islands were in sight at noon...

No reefs were in sight, nor in steering NNE and NE by N, could
any be distinguished from the masthead all the afternoon. At half
past five we tacked and bore down to the brig; and then anchored
in 31 fathoms, speckled sand and small stones, and sent a boat to
Lieutenant Murray with orders.

Our latitude here, by an observation of the moon, was 20° 10'
south; and now hoping we should not meet with any more interruption from the reefs, I resolved to send the brig back to Port
Jackson. The *Lady Nelson* sailed so ill, and had become so leewardly
since the loss of the main, and part of the after keel, that she not
only caused us delay, but ran great risk of being lost; and instead
of saving the crew of the *Investigator*, in case of accident, which was
one of the principal objects of her attendance, it was too probable
we might be called upon to render her that assistance. A good
vessel of the same size I should have considered the greatest
acquisition in Torres' Strait and the Gulf of Carpentaria; but
circumstanced as was the *Lady Nelson*, and in want of anchors and

cables which could not be spared without endangering our own safety, she was become, and would be more so every day, a burden rather than an assistant to me. Lieutenant Murray was not much acquainted with the kind of service in which we were engaged; but the zeal he had shown to make himself and his vessel of use to the voyage, made me sorry to deprive him of the advantage of continuing with us; and increased my regret at the necessity of parting from our little consort.

The stores and provisions already supplied to the brig, were returned; and Mr Murray spared us his old launch, to replace, in some sort, the cutter we had lost in Strong-tide Passage. Nanbaree, one of the two natives, having expressed a wish to go back to Port Jackson, was sent to the *Lady Nelson* in the morning, with two seamen exchanged for the same number of that vessel's crew; and Mr Denis Lacy, who had been lent, returned back to the *Investigator*. I wrote to His Excellency Governor King, an account of our proceedings and discoveries upon the east coast; and requested a new boat might be built against our return to Port Jackson, and that the brig should be repaired and equipped ready to accompany me in the following year.

I shall conclude...with some general remarks on the reefs, which form so extraordinary a barrier to this part of New South Wales; and amongst which we sought fourteen days, and sailed more than five hundred miles, before a passage could be found through them, out to sea.

The easternmost parts of the barrier seen in the *Investigator*, lie nearly in 21° south and 151° 10' east; but there can be no doubt that they are connected with the reefs lying to the southward, discovered in 1797 by Captain Campbell of the brig *Deptford*; and probably also with those further distant, which Captain Swain of the *Eliza* fell in with in the following year. If so, the Barrier Reefs will commence as far south-eastward as the latitude 22° 50' longitude about 152° 40', and possibly still further. Break-sea Spit is a coral reef, and a connection under water, between it and the barrier, seems not improbable. The opening by which we passed out, is in 18° 52', and 148° 2'; so that, did the Barrier Reefs terminate here, their extent would be near 350 miles in a straight line; and in all this space, there seems to be no large opening. Mr Swain did, indeed, get out at the latitude 22°; but it was by a long, and very tortuous channel.

Of what extent our opening may be, is uncertain; but since Captain Cook had smooth water in running to the west and northward to Cape Tribulation, where he first saw the reefs, it should seem to be not very great; certainly, as I think, not exceeding twenty, and perhaps not five leagues. I therefore assume it as a great probability, that with the exception of this, and perhaps several small openings, our Barrier Reefs are connected with the Labyrinth of Captain Cook; and that they reach to Torres' Strait and to New Guinea, in 9° south; or through 14° of latitude and 9° of longitude; which is not to be equalled in any other known part of the world...

An arm of the sea is enclosed between the barrier and the coast, which is at first twenty-five or thirty leagues wide; but is contracted to twenty, abreast of Broad Sound, and to nine leagues at Cape Gloucester; from whence it seems to go on diminishing, till, a little beyond Cape Tribulation, reefs are found close to the shore. Numerous islands lie scattered in this enclosed space; but so far as we are acquainted, there are no other coral banks in it than those by which some of the islands are surrounded; so that being sheltered from the deep waves of the ocean, it is particularly well adapted to the purposes of a coasting trade. The reader will be struck with the analogy which this arm of the sea presents to one in nearly the same latitude of the northern hemisphere. The Gulf of Florida is formed by the coast of America on the west, and by a great mass of islands and shoals on the east; which shoals are also of coral.

On the outside of the barrier, the sea appears to be generally unfathomable; but within, and amongst the reefs, there are sound-

ings everywhere. Nor is the depth very unequal, where the bottom
is sandy; but like the breadth of the reefs and the arm they enclose,
it diminishes as we advance northward, from 60 to 48, to 35, and
to 30 fathoms near our opening; and to 20 at Cape Tribulation.
The further to leeward, the shallower the water, seems to be a law
amongst coral reefs...

In the morning of the 27th, a small land bird, resembling a
linnet, was seen; at noon we were in 10° 28' south and 146° 7' east,
and the current had set WNW, three quarters of a mile an hour,
since the 25th. The wind, which had been at south-east, then
shifted suddenly to north, and blew fresh with squally weather; but
at midnight it veered to south-east again. These changes were
accompanied with thunder, lightning and rain; indications, as I
feared, of the approaching north-west monsoon. We lay to, during
a part of the night; and at daybreak bore away again upon our
north-western course...

*28 October* ~ Our latitude at noon was exactly that of the
opening by which Captain Edwards of the *Pandora* had entered
the strait in 1791; and which I call the Pandora's Entrance. This
opening appeared to be preferable to that further northward, by
which Captain Bligh and Mr Bampton had got within the reefs;
more especially as it led directly for Murray's Islands, where, if
possible, I intended to anchor. Our course was therefore steered
west; and seeing no more reefs, it was continued until eight in the
evening, at which time we hauled to the wind, having no bottom
at 105 fathoms...

*29 October* ~ Finding by the latitude that we had been set considerably to the north, and were out of the parallel of Murray's
Islands, I tacked to the SSW; and at two o'clock, the largest island
was seen bearing S38°W about five leagues. Soon afterward, a reef
came in sight to the south-east, extending in patches towards the
islands; and presently another was distinguished to the westward,
from the masthead, which took nearly a parallel direction, the
passage between them being about four miles wide. We steered

along the lee side of the eastern reef, at the distance of a mile, with
soundings from 29 to 24 fathoms, coral sand, until four o'clock; the
reef then trended more southward, and we edged away for the
islands, of which Mr Westall sketched the appearance. At half past
five, the largest island bore S36°E to 28°W, one mile and a half;
and there being more reefs coming in sight to the westward, the
anchor was immediately let go in 20 fathoms, coarse sand and
shells. The north and east sides of the island are surrounded by a
reef, which may probably include the two smaller isles on its
south-west side; but it is totally unconnected with the reefs to the
north-east. These appear to be a northern continuation of the vast
bank, on the outside of which the *Pandora* sailed as far as $11^1/_2$°
south, and in the chart of Captain Edwards' track, published by
Mr Dalrymple, it is marked as surrounding the islands; whereas it
is at least four miles distant from the reef which probably does
surround them.

A number of poles standing up in various places, more especially between the islands, appeared at a distance like the masts of
canoes, and made me apprehend that the inhabitants of the strait
had collected a fleet here; but on approaching nearer, the poles
were found to be upon the reefs, and were probably set up for some
purpose connected with fishing.

We had scarcely anchored when between forty and fifty Indians
came off, in three canoes. They would not come alongside of the
ship, but lay off at a little distance, holding up cocoa-nuts, joints of
bamboo filled with water, plantains, bows and arrows, and voci-
ferating *tooree! tooree!* and *mammoosee!* A barter soon commenced,
and was carried on in this manner: a hatchet, or other piece of iron
(*tooree*) being held up, they offered a bunch of green plantains, a
bow and quiver of arrows, or what they judged would be received
in exchange; signs of acceptance being made, the Indian leaped
overboard with his barter, and handed it to a man who went down
the side to him; and receiving his hatchet, swam back to the canoe.
Some delivered their articles without any distrust of the exchange,

but this was not always the case. Their eagerness to get *tooree* was great, and at first, anything of that same metal was received; but afterwards, if a nail were held up to an Indian, he shook his head, striking the edge of his right hand upon the left arm, in the attitude of chopping; and he was well enough understood.

At sunset, two of the canoes returned to Murray's Island, paddling to windward with more velocity than one of our boats could have rowed; the third set a narrow, upright sail, between two masts in the fore part of the canoe, and steered north-westward, as I judged, for the Darnley's Island of Captain Bligh.

I did not forget that the inhabitants of these islands had made an attack upon the *Providence* and *Assistant* in 1792; nor that Mr Bampton had some people cut off at Darnley's Island in 1793. The marines were therefore kept under arms, the guns clear, and matches lighted; and officers were stationed to watch every motion, one to each canoe, so long as they remained near the ship. Bows and arrows were contained in all the canoes; but no intention of hostility was manifested by the Indians, unless those who steered for Darnley's Island might be supposed to go for assistance.

*30 October* ~ We did not get under way in the morning until the sun was high enough for altitudes to be taken for the time keepers. Soon after daylight, the natives were with us again, in seven canoes; some of them came under the stern, and fifteen or twenty of the people ascended on board, bringing in their hands pearl-oyster shells and necklaces of cowries; with which, and some bows and arrows, they obtained more of the precious *tooree*. Wishing to secure the friendship and confidence of these islanders to such vessels as might hereafter pass through Torres' Strait, and not being able to distinguish any chief amongst them, I selected the oldest man, and presented him with a hand-saw, a hammer and nails and some other trifles; of all which we attempted to show him the use, but I believe without success; for the poor old man became frightened on finding himself to be so particularly noticed.

At this time we began to heave short for weighing, and made

signs to the Indians to go down into their canoes, which they seemed unwilling to comprehend; but on the seamen going aloft to loose the sails, they went hastily down the stern ladder and ship's sides, and shoved off; and before the anchor was up they paddled back to the shore, without our good understanding having suffered any interruption.

The colour of these Indians is a dark chocolate; they are active, muscular men, about the middle size, and their countenances expressive of a quick apprehension. Their features and hair appeared to be similar to those of the natives of New South Wales, and they also go quite naked; but some of them had ornaments of shell work, and of plaited hair or fibres of bark, about their waists, necks and ankles. Our friend Bongaree could not understand anything of their language, nor did they pay much attention to him; he seemed, indeed, to feel his own inferiority, and made but a poor figure amongst them.

The two masts of their canoes, when not wanted, are laid along the gunwales; when set up, they stand abreast of each other in the fore part of the canoe, and seemed to be secured by one set of shrouds, with a stay from one masthead to the other. The sail is extended between them; but when going with a side wind, the lee mast is brought aft by a back stay, and the sail then stands obliquely. In other words, they brace up by setting in the head of the lee mast, and perhaps the foot also; and can then lie within seven points of the wind, and possibly nearer. This was their mode, so far as a distant view would admit of judging; but how these long canoes keep to the wind, and make such way as they do, without any after sail, I am at a loss to know.

Murray's largest island is nearly two miles long, by something more than one in breadth; it is rather high land, and the hill at its eastern end may be seen from a ship's deck at the distance of eight or nine leagues, in a clear day. The two smaller isles seemed to be single hills, rising abruptly from the sea, and to be scarcely accessible; nor did we see upon them any fires, or other marks of

inhabitants. On the shores of the large island were many huts,
surrounded by palisades, apparently of bamboo; cocoa-nut trees
were abundant, both on the low grounds and the sides of the hills,
and plantains, with some other fruits, had been brought to us.
There were many Indians sitting in groups upon the shore, and the
seven canoes which came off to the ship in the morning, contained
from ten to twenty men each, or together, about a hundred. If we
suppose these hundred men to have been one half of what
belonged to the islands, and to the two hundred men, add as many
women and three hundred children, the population of Murray's
Isles will amount to seven hundred; of which nearly the whole must
belong to the larger island...

Knowing the difficulties experienced by Captain Bligh and Mr
Bampton in the northern part of the strait, I kept as much up to
the southward, for Cape York, as the direction of the reefs would
admit. On the windward side, we had a long chain of them extending WSW to a great distance; but its breadth was not great, as the
blue water was seen beyond it, from the masthead. On the north
side there was no regular chain, and but one reef of much extent;
small patches were indeed announced every now and then, from
aloft, but these did not cause us much impediment...At half past
two, we passed between reefs one mile and a half asunder, having
no ground at 25 fathoms; and then the chain which had been
followed from Murray's Isles, either terminated or took a more
southern direction. Another small, woody isle was then in sight,
nearly in our track, at four it bore N67°W, two and a half miles;
and not seeing any other island ahead to afford shelter for the
night, we bore away round the south end of its reef, and came to
an anchor in 17 fathoms, coral sand...

A boat was lowered down, and I went on shore with the botanical gentlemen, to look about the island. It is little better than a
bank of sand, upon a basis of coral rock; yet it was covered with
shrubs and trees so thickly, that in many places they were impenetrable. The north-western part is entirely sand, but there grew upon

it numbers of pandanus trees, similar to those of the east coast of New South Wales; and around many of them was placed a circle of shells of the *chama gigas*, or gigantic cockle, the intention of which excited my curiosity.

It appeared that this little island was visited occasionally by the Indians, who obtained from it the fruit of the pandanus, and probably turtle, for the marks of them were seen; and the reef furnishes them with cockles, which are of a superior size here to those we had found upon the reefs of the east coast. There being no water upon the island, they seem to have hit upon the following expedient to obtain it: long slips of bark are tied round the smooth stems of the pandanus, and the loose ends are led into the shells of the cockle, placed underneath. By these slips, the rain which runs down the branches and stem of the tree, is conducted into the shells, and fills them at every considerable shower; and as each shell will contain two or three pints, forty or fifty thus placed under different trees will supply a good number of men. A pair of these cockle shells, bleached in the sun, weighed a hundred and one pounds; but still they were much inferior in size to some I have since seen.

The fruit of the pandanus, as it is used by these Indians and by the natives of Terra Australis, affords very little nourishment. They suck the bottom part of the drupes, or separated nuts, as we do the leaves of the artichoke; but the quantity of pulp thus obtained, is very small, and to my taste, too astringent to be agreeable. In the third volume of the Asiatic Researches, the fruit of the pandanus is described as furnishing, under the name of *Mellori*, an important article of food to the inhabitants of the Nicobar Islands; and in Mauritius, one of these species is planted for its long and fibrous leaves, of which sacks, mats and bags for coffee and cotton are made.

This little island, or rather the surrounding reef, which is three or four miles long, affords shelter from the south-east winds; and being at a moderate day's run from Murray's Isles, it forms a convenient anchorage for the night to a ship passing through Torres'

Strait: I named it Half-way Island. It is scarcely more than a mile
in circumference, but appears to be increasing both in elevation
and extent. At no very distant period of time, it was one of those
banks produced by the washing up of sand and broken coral, of
which most reefs afford instances, and those of Torres' Strait a
great many. These banks are in different stages of progress: some,
like this, are become islands, but not yet habitable; some are above
high-water mark, but destitute of vegetation; whilst others are overflowed with every returning tide.

It seems to me, that when the animalcules which form the corals
at the bottom of the ocean, cease to live, their structures adhere to
each other, by virtue either of the glutinous remains within, or of
some property in salt water; and the interstices being gradually
filled up with sand and broken pieces of coral washed by the sea,
which also adhere, a mass of rock is at length formed. Future races
of these animalcules erect their habitations upon the rising bank,
and die in their turn to increase, but principally to elevate, this
monument of their wonderful labours. The care taken to work
perpendicularly in the early stages, would mark a surprising instinct
in these diminutive creatures. Their wall of coral, for the most part
in situations where the winds are constant, being arrived at the
surface, affords a shelter, to leeward of which their infant colonies
may be safely sent forth; and to this their instinctive foresight it
seems to be owing, that the windward side of a reef exposed to the
open sea, is generally, if not always the highest part, and rises
almost perpendicular, sometimes from the depth of 200, and
perhaps many more fathoms. To be constantly covered with water,
seems necessary to the existence of the animalcules, for they do not
work, except in holes upon the reef, beyond low-water mark; but
the coral sand and other broken remnants thrown up by the sea,
adhere to the rock, and form a solid mass with it, as high as the
common tides reach. That elevation surpassed, the future
remnants, being rarely covered, lose their adhesive property; and
remaining in a loose state, form what is usually called a *key*, upon

the top of the reef. The new bank is not long in being visited by
sea birds; salt plants take root upon it, and a soil begins to be
formed; a cocoa-nut, or the drupe of a pandanus is thrown on
shore; land birds visit it and deposit the seeds of shrubs and trees;
every high tide, and still more every gale, adds something to the
bank; the form of an island is gradually assumed; and last of all
comes man to take possession...

*31 October* ~ At daylight in the morning the south-east trade
blew fresh with squally weather...At two o'clock, when we passed
on the north side of the double isle, it was seen to be surrounded
with a coral reef, and there were rocks on its west and south sides.
We then hauled up SW by S for some rocky islets lying, as I
supposed, off Cape York; but finding no shelter there, bore away
round the north end of an island...I was altogether at a loss to
know what islands these were, under which we had anchored.
Supposing the flat-topped island to have been the easternmost York
Isle, the land we had in sight to the southward should have been
Cape York; but no such isles as those around us were laid down by
Captain Cook, to the north of that cape. On consulting the sketch
made by Captain Bligh in the *Bounty*'s launch, it appeared that the
first land was not the easternmost isle, but one much nearer to
Cape York; and that our anchorage was under the southern group
of the Prince of Wales' Island, the longitude of which, by Captain
Cook, is 1° 12' west of what I make it. The north-eastern isle of
this group, under which we more immediately lay, is that named
Wednesday Island by Captain Bligh; to the other isles he gave no
name; but the one westward of the ship seems to have been the
Hammond's Island of Captain Edwards, when passing here with
the *Pandora*'s boats...

*1 November* ~ This evening and all the next day, the wind blew
so strong that it was impossible to land; nor did I think it prudent
to quit the anchorage, though anxious to commence the survey of
the Gulf of Carpentaria. Upon Hammond's Island some fires were
seen; but Wednesday Island showed no signs of being inhabited,

unless some whitish, conical figures like sentry boxes, were huts; there were bushes and small trees scattered over both islands, but their general appearance was rocky and barren...

*2 November* ~ It was now ascertained, that the figures resembling sentry boxes were anthills, of eight or more feet high; Pelsaert found similar hills on the west coast, and says they might have been taken for the houses of Indians, as in fact we did take them at a distant view. They were also seen by Dampier on the north-west coast, who mistook them in the same way; but says he found them to be so many rocks, probably from not making the examination with his usual care. The insects which inhabit, and I suppose erect these structures, are small, reddish, with black heads, and seemed to be a sluggish and feeble race. We found the common black flies excessively numerous here; and almost as troublesome as Dampier describes them to be on the north-west coast...

*3 November* ~ We passed Wallis' Isles, steering southward to get in with the main coast; but the shoals forced us to run seven or eight miles to the west, out of sight of land, before regular soundings could be obtained and a southern course steered into the Gulf of Carpentaria...

I now considered all the difficulties of Torres' Strait to be surmounted, since we had got a fair entry into the Gulf of Carpentaria; and to have accomplished this, before the north-west monsoon had made any strong indications, was a source of much satisfaction, after the unexpected delay amongst the Barrier Reefs on the east coast. It was this apprehension of the north-west monsoon that prevented me from making any further examination of the Strait, than what could be done in passing through it; but even this was not without its advantage to navigation, since it demonstrated that this most direct passage, from the southern Pacific, or Great Ocean to the Indian Seas, may be accomplished in three days. It may be remembered that the reefs on the north side of Pandora's Entrance were passed at six in the morning of 29 October; and that, after lying two nights at anchor, we reached

the Prince of Wales's Islands at three in the afternoon of the 31st;
and nothing then prevented us from passing Booby Isle, had I
wished it, and clearing Torres' Strait before dusk...

*5 November* ~ When we got under way in the morning to proceed
along shore, the wind was light, off the land, and soon after nine it
fell calm; a drain of tide setting to the north-east induced me to
drop a stream anchor, four or five miles from a part of the beach
where some natives were collected round a fire. At eleven the sea
breeze came in from W by N, with dark cloudy weather, and we
steered onward, passing a small opening at one o'clock, four or five
miles south of the natives. A much larger opening came in sight at
two, into which I hoped to get the ship; but the water was so shallow
at five or six miles off, that we were obliged to tack; and after making
a second ineffectual attempt, it became dusk, and we anchored in
6¹/₂ fathoms.

*6 November* ~ In the morning we had a breeze off the land; and
the fear of the north-west monsoon preventing me from taking
time to beat up, we passed Batavia River at the distance of six
miles, with soundings from 5 to 8 fathoms. Several flocks of ducks
were seen coming from the westward, where they had probably
been to pass the night upon some island not inhabited. Our latitude at noon, from double altitudes, was 11° 56', and longitude by
time keeper 141° 50'; the clump of trees near the entrance of
Batavia River bore E1°S, the furthest extreme of the land, S11°W,
and the nearest part was distant four miles.

A light air came off the land at four in the morning, and at
daylight we again steered southward; but in two hours the wind
died off, and an anchor was dropped in 9 fathoms. There was a
small opening at E5°S, about three miles; and the botanical gentlemen being desirous of seeing the productions of this part of the
country, the whaleboat was lowered down, and we went to examine
the inlet.

On approaching the entrance, a canoe, or something like one,
passed and repassed from the north to the south side, the rower

using both hands to the paddle like the natives of Murray's Islands. We had a good deal of difficulty to get in, on account of the shoals; the channel amongst them being narrow and winding, and not more than nine to twelve feet deep. On the north side was a party of natives, and Bongaree went on shore to them, naked and unarmed; but although provided with spears, they retreated from him, and all our endeavours to bring about an interview were unsuccessful. It was not safe for the gentlemen to botanise in presence of these suspicious people; and therefore we rowed a mile higher up, to a green looking point on the same side, and landed about noon...

Whilst the botanists where making their examination and I walked along the shore to shoot some birds, several voices were heard in the wood, as of people advancing towards us; and there being too much opportunity here to creep on secretly, we assembled and retired into the boat, to wait their approach. A sea breeze had then set in; and the Indians not appearing, we rowed back to the first place, where the country was open; and the gentlemen botanised whilst sentinels kept watch on the sandy hillocks.

In the upper parts of the port the country was well covered with wood, mostly eucalyptus; but near the entrance it was little better than bare sand, with some scattered trees of the casuarina and pandanus: a stone of imperfectly concreted coral sand and shells formed the basis. Footmarks of the kangaroo were imprinted on the sand, and a dog was seen; drupes of the pandanus, which had been sucked, lay in every direction, and small cockle shells were scattered on the beaches. I sought in vain for the canoe which had landed here, nor did I find any huts of the natives.

Before quitting the shore, a hatchet was made fast to the branch of a tree, and set up conspicuously near the water side. We had scarcely shoved off, when the party of Indians, sixteen in number, made their appearance and called to us; but when the boat's head was turned towards them, they ran away. On the south side of the entrance were four other natives, who also ran at our approach; we therefore set up another hatchet for them on the beach, and returned back to the ship.

These people were all naked; and in colour, as in everything else, seemed to have a perfect resemblance to the inhabitants of the east and south coasts of Terra Australis. In Torres' Strait bows and arrows are the offensive weapons; but here we saw spears only: each man had several in his hand, and something which was supposed to be a throwing stick…Lieutenant Fowler had got the ship under way, on the sea breeze setting in, and stood off and on the entrance to Coen River, until our return at three o'clock…

*10 November* ~ At four o'clock we passed the southern extremity of Cape Keer-Weer, round which the coast falls back somewhat; the water often became more shallow, and did not admit of being safely approached nearer than four miles. An opening is laid down here in the Dutch chart, called Vereenigde River, which certainly has no existence. All this afternoon the sea breeze was fresh and favourable; and by eight o'clock, when we anchored in 5 fathoms, the distance run from noon exceeded forty miles. A fire was seen on the land about four miles off, and some smokes had been passed in the day; so that the country should seem to be at least as well peopled in this part of Carpentaria as further northward. The coast was, if possible, still lower than before; not a single hill had yet been seen; and the tops of the trees on the highest land, had scarcely exceeded the height of the ship's masthead.

*14 November* ~ There appeared to be a small opening on the south side of this little projection, which corresponds in latitude to Van Diemen's River in the old chart; but across the entrance was an extensive flat, nearly dry, and would probably prevent even boats from getting in. If this place had any title to be called a river in 1644, the coast must have undergone a great alteration since that time.

In the afternoon our course along shore was more westward; and this, with the increasing shallowness of the water, made me apprehend that the Gulf would be found to terminate nearly as represented in the old charts, and disappoint the hopes formed of a strait or passage leading out at some other part of Terra Australis...

*15 November* ~ The coast to which we approached nearest this evening, was sandy and very barren; but there were some natives collected upon the hillocks, to look at the ship; so that even here, and at the end of the dry season, fresh water may be had. These people were black and naked, and made many wild gestures. Between this part and the land set at S by W¹/₂W at noon, there was a bight falling back as far as the latitude 17° 42', or perhaps further, which appeared to be the southern extremity of the Gulf of Carpentaria.

*20 November* ~ In the morning we steered towards Allen's Isle, with the whaleboat ahead; and anchored one mile and a half from its south-east end, in 3¹/₂ fathoms, mud...Allen's Isle is between four and five miles in length, and though generally barren, there are bushes and small trees upon it, and some tolerable grass. It is altogether low land; but the south-east end is cliffy, and within two cables length of it there is 4 fathoms; no fresh water was found near the shore, nor any place where casks could be conveniently landed. After taking a set of bearings I left the gentlemen to follow their pursuits, and rowed north-westward, intending to go round the island; but an impassable reef extended so far out, that the project was given up; and after taking angles from one of the rocks, I went eastward to a smaller island two miles off, where several Indians were perceived. The water was too shallow for the boat to get near them; but we landed at a little distance, and walked after three men who were dragging six small rafts towards the extreme northern rocks, where three other natives were sitting.

These men not choosing to abandon their rafts, an interview was unavoidable, and they came on shore with their spears to wait our approach. One of us advanced towards them, unarmed; and signs being made to lay down their spears, which were understood to mean that they should sit down, they complied; and by degrees, a friendly intercourse was established. They accepted some red worsted caps and fillets, as also a hatchet and an adze, the use of which being explained, was immediately comprehended. In return, they gave us two very rude spears, and a *womerah*, or throwing stick, of nearly the same form as those used by the natives of Port Jackson.

The rafts consisted of several straight branches of mangrove, very much dried, and lashed together in two places with the largest ends one way, so as to form a broad part, and the smaller ends closing to a point. Near the broad end was a bunch of grass, where the man sits to paddle; but the raft, with his weight alone, must swim very deep; and indeed I should scarcely have supposed it could float a man at all. Upon one of the rafts was a short net, which, from the size of the meshes, was probably intended to catch turtle; upon another was a young shark; and these, with their paddles and spears, seemed to constitute the whole of their earthly riches.

Two of the three men were advanced in years, and from the resemblance of feature were probably brothers. With the exception of two chiefs at Tahiti, these were the tallest Indians I had ever seen; the two brothers being from three to four inches higher than my coxswain, who measured five feet eleven. They were not remarkable for being either stout or slender; though like most of the Australians, their legs did not bear the European proportion to the size of their heads and bodies. The third native was not so tall as the other two; and he was, according to our notions, better proportioned. Their features did not much differ from those of their countrymen on the south and east coasts; but they had each of them lost *two* front teeth from the upper jaw. Their hair was short, though not curly; and a fillet of net work, which the youngest man had wrapped round his head, was the sole ornament or clothing seen amongst them. The two old men appeared, to my surprise, to have undergone circumcision; but the posture of the youngest, who remained sitting down, did not allow of observation being made upon him.

After being five minutes with them, the old men proposed to go
to our boat; and this being agreed to, we proceeded together, hand
in hand. But they stopped halfway and, retreating a little, the eldest
made a short harangue which concluded with the word *jahree*!
pronounced with emphasis; they then returned to the rafts, and
dragged them towards their three companions who were sitting on
the furthest rocks. These I judged to be women, and that the
proposal of the men to go to our boat was a feint to get us further
from them; it did not seem, however, that the women were so much
afraid of us, as the men appeared to be on their account; for
although we walked back, past the rafts, much nearer than before,
they remained very quietly picking oysters. It was not my desire to
annoy these poor people; and therefore, leaving them to their own
way, we took an opposite direction to examine the island.

This low piece of land is between one and two miles long, and
from its form received the name of Horse-shoe Island; there is very
little soil mixed with the sand on its surface, and except the mangrove trees upon the shore, it bears nothing larger than bushes.
We did not find any huts; but the dried grass spread round two or
three neighbouring fireplaces marked the last residence of the
Indians. Near it were lying several large spiral shells, probably the
vessels in which they had brought water from the mainland;
for none was found on the island, nor was there any appearance
that it could be procured. Shells and bones of turtle, some of them
fresh, were plentifully scattered around; upon the beach also there
were turtle tracks, and several of these animals were seen in
the water during the day; but it was not our fortune to take one
of them.

In returning to the ship in the evening, I steered from Horse-
shoe, to the south-east end of Allen's Isle, and sounded the channel
between them; but had only once so much as 3 fathoms. There was
consequently no fit passage this way for the ship, and the several
low islets to the north-east precluded the expectation of finding one
anywhere to the west of Bentinck's Island; I therefore judged it

most advisable to return, and place the ship between Bentinck's and Sweers' Islands, until the necessary caulking was finished. Natives had been seen on both those islands; and this gave a hope that water might still be found to complete the holds previously to encountering the bad weather of the north-west monsoon, which I had been expecting to set in every day.

*21 November* ~ ...This anchorage between the two islands, though it may not be called a port, is yet almost equally well sheltered, and I named it Investigator's Road; it has the appearance of being exposed between NNW and NE$^1$/$_2$N; but the rocks from each shore occupy nearly one half of the space, and the water is too shallow in the remaining part to admit any surge to endanger a ship.

*22 November* ~ A boat was sent to fish with the seine upon Sweers' Island, and an officer went to the opposite shore to dig for water; the botanists divided themselves into two parties, to visit both islands, and the carpenters began caulking the starboard side of the ship. I repeated the observations under Inspection Hill, for the rates of the time keepers; and being informed on my return, that the midshipman of the seining boat had discovered a small hole containing a little muddy water, with a shell lying near it, I had the place dug out, through the sand and a stratum of whitish clay, to the depth of ten or eleven feet. Under the clay we found a bottom of stone and gravel, and the water then flowed in clear, and tolerably fast. This was a great acquisition; more especially as the spring was not far from the beach at the west point of Sweers' Island, where the casks could be conveniently landed, and where we had had great success in fishing.

The gentlemen who visited Bentinck's Island found a small lake of fresh water at no great distance from the sea side; and it appeared that the interior part of Sweers' Island, towards the northern end, was occupied by swamps. This comparative abundance of water upon such low islands, and at the end of the dry season seemed very remarkable; it may perhaps be attributed to the clayey consistence of the stratum immediately under the sand,

and to the gravelly rock upon which that stratum rests; the one preventing the evaporation of the rains, and the other obstructing their further infiltration.

Early next morning the ship was removed to within two cables' length of the west point, nearer to the spring; and Lieutenant Fowler was established on shore with a party of seamen and marines, taking tents, a seine, and other necessaries for watering the ship and supplying us with fish. The carpenters proceeded in their work of caulking; but as they advanced, report after report was brought to me of rotten places found in different parts of the ship—in the planks, bends, timbers, tree-nails, &c., until it became quite alarming. I therefore directed the master and carpenter to make a regular examination into all such essential parts, as could be done without delaying the service; and to give me an official report thereon, with answers to certain queries put to them. After two days' examination, their report was made in the following terms.

> Sir,
>
> In obedience to your directions we have taken with us the oldest carpenter's mate of the *Investigator*, and made as thorough an examination into the state of the ship as circumstances will permit, and which we find to be as under:—
>
> Out of ten top timbers on the larboard side, near the fore channel, four are sound, one partly rotten, and five entirely rotten.
>
> We have seen but one timber on the larboard quarter, which is entirely rotten.
>
> On the starboard bow, close to the stem, we have seen three timbers which are all rotten. Under the starboard fore chains we find one of the chain-plate bolts started, in consequence of the timber and inside plank being rotten; and also a preventer eye-bolt, from the same cause.

On boring into the second futtock timbers from the main hold, close under the beams of the lower deck on the larboard side, we find one sound and two rotten; and on the other side, one sound and one rotten.

On boring into one of the second futtock timbers in the cockpit, on each side, we find it to be sound on the starboard, but on the other side rotten: the inside plank on both sides is rotten. On boring into one timber of a side in the afterhold, we find them to be sound. On boring into one timber of a side from the bread-room, one is sound; but on the larboard side it is rotten.

The stem appears to be good; but the stemson is mostly decayed.

The lower breast book is decayed within side.

The transoms, sleepers, stern post, and postson are all sound.

The ends of the beams we find to be universally in a decaying state.

The tree-nails are in general rotten.

From the specimens we have seen of the top-side and bends, we expect that the insides of them are rotten, fore and aft; but that about one inch of the outside of the greater part is yet quite sound.

After the above report, and upon due consideration, we give the following answers to the four questions put to us.

1st. The ship having before made ten inches of water an hour, in a common fresh breeze, we judge from that, and that we have not seen, that a little labouring would employ two pumps; and that in a strong gale, with much sea running, the ship would hardly escape foundering; so that we think she is totally unfit to encounter much bad weather.

2nd. We have no doubt but that, if the ship should get on shore under any unfavourable circumstances, she would immediately go to pieces; but with a soft bottom and smooth

water, she might touch for a short time without any worse
consequences than to another ship, if she did not heel much;
but altogether, we judge it to be much more dangerous for
her to get aground in her present state, than if she were
sound.

3rd. It is our opinion that the ship could not bear heaving
down on any account; and that laying her on shore might so
far strain her as to start the copper and butt ends, which
would make her unable to swim without vast repair.

4th. Mr Aken [master] has known several ships of the
same kind, and built at the same place as the *Investigator*; and
has always found that when they began to rot they went on
very fast. From the state to which the ship seems now to be
advanced, it is our joint opinion, that in twelve months there
will scarcely be a sound timber in her; but that if she remain
in fine weather and happen no accident, she may run six
months longer without much risk.

I cannot express the surprise and sorrow which this statement gave
me. According to it, a return to Port Jackson was almost immediately necessary; as well to secure the journals and charts of the
examinations already made, as to preserve the lives of the ship's
company; and my hopes of ascertaining completely the exterior
form of this immense, and in many points interesting country, if
not destroyed, would at least be deferred to an uncertain period.
My leading object had hitherto been, to make so accurate an investigation of the shores of Terra Australis that no future voyage to
this country should be necessary; and with this always in view, I
had ever endeavoured to follow the land so closely, that the washing
of the surf upon it should be visible, and no opening, nor anything
of interest escape notice. Such a degree of proximity is what navigators have usually thought neither necessary nor safe to pursue...
But when circumstances were favourable, such was the plan I
pursued; and with the blessing of God, nothing of importance

should have been left for future discoverers, upon any part of these extensive coasts; but with a ship incapable of encountering bad weather—which could not be repaired if sustaining injury from any of the numerous shoals or rocks upon the coast—which, if constant fine weather could be ensured and all accidents avoided, could not run more than six months—with such a ship, I knew not how to accomplish the task.

A passage to Port Jackson at this time, presented no common difficulties. In proceeding by the west, the unfavourable monsoon was likely to prove an obstacle not to be surmounted; and in returning by the east, stormy weather was to be expected in Torres' Strait, a place where the multiplied dangers caused such an addition to be peculiarly dreaded. These considerations, with a strong desire to finish, if possible, the examination of the Gulf of Carpentaria, fixed my resolution to proceed as before in the survey, during the continuance of the north-west monsoon; and when the fair wind should come, to proceed by the west to Port Jackson, if the ship should prove capable of a winter's passage along the south coast, and if not, to make for the nearest port in the East Indies.

By the 28th, the watering and wooding of the ship were completed, the gunner had dried all his powder in the sun, and the tents and people were brought on board. All that the carpenters could do at the ship was to secure the hooding ends to the stem— shift some of the worst parts in the rotten planking—and caulk all the bends; and this they had finished...

I shall now sum up into one view, the principal remarks made during our stay amongst these islands...The soil, even in the best parts, is far behind fertility; but the small trees and bushes which grow there, and the grass in some of the less covered places, save the larger islands from the reproach of being absolutely sterile...We saw neither quadruped nor reptile upon the islands. Birds were rather numerous; the most useful of them were ducks of several species, and bustards; and one of these last, shot by Mr Bauer, weighed between ten and twelve pounds, and made us an excellent dinner. The flesh of this bird is distributed in a manner directly contrary to that of the domestic turkey, the white meat being upon the legs, and the black upon the breast. In the woody parts of the islands were seen crows and white cockatoos; as also cuckoo-pheasants, pigeons, and small birds peculiar to this part of the country. On the shores were pelicans, gulls, sea-pies, ox-birds, and sand-larks; but except the gulls, none of these tribes were numerous. The sea afforded a variety of fish; and in such abundance, that it was rare not to give a meal to all the ship's company from one or two hauls of the seine. Turtle abound amongst the islands; but it seemed to be a fatality that we could neither peg any from the boat, nor yet catch them on shore.

Indians were repeatedly seen upon both Bentinck's and Sweers' islands; but they always avoided us, and sometimes disappeared in a manner which seemed extraordinary. It is probable that they hid themselves in caves dug in the ground; for we discovered in one instance a large hole, containing two apartments (so to call them), in each of which a man might lie down. Fireplaces under the shade of the trees, with dried grass spread around, were often met with; and these I apprehend to be their fine-weather, and the caves their foul-weather residences. The fern or some similar root, appears to form a part of their subsistence; for there were some places in the sand and in the dry swamps, where the ground had been so dug up with pointed sticks that it resembled the work of a herd of swine.

Whether these people reside constantly upon the islands, or come over at certain seasons from the main, was uncertain; canoes, they seemed to have none, but to make their voyages upon rafts similar to those seen at Horse-shoe Island, and of which some were found on the shore in other places. I had been taught by the Dutch accounts to expect that the inhabitants of Carpentaria were ferocious, and armed with bows and arrows as well as spears. I found them to be timid; and so desirous to avoid intercourse with strangers, that it was by surprise alone that our sole interview, that at Horse-shoe Island, was brought about; and certainly there was then nothing ferocious in their conduct. Of bows and arrows not the least indication was perceived, either at these islands or at Coen River; and the spears were too heavy and clumsily made to be dangerous as offensive weapons: in the defensive, they might have some importance.

It is worthy of remark, that the three natives seen at Horse-shoe Island had lost the *two* upper front teeth; and Dampier, in speaking of the inhabitants of the north-west coast, says, 'the two front teeth of the upper jaw are wanting in all of them, men and women, old and young'. Nothing of the kind was observed in the natives of the islands in Torres' Strait, nor at Keppel, Hervey's, or Glass-house bays, on the east coast; yet at Port Jackson, further south, it is the custom for the boys, on arriving at the age of puberty, to have *one* of the upper front teeth knocked out, but no more; nor are the girls subjected to the same operation. At Twofold Bay, still further south, no such custom prevails, nor did I observe it at Port Phillip or King George's Sound, on the south coast; but at Van Diemen's Land it seems to be used partially...The rite of circumcision, which seemed to have been practised upon two of the three natives at Horse-shoe Island, and of which better proofs were found in other parts of the Gulf of Carpentaria, is, I believe, novel in the history of Terra Australis.

On Sweers' Island, seven human skulls and many bones were found lying together, near three extinguished fires; and a square piece of timber, seven feet long, which was of teak wood, and according to the judgment of the carpenter had been a quarter-deck carling of a ship, was thrown up on the western beach. On Bentinck's Island I saw the stumps of at least twenty trees, which had been felled with an axe, or some sharp instrument of iron; and not far from the same place were scattered the broken remains of an earthen jar. Putting these circumstances together, it seemed probable that some ship from the East Indies had been wrecked here, two or three years back; that part of the crew had been killed by the Indians and that the others had gone away,

perhaps to the mainland, upon rafts constructed after the manner
of the natives...

   *3 December* ~...At daylight, the piece of hilly land before judged
to be an island, and which still appeared so, bore N86° to 28°W,
two or three miles, with some nearer rocks lying in front; the northern land extended from behind it to N32°E, and we followed its
course at the distance of five, and from that to two miles offshore.
At noon we approached the eastern extremity, and saw a small
island two leagues further out, one of three laid down in the old
chart near Cape Van Diemen; it is thickly covered with wood, principally of that softish, white kind, whence it obtained the name of
Isle Pisonia. Another and a larger island afterwards opened from
the cape; but this could not be one of the three, for it lies so close,
that Tasman, or whoever discovered these parts, would scarcely
have observed the separation; and in fact, the other two isles
presently came in sight to the southward, nearly in the situation
assigned to them. The wind being unfavourable to doubling the
cape, we bore away for the two islands; and soon after four o'clock,
anchored on the south-east side of the outermost, in 6$^1$/$_2$ fathoms,
good holding ground.

   Turtle tracks were distinguished on the beach as we rounded the
north-east point, and afforded us the pleasurable anticipation of
some fresh food. We had explored tropical coasts for several
months, without reaping any one of the advantages usually attending it, and been frequently tantalised with the sight of turtle in the
water, and of bones and shells round the fireplaces on shore; but
we now hoped to have found a place where the Indians had not
forestalled us, and to indemnify ourselves for so many disappoint-
ments.

   In rowing to the island, we carried 5 fathoms nearly close to the
beach. Several turtle were swimming about, and some perceived
above high-water mark, which we ran to secure, but found them
dead, and rotten; they appeared to have fallen on their backs in
climbing up a steep part of the beach, and not being able to right

themselves, had miserably perished. I walked the greater part of the length of the island; and from the highest hillock set the eastern extreme of the island close to Cape Van Diemen, at N34$^3$/$_4$° W, and Isle Pisonia from N2$^3$/$_4$° to 19$^1$/$_2$°W.

During my absence from the boat, the impatient crew, not waiting for the turtle to come on shore, had been attacking them in the water; and had caught three large ones, and broken my harpoon. They had also been scratching out some of the holes, of which the upper part of the sandy beach was full; from one they filled a hat with turtles' eggs, and from another took a swarm of young ones, not broader than a crown piece, which I found crawling in every part of the boat. It was then past sunset, and numbers of turtle were collected, waiting only for our departure to take the beach; I therefore hastened to the ship, and sent Lieutenant Fowler with a party of men, to remain all night and turn them.

Next morning, two boats went to bring off the officer and people with what had been caught; but their success had been so great, that it was necessary to hoist out the launch; and it took nearly the whole day to get on board what the decks and holds could contain, without impediment to the working of the ship. They were found by Mr Brown to be nearly similar to, but not exactly the true green turtle, and he thought might be an undescribed species. We contrived to stow away forty-six, the least of them weighing 250lbs, and the average about 300; besides which, many were returned on shore and suffered to go away.

This Bountiful Island, for so I termed it, is near three miles long, and generally low and sandy; the highest parts are ridges of sand, overspread with a long, creeping, coarse grass, which binds the sand together, and preserves it from being blown away; grass of the common kind grows in the lower parts, and in one place there were some bushes and small trees. The basis consists partly of a streaked, ochrous earth, and in part of sand, concreted with particles of iron ore. Nothing bespoke this island to have been ever before visited, whence it is probable that the natives of the neighbouring lands do not possess canoes; for with them, the distance of four leagues from Cape Van Diemen would not have been too great to be passed, though too far in a tide's way for such rafts as I saw at Horse-shoe Island.

A kind of bustard, with a very strong bill, and not larger than a hen, was numerous at Bountiful Island; and appeared to subsist upon the young turtle. The effect of instinct is admirable in all cases, and was very striking in these little amphibious creatures. When scratched out from their holes, they no sooner saw the daylight than they made for the water, and with speed, as if conscious that the bustards were watching them; when placed in a direction from the sea, which was done for experiment, they turned themselves and took the straightest course to the water side. But it is not only in the bustards, nor on land alone, that they have enemies to fear; tiger sharks were numerous, and so voracious, that seven were hooked alongside the ship, measuring from five to nine feet in length. These were ready to receive such of the little animals as escape their first enemies; and even one of the full grown turtle had lost a semicircular piece, equal to the tenth part of its bulk, which had been bitten out of its side; and what seemed more extraordinary, the shell had closed, and the place was healed up...

*6 December* ~ The tide here set NNE and SSW, between the island close to the cape and Isle Pisonia; and at daylight we steered for the middle of the opening. On seeing breakers ahead, the master was sent in the whaleboat to sound, and we kept more westward, after him. There were natives upon the island nearest to the land, who seemed to wait in expectation of being visited; but our soundings diminishing to 3 fathoms, and the master having still less, we stood out and were followed by the boat. The wind was then at NE; and Isle Pisonia being brought to bear NW at nine o'clock, we tacked and weathered it nearly a mile, carrying from 9 to 33 fathoms water. Turtle tracks were very distinguishable upon the beach, but these prognostics, once so much desired, did not now interest us; however, on the wind becoming so light that we could

not weather some breakers whilst the lee tide was running, the
stream anchor was dropped in 9 fathoms, and I went to the island
with the botanical gentlemen.

More holes were scratched in the sand here by the turtle, than
even upon the island last quitted; and several of the poor animals
were lying dead on their backs. The isle is nothing more than a
high sandbank upon a basis of coral rock, which has become
thickly covered with wood, and much resembles several of the
smaller isles in Torres' Strait. There was no trace of former visitors, though it is not more than four miles from the island where
Indians had been seen in the morning; the tides probably run too
strong in a narrow, four-fathom channel, close to Isle Pisonia, to be
encountered by their rafts...

*7 December* ~ From one o'clock till four, we steered SSW past
three other small cliffy projections; and I then saw the clump of
high trees on the south-west point of this land, bearing S31°E six
miles, the same which had been set five days before from the inner
side. Our course was continued, to get in with the mainland; but
in half an hour the depth had diminished to $2^{1}/_{2}$ fathoms, and
obliged us to haul out W by N, close to the wind. The low main
coast was then in sight from the masthead to the south-westward,
and at dusk we anchored about three leagues off, in 5 fathoms,
sandy bottom.

No doubt remained that the land of Cape Van Diemen was an
island; for it had been circumnavigated, with the exception of
about three leagues, which the rocks and shoal water made imprac-
ticable. Its extent is considerable, being thirty-five miles long, and
the circumference near ninety, independently of the smaller sinuosities in the coast; I did not land upon any part, but the surface
appeared to be more rocky than sandy; and judging from the
bushes and trees with which it is mostly covered, there must be
some portion, though perhaps a small one, of vegetable soil. In any
other part of the world, this would be deemed low land; but here,
where even the tops of the trees on the main scarcely exceed a

ship's masthead in elevation, it must be called moderately high; for it may in some parts, reach three hundred feet. Several smokes and some natives were seen, and it is reasonable to suppose there are fixed inhabitants, but their number is probably small.

Had not the name of Van Diemen so often occurred in Terra Australis, as to make confusion, I should have extended it from the cape to the whole island; but such being the case, I have taken this opportunity of indulging my gratitude to a nobleman of high character and consideration; who, when governor-general of British India, humanely used his efforts to relieve me from an imprisonment which was super-added to a shipwreck in the sequel of the voyage. This large island is therefore distinguished by the name of Isle Mornington; and to the whole of the group, now discovered to exist at the head of the Gulf of Carpentaria, I have given the appellation of Wellesley's Islands...

*11 December* ~ At daylight, we steered northward with a land wind; and when the sea breeze came, stretched WSW towards the shore...

*14 December* ~ ...The north point of the island, which is the true Cape Vanderlin, bore N71°W, and was distant three or four miles: its utmost extremity lies in 15° 34½' south and 137° 8½' east. Some Indians had been seen tracking a canoe or raft, along the east side, and a body of thirty-five of them had been there collected, looking at the ship. This comparatively numerous population, and the prospect there was of this island proving more than usually interesting to the naturalists, made me desirous of finding a secure anchorage near it; and in the morning we landed at the north-east point, which is a peninsula joined to the island by a low sandy neck, and has three hummocks upon it, near the extremity. From the highest of these hummocks, I set two small islands in the offing, to the north-west, where two are laid down in the old chart; and saw more land to the west of Cape Vanderlin...

*15 December* ~ We got under way soon after ten o'clock, with a breeze from the north-westward, and were obliged to make a long

stretch to sea before Cape Vanderlin could be weathered. Towards
evening we came in with a small reef, lying N40°E two and a half
miles from the extremity of the cape; and this, with the lateness of
the hour, making it hazardous to run into the new opening, we
anchored at dusk, under the easternmost of the two small islands
in the offing, in 6 fathoms, coral sand and rock. The white beach
here seemed to be so favourable a situation for turtle, that an officer
with a party of men was sent on shore to watch them; but he
returned immediately, on finding the beach to be not sand, but
pieces of coral bleached white by the sun, which bore no traces
of turtle...

I have called this cluster of islands Sir Edward Pellew's Group.
The space occupied by these islands is thirty-four miles east and
west, by twenty-two miles of latitude; and the five principal islands
are from seven to seventeen miles in length...Where the surface is
not bare rock, it consists of sand, with a greater or less proportion
of vegetable soil, but in no case did I see any near approach to
fertility; yet all the larger islands, and more especially the western
side of Vanderlin's, are tolerably well covered with trees and
bushes, and in some low places there is grass.

As in most other parts of Terra Australis, the common trees
here are various species of the eucalyptus, mostly different from,
and smaller than those of the east and south coasts. The cabbage
palm, a new genus named by Mr Brown *Livistona inermis*, is abundant; but the cabbage is too small to be an interesting article of
food to a ship's company; of the young leaves, drawn into slips and
dried, the seamen made handsome light hats, excellent for warm
weather. The nutmeg was found principally on Vanderlin's Island,
growing upon a large spreading bush; but the fruit being unripe,
no accurate judgment could be formed of its quality. Amongst the
variety of other plants discovered by the naturalist, were two shrubs
belonging to the genus Santalum, of which the sandal wood, used
as a perfume in the east, is also one; but this affinity to so valuable
a tree being not known at the time, from the description of the

genus being imperfect, no examination was made of it with that object in view.

All the larger islands seem to possess the kangaroo; for though none were seen, their footmarks were perceptible in most of the sandy places where I landed: the species seemed to be small. In the woods were hawks, pigeons of two kinds, and some bustards; and on the shore were seen a pretty kind of duck and the usual sea fowl. Turtle tracks were observed on most of the beaches, but more especially on the smaller islands, where remains of turtle feasts were generally found.

There were traces of Indians on all the islands, both large and small, but the latter are visited only at times; these people seemed to be equally desirous of avoiding communication with strangers, as those of Wellesley's Islands, for we saw them only once at a distance, from the ship. Two canoes found on the shore of North Island were formed of slips of bark, like planks, sewed together, the edge of one slip overlaying another, as in our clincher-built boats; their breadth was about two feet, but they were too much broken for the length to be known. I cannot be certain that these canoes were the fabrication of the natives, for there were some things near them which appertained, without doubt, to another people, and their construction was much superior to that on any part of Terra Australis hitherto discovered; but their substance of bark spoke in the affirmative. The same degree of doubt was attached to a small monument found on the same island. Under a shed of bark were set up two cylindrical pieces of stone, about eighteen inches long; which seemed to have been taken from the shore, where they had been made smooth from rolling in the surf, and formed into a shape something like a nine pin. Round each of them were drawn two black circles, one towards each end; and between them were four oval black patches, at equal distances round the stone, made apparently with charcoal. The spaces between the oval marks were covered with white down and feathers, stuck on with the yolk of a turtle's egg, as I judged by the gluten and by the shell lying near the place. Of the intention in setting up these stones under a shed, no person could form a reasonable conjecture; the first idea was, that it had some relation to the dead, and we dug underneath to satisfy our curiosity; but nothing was found.

Indications of some foreign people having visited this group were almost as numerous, and as widely extended as those left by the natives. Besides pieces of earthen jars and trees cut with axes, we found remnants of bamboo lattice work, palm leaves sewed with cotton thread into the form of such hats as are worn by the Chinese, and the remains of blue cotton trousers, of the fashion called moormans. A wooden anchor of one fluke, and three boats' rudders of violet wood were also found; but what puzzled me most was a collection of stones piled together in a line, resembling a low wall, with short lines running perpendicularly at the back, dividing the space behind into compartments. In each of these were the remains of a charcoal fire, and all the wood near at hand had been cut down. Mr Brown saw on another island a similar construction, with not less than thirty-six partitions, over which was laid a rude piece of framework; and the neighbouring mangroves, to the extent of an acre and a half, had been cut down. It was evident that these people were Asiatics, but of what particular nation, or what their business here, could not be ascertained; I suspected them, however, to be Chinese, and that the nutmegs might possibly be their object. From the traces amongst Wellesley's Islands, they had been conjectured to be shipwrecked people; but that opinion did not now appear to be correct.

The barometer stood here from 29.96 to 29.62 inches, being highest with the winds at north-east, and lowest with those from the southward; in the heavy squalls of wind, rain, thunder, and lightning from the north-west, the mercury stood at a medium elevation. On board the ship, the average standard of the thermometer was nearly 85°. On shore it was hotter, yet the mosquitoes were not very troublesome; but the common black flies, from their extraordinary numbers and their impudence, were scarcely less annoying than mosquitoes; they get into the mouth and nose, and settle upon the face or any other part of the body, with as much unconcern as they would alight on a gum tree; nor are they driven away easily. This was the case on shore, and on board the ship whilst lying at anchor, and for a day or two afterwards; but the society of man wrought a change in the manners even of these little animals. They soon became more cautious, went off when a hand was lifted up, and in three or four days after quitting the land, behaved themselves orderly, like other flies; and though still numerous on board, they gave little molestation. Dampier found these insects equally troublesome on the north-west coast; for he says, speaking of the natives, 'Their eyelids are always half closed, to keep the flies out of their eyes; they being so troublesome here, that no fanning will keep them from coming to one's face; and without the assistance of both hands to keep them off, they will creep into one's nostrils, and mouth too, if the lips are not shut very close.'

[The *Investigator*]
January–June 1803

*January 4, 1803* ~ The weather remained squally, and wind unsettled during the night. In the morning our course was continued to the northward, leaving extensive land, which I supposed to be the Groote Eylandt of the old charts, six or eight leagues on the starboard hand. Before commencing the investigation of that island, I wished to trace the main coast further on, and if possible, give the botanists an opportunity of examining its productions; for it was upon the main that they usually made the most interesting discoveries, and only once, since entering the Gulf of Carpentaria, had we been able to land there. At seven o'clock we edged in for the coast; and on coming into 3 fathoms, dropped the anchor on a bottom of blue mud, within a mile of the shore. No part of Groote Eylandt was in sight; but an island of considerable extent and elevation, not noticed in the old chart, lay six or seven miles to the ENE; and I have called it Bickerton's Island.

Whilst the botanical gentlemen landed abreast of the ship, I took the whaleboat to a woody islet, five miles off, close to Bickerton's Island...The islet is about half a mile long, and though many bushes and some trees grow upon it, is little more than a bed of sand. There were holes in the beach, made by turtle; and besides other proofs of the islet being sometimes visited by the Indians, I found four human skulls lying at the back of the shore.

From the woody islet I crossed over to the mainland near the ship, and took another set of bearings for the survey. Upon the shore

were pieces of bamboo, and other traces of the same foreign people
of whom mention has frequently been made; and three small huts
were found, so entirely covered with grass that no opening was left;
but they were empty, and nothing was buried underneath. On the
borders of a small fresh lake the botanists reaped a harvest of new
plants, without molestation; indeed no natives were seen anywhere;
but several skeletons were found, standing upright in the hollow
stumps of trees; and the skulls and bones being smeared or painted,
partly red and partly white, made a very strange appearance. Some
kangaroos were perceived at a distance; and judging by their footmarks on the sand, they were rather numerous...

*5 January* ~ In the morning we got under way and steered eastward for Groote Eylandt, which I now intended to circumnavigate...

Between the nearest parts of Groote and Bickerton's Islands is
a space of eight miles, which seemed to offer a perfectly safe
passage, with soundings, if I may judge from what we had in crossing the south side, between 13 and 17 fathoms; nor can the rather
high and woody isle, which lies almost exactly in the middle of the
opening, be considered as presenting any obstacle...I call it
Connexion Island; because my survey round Groote Eylandt was
connected by its means, and made in a great measure independent
of the time keepers...

*12 January* ~...The land was better distinguished than before,
and many straggling rocks and two islets were seen to lie off the
north end of Groote Eylandt. In the morning of the 14th we
weathered all these, and on the wind dying away, anchored in 11½
fathoms, blue mud; the outer North-point Islet, which lies in 13°
37' south and 136° 45' east, then bore E3°S five miles, and the
furthest extreme of a higher cliffy island, S38°W three miles.

I went in a boat to this last island with the botanical gentlemen,
intending to take bearings from the uppermost cliffs; but the many
deep chasms by which the upper parts are intersected, made
it impossible to reach the top in the short time we had to spare,
and a few bearings from the eastern low point were all that could

be obtained. This was called Chasm Island; it lies one mile and a half from a low point of Groote Eylandt, where the shore trends southward and seemed to form a bay, into which I proposed to conduct the ship.

We found upon Chasm Island a fruit which proved to be a new species of *eugenia*, of the size of an apple, whose acidity of taste was agreeable; there were also many large bushes covered with nutmegs, similar to those seen at Cape Vanderlin; and in some of the chasms the ground was covered with this fruit, without our being able, for some time, to know whence it came. Several trees shot up in these chasms, thirty or forty feet high, and on consider- ing them attentively, these were found to be the trees whence the nutmegs had fallen; thus what was a spreading bush above, became, from the necessity of air and light, a tall, slender tree, and showed the admirable power in nature to accommodate itself to local circumstances. The fruit was small, and not of an agreeable flavour; nor is it probable that it can at all come in competition with the nutmeg of the Molucca Islands...

In the steep sides of the chasms were deep holes or caverns, undermining the cliffs; upon the walls of which I found rude draw- ings, made with charcoal and something like red paint upon the white ground of the rock. These drawings represented porpoises, turtle, kangaroos, and a human hand; and Mr Westall, who went afterwards to see them, found the representation of a kangaroo, with a file of thirty-two persons following after it. The third person of the band was twice the height of the others, and held in his hand something resembling the *whaddie*, or wooden sword of the natives of Port Jackson; and was probably intended to represent a chief. They could not, as with us, indicate superiority by clothing or ornament, since they wear none of any kind; and therefore, with the addition of a weapon, similar to the ancients, they seem to have made superiority of person the principal emblem of superior power, of which, indeed, power is usually a consequence in the very early stages of society.

A sea breeze had sprung up from the eastward, and the ship was under way when we returned on board at three in the afternoon. At five we hauled round Chasm Island with 12 fathoms water, which diminished gradually as we proceeded up the bay...

Early next morning the botanists landed on Groote Eylandt, and I went to Finch's Island with the second lieutenant, to take bearings and astronomical observations. From the western head, I saw that the bay extended six or eight miles above the ship, to the southward, and that the southern outlet, beyond Winchilsea Island, was about one mile wide; but the whole seemed to be too shallow for anything larger than boats...

*16 January* ~ The botanists landed upon Winchilsea Island, and further astronomical observations were taken upon that of Finch; where also a part of the ship's company went to divert themselves, and to wash their linen; and in the evening we prepared to quit North-west Bay.

*18 January* ~...I went immediately, with the botanical gentlemen, to the northern and largest of the two sandy isles; and after observing the latitude 13° 42' 17" on the south-west point, ascended the highest hillock, which, from the clump of trees upon it, was called Pandanus Hill. Some of the trees being cut down, I had a tolerably extensive view of points and islands before passed...One of these I have called Burney's Island, in compliment to Captain James Burney of the navy, and another Nicol's Island, after His Majesty's bookseller, the publisher of this work. Beyond these was a more extensive land, which also proved to be an island; and its form having some resemblance to the *whaddie* or *woodah*, or wooden sword used by the natives of Port Jackson, it was named Isle Woodah.

*20 January* ~ In the morning, we steered SW to take up the survey of the main coast at Cape Barrow, between which and Isle Woodah was an opening...A higher island, two or three miles long, then showed itself to the NNW; and on the water shoaling to $3^1/_2$ fathoms, the anchor was dropped at four in the afternoon, one mile

and a half from its south side, on a bottom of blue mud. The mainland was in sight to the westward, forming a large bay with Isle
Woodah, and Bickerton's Island covered the entrance, so that the
ship was in complete shelter.

On landing with the botanical gentlemen, I ascended a
hummock at the east end of the island, where alone the view was
not impeded by wood. Many of my former fixed points were visible
from thence, and the mainland was traced round to the northward,
to a hill named Mount Grindall, near which was another round hill
upon an island; and behind them the main extended eastward,
nearly as far as over the middle of Isle Woodah...

A party of men was sent to cut wood on the following morning,
and another to haul the seine; the botanists also landed, and I went
to observe the latitude and take bearings from the west end of the
island; every person was armed, for marks of feet had been
perceived, so newly imprinted on the sand, that we expected to
meet with Indians. After accomplishing my objects, I walked with
a small party round the north-west end of the island; and then
returned over the high land, through a most fatiguing brush wood,
towards the wooders and the boat.

On clearing the wood, four or five Indians were seen on a hill,
half a mile to the left, and some of the wooding party advancing
towards them. The sight of us seemed to give the natives an apprehension of being surrounded, for they immediately ran; but our
proceeding quietly down to the boat, which I did in the hope that
our people might bring on an interview, appeared to satisfy them.
The scientific gentlemen accompanied me on board to dinner; and
I learned from Mr Westall, that whilst he was taking a sketch at the
east end of the island, a canoe, with six men in it, came over from
Woodah. He took little notice of them until, finding they saw him
and landed not far off, he thought it prudent to retreat with his
servant to the wooding party. The natives followed pretty smartly
after him; and when they appeared on the brow of the hill, Mr
Whitewood, the master's mate, and some of his wooders went to

meet them in a friendly manner. This was at the time that the appearance of my party caused them to run; but when we left the shore they had stopped, and our people were walking gently up the hill.

The natives had spears, but from the smallness of their number, and our men being armed, I did not apprehend any danger; we had, however, scarcely reached the ship, when the report of muskets was heard; and the people were making signals and carrying someone down to the boat, as if wounded or killed. I immediately despatched two armed boats to their assistance, under the direction of the master; with orders, if he met with the natives, to be friendly and give them presents, and by no means to pursue them into the wood. I suspected, indeed, that our people must have been the aggressors; but told the master, if the Indians had made a wanton attack, to bring off their canoe by way of punishment; intending myself to take such steps on the following day, as might be found expedient.

At five o'clock Mr Whitewood was brought on board, with four spear wounds in his body. It appeared that the natives, in waiting to receive our men, kept their spears ready, as ours had their muskets. Mr Whitewood, who was foremost, put out his hand to receive a spear which he supposed was offered; but the Indian, thinking perhaps that an attempt was made to take his arms, ran the spear into the breast of his supposed enemy. The officer snapped his firelock, but it missed, and he retreated to his men; and the Indians, encouraged by this, threw several spears after him, three of which took effect. Our people attempted to fire, and after some time two muskets went off, and the Indians fled; but not without taking away a hat which had been dropped. Thomas Morgan, a marine, having been some time exposed bare-headed to the sun, was struck with a *coup-de-soleil*; he was brought on board with Mr Whitewood and died in a state of frenzy the same night.

So soon as the master had learned what had happened, he went round in the whaleboat to the east end of the island, to secure the canoe; and forgetting the orders I had given him, sent Mr Lacy with the wooders overland, to intercept the natives on that side. Their searches were for some time fruitless; but in the dusk of the evening three Indians were seen by the wooders, and before they could be intercepted had pushed off in the canoe. A sharp fire was commenced after them; and before they got out of reach, one fell and the others leaped out and dived away. A seaman who gave himself the credit of having shot the native, swam off to the canoe, and found him lying dead at the bottom, with a straw hat on his head which he recognised to be his own. Whilst displaying this in triumph, he upset the ticklish vessel, and the body sunk; but the canoe was towed to the shore, and the master returned with it at nine o'clock.

I was much concerned at what had happened, and greatly displeased with the master for having acted so contrary to my orders; but the mischief being unfortunately done, a boat was sent in the morning to search for the dead body, the painter being desirous of it to make a drawing, and the naturalist and surgeon for anatomical purposes. The corpse was found lying at the water's edge, not lengthwise as a body washed up, but with the head on shore and the feet touching the surf. The arms were crossed under the head, with the face downward, in the posture of a man who was just able to crawl out of the water and die; and I very much apprehend this to have been one of the two natives who had leaped out of the canoe, and were thought to have escaped. He was of the middle size, rather slender, had a prominent chest, small legs, and similar features to the inhabitants of other parts of this country; and he appeared to have been circumcised! A musket ball had passed through the shoulder blade, from behind; and penetrating upwards, had lodged in the neck.

The canoe was of bark, but not of one piece, as at Port Jackson; it consisted of two pieces, sewed together lengthwise, with the seam on one side; the two ends were also sewed up, and made tight with gum. Along each gunwale was lashed a small pole; and these were spanned together in five places, with creeping vine, to preserve the shape, and to strengthen the canoe. Its length was thirteen and a half, and the breadth two and a half feet; and it seemed capable of carrying six people, being larger than those generally used at Port Jackson.

It does not accord with the usually timid character of the natives of Terra Australis, to suppose the Indians came over from Isle Woodah for the purpose of making an attack; yet the circumstance of their being without women or children, their following so briskly after Mr Westall, and advancing armed to the wooders all imply that they rather sought than avoided a quarrel. I can account for this unusual conduct only by supposing, that they might have had differences with, and entertained no respectful opinion of the Asiatic visitors, of whom we had found so many traces, some almost in sight of this place.

The body of Thomas Morgan who died so unfortunately, was this day committed to the deep with the usual ceremony; and the island was named after him, Morgan's Island...

*27 January* ~ We steered westward, with a fair wind, to explore the main coast up to Mount Grindall, and see the northern part of Blue-mud Bay. At three leagues from Cape Shield, we passed a projecting point to which I gave the name of Point Blane, in compliment to Dr (now Sir Gilbert) Blane, of the naval medical board...We then worked up to a large bight on the west side of Point Blane; and the water being shallow towards the head, anchored in 3 fathoms, muddy ground, with the extremity of the point bearing S41°E two and a half miles.

An officer was sent on shore to search for fresh water and examine the beach with a view to hauling the seine, but had no success; the naturalist accompanied him, to botanise, and not coming down to the boat at dusk, the officer left a man with a fire on the beach, to wait his arrival. At ten o'clock a gun was fired and the boat sent back; but nothing had been heard of the naturalist, or the seaman who carried his specimen boxes, and some apprehensions began to be entertained. Soon after daylight we had the satisfaction to see Mr Brown on the shore. It appeared that from one of those mistakes which so frequently occur in thick woods and dull weather, when without a compass, the east had been mistaken for west; and Mr Brown reached the water side at dusk, but on the wrong side of the point. He thought it more prudent to remain there all night, than to re-enter the wood in the dark; and the report of the gun having given him the true direction, he had no difficulty in the morning. No natives were seen; but the howling of dogs was heard not far off...

*3 February* ~ In the morning, there being no wind to move the ship, I sent the master up the bay with the whaleboat, to search for fresh water and a secure anchorage; and on his making the signal to follow, a little before noon, we steered for Point Middle. A shoal was seen to extend from it, down the bay; and the depth having diminished to 4 fathoms, we hauled up into the eastern branch, and anchored under Point Alexander in $4^1/_2$ fathoms... Several natives were seen on the shore abreast of the ship, and Lieutenant Fowler was sent to communicate with them, and to search for fresh water. They stayed to receive him, without showing that timidity so usual with the Australians; and after a friendly intercourse in which mutual presents were made, Mr Fowler returned with the information that fresh water was plentiful.

*4 February* ~ Having given directions for two tents, a seine, and a corporal's guard, to be sent on shore under the command of the first lieutenant, I landed with the botanical gentlemen; the natives running from their night residences to meet us. There were twelve middle-aged and young men, all of whom expressed much joy, especially at seeing Bongaree, our good-natured Indian from Port Jackson. On the arrival of two other boats, the natives retreated into the wood, except two, who assisted in hauling the seine; and the others came back by degrees, without arms as before, and received a portion of the fish. A situation was chosen for the tents, and confidence seeming to be established, I went into the wood, towards some sandhills, for the purpose of taking bearings; but whilst making the circuit of a salt swamp which lay in the way, the natives were heard running in the wood, and calling to each other. This happened twice, and at length a musket was fired; upon which I returned to the tents with all expedition.

When the botanical gentlemen had entered the wood with their attendants, the greater part of the natives followed them; and one took an opportunity of snatching a hatchet from the hand of a servant. The Indians then ran off; but seeing no pursuit, nor much notice taken, soon returned, and became more friendly than ever. Each of our party had a native with him, walking arm in arm, and Mr Brown's servant had two, who paid him particular attention; so much so, that whilst one held him by the arm, the other snatched the musket off his shoulder, and they all again ran off; that is, all who remained, for several had previously withdrawn themselves. A musket was fired after the thief; but he had already got some distance, and it produced no other visible effect than that of making him run faster. The botanists then judged it imprudent to follow their pursuit, and returned to the tents.

Two hours passed before anything more was heard of the natives; some were then seen in the wood, and an interview was obtained with two, who being made to understand that a hatchet would be given on the musket being returned, they went off to fetch it. In a little time it was actually brought, with the stock broken and ram-rod gone, and the hatchet was paid; after which the natives came to the tents with confidence, and some would have remained all night, had they been permitted.

This afternoon and the following morning, I took bearings from two stations on Point Middle, and others from a sandy hummock on Point Alexander. The natives came early to the tents, and behaved themselves tranquilly until noon; when one of those who had been most kindly treated, ran off with a wooding axe, and from the thickness of the forest, eluded the pursuit made after him. The corporal and another marine, who had run after the Indian without their hats, received a *coup-de-soleil*, and were sent on board in a state nearly approaching to delirium; but they happily recovered.

Finding these people so determinately bent upon stealing everything within their reach, I ordered Lieutenant Fowler to watch an opportunity of seizing two of them; and after a while to release one, making him understand that the other would be carried away in the ship, if the stolen axe were not returned. In the evening, I went over with two of the gentlemen to the south side of the bay; for the purpose of taking a station upon a hill there named Mount Caledon, whose height exceeded that of any other near the water side...

We returned to the ship in the afternoon, and the natives had not then approached the tents since the theft of the axe; but next morning two of them advanced, bringing some small fruits; and on being invited to eat fish, they sat down and were immediately seized, some others who followed, running away on hearing their cries. In a little time the eldest and most intelligent of them was liberated; on his promising by signs to restore the axe, and being made to understand that his companion would be carried off, should he fail. We observed from the ship much running of the natives amongst the bushes and peeping about the tents; and lest they should attempt any mischief, a spring was put upon the cable, and a six-pounder, with grape-shot, kept ready; but after one of the prisoners was released they seemed to have less anxiety, and several swam back across a salt creek, to their usual place of residence.

In the evening I landed at the tents; and taking the native, a youth of fourteen named Woga, into the boat, rowed to the place most frequented by the Indians, many of whom were seen behind the bushes. Two came forward, bringing a young girl in their arms; and by expressive signs they offered her to Bongaree, in order to entice him on shore, for the purpose, apparently, of seizing him by way of retaliation. We demanded the restoration of the axe, and our prisoner seemed to use all his powers to enforce it; but the constant answer was, that the thief Yehangeree had been beaten and was gone away; and finding no axe likely to be brought, Woga was carried on board the ship, through a great deal of crying, entreating, threatening, and struggling on his part. He there ate heartily, laughed, sometimes cried, and noticed everything; frequently expressing admiration at what he saw, and especially at the sheep, hogs and cats. We had not seen any bows and arrows in the Gulf of Carpentaria, nor in any part of Terra Australis; but some of those from Murray's Islands being shown to Woga, he knew the use of them, and gave their names in his language...

*8 February* ~ After breakfast next morning, I took our prisoner to the tents. On approaching the shore, he was preparing to make a spring out of the boat, which made it necessary to bind him again, for he had been loosed on board the ship. He struggled much, calling upon Bongaree to assist him; but after a while, became quiet, and I left him bound to a tree, eating rice and fish.

A party of the gentlemen landed near the head of the bay, hoping to botanise without interruption; but a number of natives had collected there, two of whom advanced, and sought to entice them into the wood by explaining how many animals might be there shot. The gentlemen were aware of the treachery and soon thought it advisable to return to the boat; upon which the natives closed in upon them, with poised spears and every appearance of intended mischief. The pointing of muskets stopped their forwardness for a moment; but they came on again, and a shot was fired at each of the two foremost, which put them to flight, and they were not seen afterwards; but the gentlemen thought it unsafe to proceed in their occupation and returned to the ship. Neither of the two natives dropped; but the muskets being loaded with buck-shot, it was supposed that one or both, must have been wounded.

The second evening of Woga's captivity came, and there was no appearance of the axe being restored; his detention, on the contrary, had caused some annoyance to us, and mischief to his countrymen; and if persevered in to the extent of carrying him away, might be an injury to those who should come after us, especially to Captain Baudin, whom we daily expected to meet, according to what he had said at Port Jackson. Had the consequences affected ourselves alone, the time of our departure was so near that I should have been glad to have kept Woga; for he was a sprightly lad, whom our treatment would soon have reconciled, and in any future intercourse with his countrymen, as also in furnishing information upon many interesting points, he might have been of service. But for the above reason, and that it was not altogether just to do otherwise, I determined to release the poor prisoner though the axe should not be restored, and went to the tents for that purpose. Woga appeared to be a little melancholy in his bondage, but upon the whole, had not fared amiss, having been eating the greater part of the morning and afternoon. He begged hard to be released, promising, with tears in his eyes, to bring back the axe; and after giving him some clothing and presents, he was suffered to depart. As far as two hundred yards, he walked away leisurely; but then, looking first behind him, took to his heels with all his might, leaving us no faith in the fulfilment of his pathetic promises.

At this time the holds were completed with water and wood, and on the following morning the last observations for the time keepers were taken; after which the shore establishment was embarked, and we prepared for sea. The botanists made an excursion upon Point Middle, and pursued their researches without disturbance; and neither Woga nor any of his countrymen were seen during the whole day.

It has been said, that an opening of a river-like form is laid down in the Dutch chart, in the situation of this bay. No name is there given to it; and as I conceive our examination to confer the right of bestowing one, I have distinguished it by the title of

Caledon Bay, as a mark of respect to the worthy nobleman, lately governor of the Cape of Good Hope, after whom the mount on the south side was also named...

The natives of Caledon Bay are the same race of men as those of Port Jackson and King George's Sound, places at nearly the two opposite extremities of Terra Australis; in personal appearance they were behind some tribes we had seen, but the difference did not go beyond what a less abundant supply of food might produce. All those who came to the tents had lost the upper front tooth on the left side, whereas at Port Jackson it is the right tooth which is knocked out at the age of puberty; whether the women undergo the same operation, contrary to the usage at Port Jackson, we had no opportunity of knowing, having seen only one female, and that at a distance. This girl wore a small piece of bark, in guise of a fig leaf, which was the sole approximation to clothing seen among them. Above the elbow the men usually wore a bandage of net work, in which was stuck a short piece of strong grass, called *tomo*, and used as a toothpick; but the most remarkable circumstance in their persons was, that the whole of them appeared to have undergone the Jewish and Mahometan rite of circumcision. The same thing was before noticed in a native of Isle Woodah, and in two at Wellesley's Islands; it would seem, therefore, to be general on the west side of the Gulf of Carpentaria; but with what view it may be done, or whence the custom were received, it is not in my power to state. No such practice was found on the south or east coasts, nor was it observed in the natives of the islands in Torres' Strait, who however, go naked as the Australians.

No other weapons than spears were seen amongst these people; but they were not unacquainted with bows and arrows. It is probable that they have bark canoes, though none were seen, for several trees were found stripped, as if for that purpose; yet when Bongaree made them a present of the canoe brought from Blue-mud Bay, they expressed very little pleasure at the gift, and did not seem to know how to repair it.

That this bay had before received the visits of some strangers, was evinced by the knowledge which the natives had of firearms; they imitated the act of shooting when we first landed, and when a musket was fired at their request, were not much alarmed. A quantity of posts was lying near the water, which had been evidently cut with iron instruments; and when we inquired of the inhabitants concerning them, they imitated with their hands the motion of an axe cutting down a tree, and then stopping, exclaimed *Poo*! Whence we understood that the people who cut the wood had firearms. This was all that could be learned from the natives; but from the bamboos and partitions of framework found here, similar to those at Pellew's Group, they were doubtless the same Asiatic nation, if not the same individuals, of whom so many traces had been seen all the way from the head of the Gulf.

The propensity shown by the natives to steal, especially our axes, so contrary to all I have known and heard of their country-men, is not only a proof that they had been previously visited by people possessing iron implements, but from their audacity it would appear, that the effect of firearms was either not very certain in the hands of the strangers, or had seldom been resorted to in the punishment of aggression; and from the circumstance of the Indians bringing us a few berries, as a recompense for the last stolen axe, it should seem that they had been accustomed to make very easy atonements for their thefts. I have some hope that those who may follow us will not be robbed, at least with so much effrontery; and at the same time, that the inhabitants of Caledon Bay will not avoid, but be desirous of further communication with Europeans.

I do not know that the language at any two parts of Terra Australis, however near, has been found to be entirely the same; for even at Botany Bay, Port Jackson and Broken Bay, not only the dialect, but many words are radically different; and this confirms one part of an observation, the truth of which seems to be gener-ally admitted: that although similarity of language in two nations

proves their origin to be the same, yet dissimilarity of language is
no proof of the contrary position. The language of Caledon Bay
may therefore be totally different to what is spoken on the east and
south coasts, and yet the inhabitants have one common origin; but
I do not think that the language is absolutely and wholly different,
though it certainly was no better understood by Bongaree than by
ourselves. In three instances I found a similarity: the personal
pronoun of Port Jackson, *gni-a* (I), was used here, and apparently
in the same sense; when inquiry was made after the axe, the natives
replied '*Yehangeree py*,' making signs of beating; and *py* signifies to
beat, in the Port Jackson language; the third instance was of the
lad Woga calling to Bongaree in the boat, which after he had done
several times without being answered, he became angry, and
exclaimed *Bongaree-gah*! in a vehement manner, as Bongaree himself
would have done in a similar case...

On board the ship, the range of the thermometer was from 83°
to 87°, nearly as it had been from first entering the Gulf of
Carpentaria; and on shore it was probably 10° higher. Several of
our people were ill of diarrhoeas at this time, accompanied with
some fever, which was attributed by the surgeon to the heat and the
moist state of the atmosphere; for since December, when the
north-west monsoon began, not many days had passed without
rain, and thunder squalls were frequent. Exposing the head uncov-
ered to the sun, more especially if engaged in strong exercise, was
proved to be very dangerous here; I lost one man in Blue-mud Bay
from a want of due precaution in this particular, and at this place
two others very narrowly escaped...

*11 February* ~ At eight in the morning we passed Cape Arnhem,
a smooth grassy projection which rises gently from the water's edge
into the country, but is nowhere of much elevation; a broad rock
lies near the south-eastern extremity, and its position was ascertained to be 12° 19' south, and 187° 1' east...The furthest land
visible at noon was a flat-topped hill which I call Mount Saunders,
and nearer to us was a higher and more woody hill, also flat-topped

and steep at its north end, to which is given the name of Mount Dundas...

We tacked to the westward in the afternoon, and an island came in sight, lying to the north of the two mounts, with several rocks and islets scattered on its north-east side. At sunset the wind died away, and a stream anchor was dropped in 16 fathoms sandy ground; our situation being five miles from the shore under Mount Dundas, and three from the nearest rocky islets to the north-west. The flood tide set gently to the westward, and induced me to suppose there might be a passage within the island and rocks, and in the morning our endeavours were used to reach it; but the winds being light and mostly contrary, the evening came before we got through. An anchor was then dropped in 4 fathoms, coarse sand, one mile and a half from the sandy shore under Mount Saunders...

Two natives, with a canoe, had been seen upon the island; and as our boat stood that way, sounding ahead of the ship, they waved and called to the people. The island is about five miles long, and between one and two in breadth; it is low, mostly destitute of wood, and the shores in general are sandy; and not being laid down in the Dutch chart, I distinguish it, with the islets and rocks to the north and north-east, by the name of Melville Isles...

*16 February* ~ Coasting along the mangrove shore from thence northward, and after landing at one other place, we came to the isthmus which connects Drimmie Head to the land of Point Dundas; and it being near high water, the boat was got over the isthmus by a small passage through the mangroves, and we reached the ship at one o'clock, where everything was prepared for weighing the anchor.

This bay is unnoticed in the Dutch chart, and I name it Melville Bay...No inhabitants were perceived, nor any fresh traces of them; but as dogs were seen twice, it is probable the natives were watching us at no great distance; they had visited all the places where I landed, and should therefore seem to possess canoes. Traces of the same strangers, of whom mention has been so often made, were found here; and amongst others were partitions of framework and part of a large earthen jar. Kangaroos appeared to be rather numerous in the woods, brown doves and large white pigeons were tolerably plentiful, and a bird nearly black, of the size and appearance of a hen, was shot; there were also cockatoos, both black and white, and a beautiful species of parakeet not known at Port Jackson. The aquatic birds were blue and white cranes, sea-pies, and sand-larks. Besides fish, our seine usually brought on shore many of the grey slugs or sea cucumbers, but not so abundantly as in Caledon Bay.

We were not here pestered so much with the black flies as before; but the mosquitoes and sandflies were numerous and fierce. Most of the bushes contained nests made by a small green ant; and if the bush were disturbed, these resentful little animals came out in squadrons, and never ceased to pursue till the disturber was out of sight. In forcing our way amongst the underwood, we sometimes got our hair and clothes filled with them; and as their bite is very sharp, and their vengeance never satisfied, there was no other resource than stripping as expeditiously as possible...

At two in the afternoon of the 16th, the wind being moderate at NNW, we worked out of Melville Bay; and anchored at dusk, five miles from the entrance in 13 fathoms, sand and mud. Next morning, in following the line of the western shore with a breeze off the land, we passed three rocks lying out from a point under Mount Bonner; and further on, six or seven miles short of Cape Wilberforce, there was a small shallow opening. From the north part of this cliffy cape, a chain of islands and rocks extends out three or four leagues to the ENE, which I call Bromby's Isles...

*17 February* ~ At this time the weather became squally with much rain; but after numberless tacks, made under double-reefed top sails and courses in the narrow passage, with soundings from 10 to 18 fathoms, we cleared it at two o'clock, and stretched south-westward as the main coast was found to trend; and thus was

the examination of the Gulf of Carpentaria finished, after employ-
ing one hundred and five days in coasting along its shores and
exploring its bays and islands...Henceforward, the Gulf of
Carpentaria will take its station amongst the conspicuous parts of
the globe in a decided character.

After clearing the narrow passage between Cape Wilberforce
and Bromby's Isles, we followed the main coast to the SW; having
on the starboard hand some high and large islands, which closed
in towards the coast ahead so as to make it doubtful whether
there were any passage between them. Under the nearest island
was perceived a canoe full of men; and in a sort of roadstead, at
the south end of the same island, there were six vessels covered
over like hulks, as if laid up for the bad season. Our conjectures
were various as to who those people could be, and what their
business here; but we had little doubt of their being the same,
whose traces had been found so abundantly in the gulf. I had
inclined to the opinion that these traces had been left by Chinese,
and the report of the natives in Caledon Bay that they had
firearms, strengthened the supposition; and combining this with
the appearance of the vessels, I set them down for piratical
Ladrones who secreted themselves here from pursuit, and issued
out as the season permitted, or prey invited them. Impressed with
this idea, we tacked to work up for the road; and our pendant and
ensign being hoisted, each of them hung out a small white flag.
On approaching, I sent Lieutenant Flinders in an armed boat, to
learn who they were; and soon afterward we came to an anchor
in 12 fathoms, within musket shot; having a spring on the cable,
and all hands at quarters.

Every motion in the whaleboat, and in the vessel alongside
which she was lying, was closely watched with our glasses, but all
seemed to pass quietly; and on the return of Lieutenant Flinders,
we learned that they were prows from Macassar, and the six Malay
commanders shortly afterwards came on board in a canoe. It
happened fortunately that my cook was a Malay, and through his

means I was able to communicate with them. The chief of the six prows was a short, elderly man, named Pobassoo; he said there were upon the coast, in different divisions, sixty prows, and that Salloo was the commander-in-chief. These people were Mahometans, and on looking into the launch, expressed great horror to see hogs there; nevertheless they had no objection to port wine, and even requested a bottle to carry away with them at sunset. The weather continued squally all night, with frequent heavy rain, and the wind blew strong; but coming off the islands, the ship rode easily.

In the morning, I went on board Pobassoo's vessel, with two of the gentlemen and my interpreter, to make further inquiries; and afterwards the six chiefs came to the *Investigator*, and several canoes were alongside for the purpose of barter. Before noon, five other prows steered into the road from the SW, anchoring near the former six; and we had more people about the ship than I chose to admit on board, for each of them wore a short dagger or cress by his side. My people were under arms, and the guns were exercised and a shot fired at the request of the chiefs; in the evening they all retired quietly, but our guns were kept ready and half the people at quarters all night. The weather was very rainy; and towards morning, much noise was heard amongst the prows. At daylight they got under sail, and steered through the narrow passage between Cape Wilberforce and Bromby's Isles, by which we had come; and afterwards directed their course south-eastward into the Gulf of Carpentaria.

My desire to learn everything concerning these people, and the strict lookout which it had been necessary to keep upon them, prevented me attending to any other business during their stay. According to Pobassoo, from whom my information was principally obtained, sixty prows belonging to the Rajah of Boni, and carrying one thousand men, had left Macassar with the north-west monsoon, two months before, upon an expedition to this coast; and the fleet was then lying in different places to the westward, five or six together, Pobassoo's division being the foremost. These prows seemed to be about twenty-five tons, and to have twenty or twenty-five men in each; that of Pobassoo carried two small brass guns, obtained from the Dutch, but the others had only muskets; besides which, every Malay wears a cress or dagger, either secretly or openly. I inquired after bows and arrows, and the *ippo* poison, but they had none of them; and it was with difficulty they could understand what was meant by the ippo.†

The object of their expedition was a certain marine animal, called *trepang*. Of this they gave me two dried specimens; and it proved to be the *bêche-de-mer*, or sea cucumber which we had first seen on the reefs of the east coast, and had afterwards hauled on shore so plentifully with the seine, especially in Caledon Bay. They get the trepang by diving, in from 3 to 8 fathoms water; and where it is abundant, a man will bring up eight or ten at a time. The mode of preserving it is this: the animal is split down one side, boiled, and pressed with a weight of stones; then stretched open by slips of bamboo, dried in the sun, and afterwards in smoke, when it is fit to be put away in bags, but requires frequent exposure to the sun. A thousand trepang make a *picol*, of about 125 Dutch pounds; and one hundred picols are a cargo for a prow. It is carried to Timor, and sold to the Chinese, who meet them there; and when all the prows are assembled, the fleet returns to Macassar...‡

Pobassoo had made six or seven voyages from Macassar to this coast, within the preceding twenty years, and he was one of the first who came; but had never seen any ship here before. This road was the first rendezvous for his division, to take in water previously to going into the gulf. One of their prows had been lost the year before, and much inquiry was made concerning the pieces of

† During the nineteenth century it was widely believed that poisoned arrows were in use in Australasia, probably because several Europeans wounded by arrows had died soon after from tetanus.

‡ The trepang was actually taken to Timor-laoet, off Ceram.

wreck we had seen; and a canoe's rudder being produced, it was recognised as having belonged to her. They sometimes had skirmishes with the native inhabitants of the coast; Pobassoo himself had been formerly speared in the knee, and a man had been slightly wounded since their arrival in this road: they cautioned us much to beware of the natives.*

They had no knowledge of any European settlement in this country; and on learning the name Port Jackson, the son of Pobassoo made a memorandum of it as thus, ﺳﯩﺭﺟﺭﻭﺳ, writing from left to right. Until this time, that some nutmegs were shown to them, they did not know of their being produced here; nor had they ever met with cocoa-nuts, bananas, or other edible fruits or vegetables; fish, and sometimes turtle, being all they procured. I inquired if they knew of any rivers or openings leading far inland, if they made charts of what they saw, or used any charts? To all which Pobassoo answered in the negative. There was a river at Timor, into which the ship could go; and he informed me of two turtle islands, one of them not far to the north-west of our situation in the road; the other would be seen from the masthead as we sailed along the shore.

I could find no other nautical instrument amongst them than a very small pocket compass, apparently of Dutch manufacture; by this their course is directed at sea, without the aid of any chart or astronomical observation. They carry a month's water, in joints of bamboo; and their food is rice, cocoa-nuts, and dried fish, with a few fowls for the chiefs. The black *gummotoo* rope, of which we had found pieces at Sir Edward Pellew's Group, was in use on board the prows; and they said it was made from the same palm whence the sweet sirup, called *gulah*, is obtained.

---

* A question suggests itself here: could the natives of the west side of the Gulf of Carpentaria have learned the rite of circumcision from these Malay Mahometans? From the short period that the latter had frequented the coast, and the nature of the intercourse between the two people, it seems to me very little probable.

My numberless questions were answered patiently, and with apparent sincerity; Pobassoo even stopped one day longer at my desire than he had intended, for the north-west monsoon, he said, would not blow quite a month longer, and he was rather late. I rewarded his trouble and that of his companions with several presents, principally iron tools, which they seemed anxious to possess; and he begged of me an English Jack, which he afterwards carried at the head of his squadron. He also expressed a desire for a letter, to show to any other ship he might meet; and I accordingly wrote him a note to Captain Baudin, whom it seemed probable he might encounter in the gulf, either going or returning.

So soon as the prows were gone, the botanical gentlemen and myself proceeded to make our examinations. The place where the ship was anchored, and which I call Malay Road, is formed by two islands: one to the SW, now named Pobassoo's Island, upon which was a stream of fresh water behind a beach; the other to the north, named Cotton's Island, after Captain Cotton of the India directory...Cotton's Island extends six or seven miles to the north, and beyond it, to the north-east, was another large island, which I called Wigram's, whose south-east part is also a high cliff. Further off were two small isles; and at a greater distance another, named Truant Island, from its lying away from the rest. Pobassoo's Island intercepted my view to the SW; but on moving back to a higher station, two other islands were seen over it, close to each other; to the furthest and largest I gave the name of Inglis, and to the nearer that of Bosanquet. In the west also, and not more than three miles distant, was an island of considerable size, which was distinguished by the name of Astell. The general trending of all these islands is nearly NE by E, parallel with the line of the main coast and of Bromby's Isles. In the Dutch chart, if they be marked at all, it is as mainland, and without distinctive appellation; I have therefore applied names to each, mostly after gentlemen in the East-India directory; and in compliment to that respectable body of men, whose liberal attention to this voyage was useful to us and honourable to them, the whole cluster is named the English Company's Islands...

From the 19th to the 22nd February, the weather was frequently rainy, with thunder and lightning; and the wind blew strong in squalls, generally between the north and west, and made it unsafe to move the ship. During these days, the botanical gentlemen over-ran the two islands which form Malay Road; and I made a boat excursion to Astell's, and another to the north end of Cotton's Island, to sound and take bearings for the survey. In the latter excursion, three black children were perceived on the north-east beach; and on walking that way we saw two bark huts, and an elderly man was sitting under a tree, near them. He smiled on finding himself discovered, and went behind a bush, when a confused noise was heard of women and children making off into the wood; the man also retreated up the hill, and our friendly signs were ineffectual to stop him. In one of the huts was a net bag, containing some pieces of gum, bone, and a broken spike nail; and against a neighbouring bush were standing three spears, one of which had a number of barbs, and had been wrought with some ingenuity. This I took away; but the rest of the arms, with the utensils and furniture of the huts, consisting of the aforesaid net bag and a shell to drink out of, were left as we found them, with the addition of a hatchet and pocket handkerchief.

Cotton's, Pobassoo's, and Astell's Islands, to which our examinations were limited, are moderately high, woody land; they slope down nearly to the water on their west sides, but on the east, and more especially the south-east, they present steep cliffs...On breaking some pieces out of the cliffs, I found them curiously marked with the representation of flowers and trees, owing, as I am told, to manganese or iron ore inserting itself partially into the fissures. The layers are of a reddish colour, resembling flat tiles, and might, I conceive, be used as such, almost without any preparation; there are enough of them to cover a whole town, and the sand stone at the top of the cliffs is equally well calculated for building the walls of the houses.

The upper surfaces of these islands are barren; but in the valleys, down which ran streams of water at this time, there is a tolerable soil. One of these valleys, at the south end of Cotton's Island, might be made a delightful situation to a college of monks, who could bear the heat of the climate, and were impenetrable to the stings of mosquitoes. Here grew the wild nutmeg, in abundance, the fig which bears its fruit on the stem, two species of palm, and a tree whose bark is in common use in the east for making ropes...

The weather was still squally on the 23rd, but in the afternoon became finer; and at three o'clock we steered south-westward, between the islands and the main, with a flood-tide in our favour and the whaleboat sounding ahead...At dusk in the evening we came to, in 5 fathoms muddy ground, in a place much like Malay Road; it is formed by Inglis' and Bosanquet's Islands, and except in a space between them, of half a mile wide, we had land at various distances all round.

Inglis' Island forms here a pretty-looking cove, in which is a woody islet. In the morning I sounded the cove; and finding it to be shallow, went on, accompanied by the landscape painter, to take bearings from the steep north-east head of the island...

We had not brought any provision in the boat; but Inglis' Island appearing to terminate three or four miles further on, I hoped to make the circuit, and reach the ship to a late dinner. An Indian followed along the shore, inviting us by signs to land; but when the boat's head was turned that way, he retreated into the wood, and we had no time to follow, or to wait his pleasure to come down; for a good deal of delay had been caused by the tide, and the island was found to extend several miles further than was expected, to another steep head, from which I was desirous to obtain a set of bearings. At five o'clock, when we reached the head, it rained fast, which deterred me from attempting the steep ascent, and we pushed onward; but the island, instead of terminating here, extended four miles further in a west direction, to a low point, where sunset and the bad weather obliged us to stop for the night. No wood could be found to make a fire, nor had we any tent; and from the rain, the cold, and mosquitoes, and our want of dinner, the night passed uncomfortably.

*25 February* ~ At daylight, I took bearings from the low south-west point, whilst Bongaree speared a few fish...Bongaree was busily employed preparing his fish, when my bearings were concluded. The natives of Port Jackson have a prejudice against all fish of the ray kind, as well as against sharks; and whilst they devour with eager avidity the blubber of a whale or porpoise, a piece of skate would excite disgust. Our good natured Indian had been ridiculed by the sailors for this unaccountable whim, but he had not been cured; and it so happened, that the fish he had speared this morning were three small rays and a mullet. This last, being the most delicate, he presented to Mr Westall and me, so soon as it was cooked; and then went to saunter by the water side, whilst the boats' crew should cook and eat the rays, although, having had nothing since the morning before, it may be supposed he did not want appetite. I noticed this in silence till the whole were prepared, and then had him called up to take his portion of the mullet; but it was with much difficulty that his modesty and forbearance could be overcome, for these qualities, so seldom expected in a savage, formed leading features in the character of my humble friend. But there was one of the sailors also, who preferred hunger to ray-eating! It might be supposed he had an eye to the mullet; but this was not the case. He had been seven or eight years with me, mostly in New South Wales, had learned many of the native habits, and even imbibed this ridiculous notion respecting rays and sharks; though he could not allege, as Bongaree did, that 'they might be very good for white men, but would kill him'. The mullet accordingly underwent a further division; and Mr Westall and myself, having no prejudice against rays, made up our proportion of this scanty repast from one of them.

We rowed northward, round the west end of Inglis' Island,

leaving a hummocky isle and a sandy islet to the left; but on coming
to a low point with a small island near it, the rapidity of the flood
tide was such, that we could not make headway, and were obliged
to wait for high water. I took the opportunity to get another set of
bearings, and then followed the example of the boats' crew, who,
not finding oysters or anything to eat, had fallen asleep on the
beach to forget the want of food...

*6 March* ~ For the last several days the wind had inclined from
the eastward, and at this time blew a steady breeze at E by S, with
fine weather; as if the north-west monsoon were passed and the
south-east trade had resumed its course. We had continued the
survey of the coast for more than one-half of the six months which
the master and carpenter had judged the ship might run without
much risk, provided she remained in fine weather and no accident
happened; and the remainder of the time being not much more
than necessary for us to reach Port Jackson, I judged it imprudent
to continue the investigation longer.

In addition to the rottenness of the ship, the state of my own
health and that of the ship's company were urgent to terminate the
examination here; for nearly all had become debilitated from the
heat and moisture of the climate—from being a good deal
fatigued—and from the want of nourishing food. I was myself
disabled by scorbutic sores from going to the masthead, or making
any more expeditions in boats; and as the whole of the surveying
department rested upon me, our further stay was without one of
its principal objects. It was not, however, without much regret that
I quitted the coast; both from its numerous harbours and better
soil, and its greater proximity to our Indian possessions having
made it become daily more interesting; and also, after struggling
three months against foul winds, from their now being fair as could
be wished for prosecuting the further examination. The accom-
plishment of the survey was, in fact, an object so near to my heart,
that could I have foreseen the train of ills that were to follow the
decay of the *Investigator* and prevent the survey being resumed—

and had my existence depended upon the expression of a wish, I
do not know that it would have received utterance; but Infinite
Wisdom has, in infinite mercy, reserved the knowledge of futurity
to itself...

*26 March* ~ The winds had hung so much in the south-west,
and retarded our passage as well as driven us near to the island
Timor, that I judged it advisable to obtain refreshments there for
my ship's company; under the apprehension that, as the winter
season was fast advancing on the south coast of Terra Australis, the
bad state of the ship might cause more labour at the pumps than
our present strength was capable of exerting. Some of the smaller
articles of sea provision, such as peas, rice and sugar, which formed
a principal part of our little comforts, were also become deficient,
in consequence of losses sustained from the heat and moisture of
the climate, and leakiness of the ship's upper works; and these I
was anxious to replenish.

Coepang is a Dutch settlement at the south-west end of Timor;
and the determination to put in there being made, I resolved in my
mind the possibility of afterwards returning to the examination of
the north and north-west coasts of Terra Australis, during the
winter six months, and taking the following summer to pass the
higher latitudes and return to Port Jackson. There was little chance
of obtaining salt provisions at Coepang, but there might be a ship
or ships there, capable of furnishing a supply, and by which an
officer might be conveyed to England; for it was a necessary part
of my project to despatch Lieutenant Fowler to the Admiralty, with
an account of our proceedings, and a request that he might return
as speedily as possible, with a vessel fit to accomplish all the objects
of the voyage; and I calculated that six months employed upon the
north and north-west coasts, and the subsequent passage to Port
Jackson, would not leave much more than the requisite time for
refreshing the ship's company before his arrival might be expected.

It is to be observed, that the ship had leaked very little in her
sides since the caulking done at the head of the Gulf; and the

carpenter being now directed to bore into some of the timbers then examined, did not find them to have become perceptibly worse; so that I was led to hope and believe that the ship might go through this service, without much more than common risk, provided we remained in fine-weather climates, as was intended...

*31 March* ~ At daylight, the north-east point of Rottee was distant two miles, and we steered along the shore, looking for boats and people to obtain intelligence, and if possible some refreshments; but none were seen, although we passed close to a deep and well-sheltered cove. At ten o'clock, when the sandy north point of Rottee was distant one mile and a half, we hauled up north-eastward, across the passage of about six miles wide, between it and the northern lands; for the purpose of entering Samow Strait, which was then open...

Two vessels were lying under the north-east end of Samow; and on our ensign and pendant being hoisted, the one showed American, and the other Dutch colours. An officer was sent to them for information, as well of the propriety of going into Coepang Bay at this season, as of the political state of Europe; for although the intelligence of peace had arrived before we left Port Jackson, it seemed to be doubtful how long it might last. On his return with favourable intelligence, I steered through the northern outlet of the strait...

I sent the second lieutenant to present my respects to the Dutch governor, and inform him of our arrival and wants, with an offer of saluting the fort provided an equal number of guns should be returned; and the offer being accepted, mutual salutes of thirteen guns passed, and the same evening we received a boat-load of refreshments. Next day, I went with three officers and gentlemen to wait upon Mynheer Giesler, the governor, who sent the commandant of the fort and surgeon of the colony to receive us at the water side. The governor did not speak English, nor I any Dutch; and our communications would have been embarrassed but for the presence of Captain Johnson, commander of the Dutch brig, who interpreted with much polite attention.

Coepang is dependent on Batavia for a variety of articles, and amongst others, for arrack, rice, sugar, &c. Mr Johnson had arrived not long before with the annual supply, yet I found some difficulty in obtaining from the governor the comparatively small quantities of which we stood in need; and I had no resource but in his kindness, for there were no merchants in Coepang, nor any other who would receive bills in payment. Having made an agreement for the provisions, I requested permission for our botanists and painters to range the country, which was readily granted; with a caution not to extend their walks far from the town, as they might be there liable to insults from the natives, over whom the governor had no power...

A part of the ship's company was permitted to go on shore so soon as our work was completed; and two men, my Malay cook and a youth from Port Jackson, being absent in the evening, the town was searched for them, but in vain. We got under way early next morning, before the sea breeze set in, and stood off and on until Lieutenant Fowler again went after the men. On his return without success, we stretched out of the bay; but the wind being light, and the governor having promised to send off the men, if found before the ship was out of sight, I still entertained a hope of receiving my deserters...

I made many inquiries concerning the Malay trepang fishers, whom we had met at the entrance of the Gulf of Carpentaria, and learned the following particulars. The natives of Macassar had been long accustomed to fish for the trepang amongst the islands in the vicinity of Java, and upon a dry shoal lying to the south of Rottee; but about twenty years before, one of their prows was driven by the north-west monsoon to the coast of New Holland, and finding the trepang to be abundant, they afterwards returned; and had continued to fish there since that time. The governor was of opinion that the Chinese did not meet them at Timor-laoet, but at Macassar itself, where they are accustomed to trade for birds

nests, trepang, sharks fins, &c; and it therefore seems probable that
the prows rendezvous only at Timor-laoet, on quitting Carpentaria,
and then return in a fleet with their cargoes.

About ten days before our arrival, a homeward-bound ship
from India had touched at Coepang; and had we been so fortunate as to meet with her, it might have enabled me to put in
execution the plan I had formed of sending an officer to England,
and returning to the examination of the north and north-west
coasts of Terra Australis. This plan was now frustrated; and the
sole opportunity of writing to Europe was by Captain Johnson,
who expected to sail for Batavia in May, and promised to forward
our letters from thence. I committed to his care an account of our
examinations and discoveries upon the east and north coasts, for
the Admiralty; with the report of the master and carpenter upon
the state of the ship, and the information I had obtained of the
trepang fishery.

Our supplies for the ship, procured at Coepang, were rice,
arrack, sugar and the palm syrup called *gulah*; with fresh meat,
fruit and vegetables during our stay, and for ten days afterwards.
The animal food consisted of young *karabow*, a species of buffalo,
and of small pigs and kids; the karabow being charged at eight,
the pigs at five, and kids at two rix dollars each. Vegetables were
dear and not good, and for many of the fruits we were too early
in the season; but cocoa-nuts, oranges, limes, bananas and shad-
docks were tolerably plentiful. Tea, sugar candy, and some other
articles for our messes, were purchased at the little shops kept by
the Chinese-Malays; and poultry was obtained alongside
by barter.

To judge from the appearance of those who had resided any
length of time at Coepang, the climate is not good; for even in
comparison with us, who had suffered considerably, they were sickly
looking people. Yet they did not themselves consider the colony as
unhealthy, probably from making their comparison with Batavia;
but they spoke of Diely, the Portuguese settlement, as very bad in

this respect.† Captain Baudin had lost twelve men from dysentery, during his stay at Coepang, and I found a monument which he had erected to his principal gardener; but it was even then beginning to decay…

When we stretched out of Coepang Bay on the 8th of April, the wind was light from the westward; in the afternoon we tacked towards Pulo Samow, hoping that a canoe seen under the land might have the two deserters on board; but this not being the case, they were given up…

*21 April* ~…Dull weather, with frequent heavy rain, thunder and lightning, had prevailed from the time of leaving Coepang, and it produced the same effect upon the health of the ship's company as similar weather had before done in the Gulf of Carpentaria; for we had at this time ten men in the sick list with diarrhoea, and many others were slightly affected. It seemed possible that the change of food from salt provisions to the fresh meat, fruit and vegetables of Timor—a change by which I hoped to banish every appearance of scurvy, might have had an influence in producing the disease; and if so, it was avoiding Scylla to fall upon Charybdis, and was truly unfortunate…

From the 27th of April we steered eight days to the SSW, mostly with south-eastern winds; they were sometimes light, but occa-sionally fresh, and at these times the ship made five inches of water in the hour. The diarrhoea on board was gaining ground, notwith-standing all the attention paid to keeping the ship dry and well aired, and the people clean and as comfortable as possible. Some of the officers began to feel its attack; and in order to relieve them and the people, now that we had no expectation of meeting danger, I directed the ship's company to be divided into three watches, and put the officers to four; giving Mr Denis Lacy, master's mate, the charge of acting lieutenant in the fourth watch.

On 5 May, in latitude 26° 24' and longitude 103° 21', the south-

† Diely: Dili

east wind died away, and a breeze sprung up from the opposite quarter, which veered afterwards to the SW, blowing fresh with squally, moist weather. Our course was then directed for Cape Leeuwin, with the wind usually abeam; the sea being too high for the ship to make good way any nearer. In this passage we were accompanied by several petrels, and amongst them by the albatross, the first of which had been seen in the latitude 23°.

On the 13th, we had reached the parallel of Cape Leeuwin, and were steering E by S, to make it...

*16 May* ~ My intention in coming so near the south coast, was to skirt along the outer parts of the Archipelago of the Recherche, which had before been seen imperfectly; and to stop a day or two in Goose-Island Bay, for the purposes of procuring geese for our sick people, seal oil for our lamps, and a few casks of salt from the lake on Middle Island. It was night when we approached the archipelago, and I therefore steered to make Termination Island, which is the outermost part; at four in the morning of the 17th, it was seen about two leagues to the NE, and we had 62 fathoms on a bottom of white sand. Mondrain Island was set at daylight, and the positions of many other places were either verified or corrected, during the run to noon...

*17 May* ~ At one o'clock, in steering for Douglas's Isles, a single breaker was seen right ahead of the ship...We passed to the northward of it, having no ground at 25 fathoms; and as we approached to do the same by the isles, Mr Charles Douglas, the boatswain, breathed his last; and I affixed his name to the two lumps of land, which seemed to offer themselves as a monument to his memory. We hauled up close along the east side of Middle Island with the wind at west; and at six in the evening anchored in Goose-Island Bay...

In the morning, a party of men was sent to kill geese and seals upon the rocky islets to the eastward, and another upon Middle Island to cut wood and brooms. There was now so much more surf upon the shores of the bay than in January of the former year that

we could not land at the eastern beach, behind which lies the salt
lake. I therefore went with the master to the middle beach, and
being scarcely able to get out of the boat from scorbutic sores, sent
him to examine the lake and make choice of a convenient place for
filling some casks; but to my surprise he reported that no good salt
could be procured, although it had been so abundant before that
according to the testimony of all those who saw the lake, it would
have furnished almost any quantity: this alteration had doubtless
been produced by the heavy rains which appeared to have lately
fallen. I caused a hole to be dug in a sandy gully, in order to fill a
few casks of water, thinking it possible that what we had taken in
at Timor might have been injurious; but the water was too salt to
be drinkable, although draining from land much above the level of
the sea. This may afford some insight into the formation of salt in
the lake; and it seems not improbable that rock salt may be
contained in some part of Middle Island.

We remained here three days, cutting wood, boiling down seal
oil and killing geese; but our success in this last occupation was very
inferior to what it had been in January 1802—no more than twelve
geese being now shot, whereas sixty-five had then been procured.
Mr Douglas was interred upon Middle Island, and an inscription
upon copper placed over his grave; William Hillier, one of my best
men, also died of dysentery and fever before quitting the bay, and
the surgeon had fourteen others in his list unable to do any duty. At
his well-judged suggestion I ordered the cables, which the small size
of the ship had made it necessary to coil between decks, to be put
into the holds, our present light state permitting this to be done on
clearing away the empty casks. By this arrangement more room was
made for the messing and sleeping places; and almost every
morning they were washed with boiling water, aired with stoves, and
sprinkled with vinegar, for the surgeon considered the dysentery on
board to be approaching that state when it becomes contagious.

*21 May* ~ At daylight, having a fresh breeze at NW, we prepared
to depart, and hove short; but the ship driving before the sails were

loosed, and there being little room astern, a second bower was dropped and a kedge anchor carried out. This last not holding after the bowers were weighed, a stream anchor was let go; and before the ship brought up, it was again necessary to drop the best bower. At this time we were not more than a cable's length from the rocks of Middle Island; and the ship being exposed to great danger with the least increase of wind, we got a spring on the stream cable and began to heave on the best bower. In the meantime the ship drove with both anchors ahead, which obliged me, on the instant, to cut both cables, heave upon the spring, and run up the jib and stay-sails; and my orders being obeyed with an alacrity not to be exceeded, we happily cleared the rocks by a few fathoms, and at noon made sail to the eastward...

*23 May* ~ This day James Greenhalgh, sergeant of marines, died of the dysentery; a man whom I sincerely regretted, from the zeal and fidelity with which he had constantly fulfilled the duties of his situation.

The winds continued to blow strong, usually between south and WSW; but the ship did not at any time leak more than five inches an hour. On the 29th, when approaching Bass' Strait, the breeze died away, and after some hours calm sprung up from the northward...

It was a great mortification to be thus obliged to pass Hunter's Isles and the north coast of Van Diemen's Land, without correcting their positions in longitude from the errors which the want of a time keeper in the *Norfolk* had made unavoidable; but when I contemplated eighteen of my men below, several of whom were stretched in their hammocks almost without hope, and reflected that the lives of the rest depended upon our speedy arrival in port, every other consideration vanished; and I carried all possible sail, day and night, making such observations only as could be done without causing delay...

On the 2nd of June we lost John Draper, quarter-master, one of the most orderly men in the ship; and it seemed to be a fatality, that the dysentery should fall heaviest on the most valuable part of the

crew...We steered a due north course, closing a little in with the
land; at sunset Mount Dromedary bore N45°W, and at eight next
morning it was seen bearing S30°W, at the distance of twenty
leagues, although the weather was hazy...Whilst beating against
this foul wind the dysentery carried off another seaman, Thomas
Smith, one of those obtained from Governor King; and had the
wind continued long in the same quarter, many others must have
followed. Happily it veered to the southward at midnight, we
passed Botany Bay at three in the morning, and at daybreak tacked
between the heads of Port Jackson, to work up for Sydney Cove.

I left the ship at noon, above Garden Island, and waited upon
His Excellency Governor King, to inform him of our arrival and
concert arrangements for the reception of the sick at the colonial
hospital. On the following day they were placed under the care of
Thomas Jamison, Esq., principal surgeon of the colony; from
whom they received that kind attention and care which their
situation demanded; but four were too much exhausted, and died
in a few days. The first of them was Mr Peter Good, botanical
gardener, a zealous, worthy man, who was regretted by all.

Lieutenant Murray had arrived safely with the *Lady Nelson*, after
a somewhat tedious passage from the Barrier Reefs; he made
himself an anchor of heavy wood on the coast, for fear of accident
to his sole remaining bower, but fortunately had no occasion to use
it. Besides the *Lady Nelson*, we found lying in Sydney Cove H.M.
armed vessel *Porpoise*, the *Bridgewater* extra-Indiaman, the ships *Cato*,
*Rolla*, and *Alexander*, and brig *Nautilus*. The *Géographe* and *Naturaliste*
had not sailed for the south coast till some months after I left Port
Jackson to go to the northward, and so late as the end of
December, Captain Baudin was lying at King's Island in Bass'
Strait; it was therefore not very probable that he should reach the
Gulf of Carpentaria by the middle of February, when I had
finished its examination, nor even at the beginning of March, when
the south-west monsoon would set in against him.

We found also at Port Jackson Mr James Inman (the present

professor of mathematics at the Royal Naval College, Portsmouth), whom the Board of Longitude had sent out to join the expedition as astronomer, in the place of Mr Crosley who had left us at the Cape of Good Hope. To this gentleman's care I committed all the larger astronomical instruments, and also the time keepers, after observations had been taken to compare their longitudes with that of Cattle Point...

In order to re-establish the health of the ship's company, I contracted for a regular supply of vegetables and fresh meat; and such was the favourable change in the state of the colony in one year, that the meat, pork one day and mutton another, was obtained at the average price of 10d per pound, which before, if it could have been obtained, would have cost nearly double the sum. On my application to the governor, the commissary was ordered to supply us with two pipes of port wine; and a pint was given daily to all those on board, as well as on shore, whose debilitated health was judged by the surgeon to require it.

The arrangements being made which concerned the health of the ship's company, I enclosed to the governor the report of the master and carpenter upon the state of the ship when in the Gulf of Carpentaria; and requested that he would appoint officers to make a survey of her condition. A plank was ripped off all round, a little above the water's edge; and on the 14th, the officers appointed by His Excellency made the survey, and their report was as follows:

Pursuant to an order from His Excellency
Philip Gidley King...

We whose names are hereunto subscribed, have been on board His Majesty's ship *Investigator*, and taken a strict, careful, and minute survey of her defects, the state of which we find to be as follows.

One plank immediately above the wales being ripped off all round the ship, we began the examination on the larboard

side forward; and out of ninety-eight timbers we find eleven
to be sound, so far as the ripping off of one plank enables us
to see into them, ten of which are amongst the aftermost
timbers. Sixty-three of the remaining timbers are so far
rotten as to make it necessary to shift them; and the remaining twenty-four entirely rotten, and these are principally in
the bow and the middle of the ship.

On the starboard side forward we have minutely examined eighty-nine timbers, out of which we find only five
sound; fifty-six are so far decayed as to require shifting, and
the remaining twenty-eight are entirely rotten. The sound
timbers are in the after part of the ship, and those totally
decayed lie principally in the bow...

The above being the state of the *Investigator* thus far, we
think it altogether unnecessary to make any further examination; being unanimously of opinion that she is not worth
repairing in any country, and that it is impossible in this
country to put her in a state fit for going to sea.

And we do further declare, that we have taken this survey
with such care and circumspection, that we are ready, if
required, to make oath to the veracity and impartiality of our
proceedings.

Given under our hands on board the said ship in Sydney
Cove, this 14th June 1803.

(Signed) W. Scott, Commander of HM armed vessel *Porpoise*.
E. H. Palmer, Commander of the Hon. East-India-
Company's extra ship *Bridgewater*.
Thomas Moore, Master builder to the Territory of New
South Wales.

I went round the ship with the officers in their examination,
and was excessively surprised to see the state of rottenness in
which the timbers were found. In the starboard bow there were

thirteen close together, through any one of which a cane might have been thrust; and it was on this side that the ship had made twelve inches of water in an hour, in Torres' Strait, before the first examination. In the passage along the south coast, the strong breezes were from the southward,,and the starboard bow being out of the water, the leaks did not exceed five inches; had the wind come from the northward, the little exertion we were then capable of making at the pumps could hardly have kept the ship up; and a hard gale from any quarter must have sent us to the bottom.

The *Investigator* being thus found incapable of further service, various plans were suggested, and discussed with the governor, for prosecuting the voyage; but that which alone could be adopted without incurring a heavy expense to government was to employ the armed vessel *Porpoise*; and as this ship was small to carry all my complement, with the necessary provisions, to put the remainder into the *Lady Nelson*, under the command of my second lieutenant. Both vessels were at this time required for a few weeks colonial service to Van Diemen's Land; and my people not being in a state to fit out a new ship immediately, our final arrangements were deferred until their return. I took this opportunity of making an excursion to the Hawkesbury settlement, near the foot of the back mountains; and the fresh air there, with a vegetable diet and medical care, soon made a great alteration in the scorbutic sores which had disabled me for four months; and in the beginning of July I returned to the ship, nearly recovered.

~

Following is a letter Matthew wrote to his wife Ann after returning
to Port Jackson.

25 June, 1803

Grateful for thy recovered health, my dearest love, and grateful to thee for thy many long and most dear remembrances of
me, which I have received on our arrival here some days
since. How shall I express the anguish of my heart at the
dreadful havock that death is making all around? How dear
is the name of father to an affectionate son, and how sweet
the idea of being soon able to console and assist him in his
every want and wish. When parting with the hope of soon
showing that my actions should prove better than my words
how much I loved him, how dreadful is this blow. Tis too
painful to be dwelt upon, although, alas, I have lately had too
much experience of death's power, for my eyes can scarcely
be turned where some victim does not die. Douglas, the
boatswain is gone—the sergeant, two quarter-masters and
another followed before we got into this port; and since, the
gardener and three others are laid in earth. Death's hand is
now stayed, and his envious eye which had been cast upon
more of us seems to be turning away.

But little indeed can be boasted of our state and condition, but thou shalt have some brief account of us; and first
of the ship: a survey has been held upon her and which
proves her to be so very much decayed as to be totally
irreparable. It was the unanimous opinion of the surveying
officers that had we met a severe gale of wind in the passage
from Timor, that she must have been crushed like an egg and
gone down. I was partly aware of her bad state and returned
sooner to Port Jackson on that account, before the worst
weather came. For me, whom this obstruction in the voyage
and the melancholy state of my poor people have much

distressed, I have been lame about four months and was much debilitated in health, and I fear in constitution, but am now recovering and shall soon be altogether well.

Trim, like his master, is becoming grey; he is at present fat and frisky, and takes meat from our forks with his former dexterity: he is commonly my bedfellow.[†] The master we have in poor Thistle's place, is an easy good-natured man.

As I shall be better able in a few weeks to say how the voyage will be prosecuted, and how soon we may probably return, I will leave Port Jackson and return to thy dear and kind letters. I have now before me the following—two dated in December 1801, one in January 1802, and others in Feb., June and September 1802. All these I found on our arrival, and for which I am most grateful to thee, and also to thy father and mother for their enclosures. Thou hast shown me how very ill I have requited thy tender love in several instances. I cannot excuse myself, but plead for respite until my return when in thy dear arms I will beg for pardon, and if thou canst forgive me at all, will have it sealed—oh, with ten thousand kisses. If I could laugh at the effusions of thy tenderness it would be to me the idolatrous language thy frequently usest to me. Thou makest an idol, and then worshippest it; and like some of the inhabitants of the east thou also bestoweth a little castigation occasionally, just to let the ugly deity know the value of thy devotion. Thinkest thou not, my dearest love, that I shall be spoiled by thy endearing flatteries? I fear it, and yet can hardly part with one, so dear to me is thy affection in whatever way expressed. I am indeed far behind thee in expressions of tenderness, yet I cannot allow that my love is far behind thine. Measure me not by the abundance of profession, but believe, my dearest and only love, that very very often my thoughts which are never

† Trim: Flinders' cat.

expressed are devoted to thee. In torture at the great distance from me, I lay musing upon thee, whilst sighs of fervent love, compassion for thy suffering health, and admiration of thy excellencies in turn get utterance.

I would not my dear Ann, have the ambitions, for was that the case, and instead of restraining me thou wast to add fuel to the fire, I know not what might be aimed [at], even to sovereign power; but my heart is with thee, and so soon as I can ensure for us a moderate portion of the comforts of life, thou wilt see whether love or ambition have the greater power over me.

Before thou wast mine, I was engaged on this voyage—without it we could not live. Thou knowest not the struggle in my bosom, before I consented to the necessity. There was no prospect of a permanent subsistence but in pursuing what I had undertaken, and I doubt not but that it will answer its end.

[The *Porpoise*]
July–December 1803

On 4 July the *Porpoise* arrived from Van Diemen's Land, and I requested the governor would order her to be surveyed, that it might be duly known whether she were, or could be in a short time made, capable of executing the service which remained to be done. I had heard some reports of her being unsound; and it seemed worse than folly to be at the trouble and expense of fitting out a ship which, besides causing a repetition of the risk we had incurred in the *Investigator*, might still leave the voyage unfinished. His Excellency, with that prompt zeal for His Majesty's service which characterised him, and was eminently shown in everything wherein my voyage was concerned, immediately ordered the survey to be made; and it appeared that the repairs necessary to make her fit for completing what remained of the voyage, could not be done in less than twelve months; and even then this ship was, from her small size and sharp construction, very ill-adapted to this service. Other arrangements were therefore suggested; and I received the following letter of propositions from the governor.

Government House, Sydney,
10 July, 1803.

Sir,
I enclose the report of the survey on the *Porpoise*, and am much concerned that the repairs and alterations of that ship

will require so much time to complete her fit for the service you have to execute. This being the case, I can see no other alternatives than the following:

1. To wait the *Porpoise* being repaired and refitted.

2. To purchase the *Rolla*, and fit her.

3. To take the *Lady Nelson* and colonial schooner *Francis*.

4. Wait for the *Buffalo*'s return from India, which will be about the next January; or

5. Return to England and solicit another ship to complete what you have so successfully begun.

On the first point, you will be the best able to determine how far it would be advisable to wait so long a time for the *Porpoise*'s repairs, nor do I think they can be completed in a less time here.

The builder and your carpenter report to me, that the *Rolla* cannot be put into the least convenient state to receive your establishment, stores and provisions, in less than six months...

If you think the *Lady Nelson* and *Francis* schooner equal to execute what you have to finish, they are at your service. The latter being absent getting coals and cedar, I cannot say what state she may be in; although she will require considerable repairs to make her fit for a long voyage.

The *Buffalo* is now inspecting the islands to the eastward of Java, to ascertain whether breeding stock can be procured among them. That service performed, she proceeds to Calcutta for a cargo of cows, and may be expected about January, when she may want some repairs, and of course fitting. It is my intention, if you do not fix on her, to profit by your discovery in stocking this colony with breeding animals, by the safe and expeditious channel you have opened through Torres' Strait.

If you do not consider waiting for the *Porpoise*'s repairs advisable, it is my intention to send her to England by a

summer's passage round Cape Horn; which it is thought she
may perform in her present state. But should you conceive it
may ultimately forward the service you are employed on, to
go to England in her, leaving this port when you judge proper,
and taking the route most conducive to perfectioning any part
of the surveys you have commenced; I shall direct the
commander of that ship to receive you and as many of your
officers and people as can be accommodated, as passengers;
and to follow your directions and give you every assistance in
every circumstance connected with the execution of the
orders you have received from my Lords Commissioners of
the Admiralty.

You will, Sir, have the goodness to consider of the above;
and whatever the result of your deliberation may be, I will
most cheerfully give my concurrence and assistance; knowing
that your zealous perseverance in wishing to complete the
service you have so beneficially commenced, could only be
impeded by unforeseen and distressing circumstances; but
which I hope, for the benefit of science and navigation, will
only be a temporary delay.

I am, &c.
(Signed), Philip Gidley King.

Each of the plans proposed in the governor's letter were attended
with one common disadvantage: a delay in the completion of the
surveys. Against the last proposition there did not seem to be any
other objection; but the four first included so many more incon-
veniences and difficulties, either to the voyage, or to the colony, that
I saw the necessity of concurring with the governor's opinion;
notwithstanding the reluctance I felt at returning to England
without having accomplished the objects for which the *Investigator*
was fitted out. My election was therefore made to embark as a
passenger in the *Porpoise*; in order to lay my charts and journals

before the Lords Commissioners of the Admiralty, and obtain, if such should be their pleasure, another ship to complete the examination of Terra Australis...

Of the nine convicts who had been received into the *Investigator*, one had died; another had behaved himself so improperly, that I could not recommend him to the governor; and the remaining seven were fully emancipated by His Excellency from their sentence of transportation, their conduct having been such throughout, as to receive my approbation. Four of these were entered into the complement of the *Porpoise*; but I am sorry to add, that the subsequent behaviour of two was different to what it had been when their liberty was at stake, and that a third was condemned to the hulks not very long after he reached England.

Being about to take leave of Port Jackson, it might be expected that I should give some account of our colony there, and could this voyage have appeared in due time, a chapter would have been devoted to it; but a much later account being now before the public, dispenses me from speaking of it in other than a few general terms. In 1803, it was progressively advancing towards a state of independence on the mother country for food and clothing; both the wild and tame cattle had augmented in a proportion to make it probable that they would, before many years, be very abundant; and manufactures of woollen, linen, cordage and leather, with breweries and a pottery, were commenced. The number of inhabitants was increasing rapidly; and that energetic spirit of enterprise which characterises Britain's children, seemed to be throwing out vigorous shoots in this new world. The seal fishery in Bass' Strait was carried on with ardour, many boats were employed in catching and preparing fish along the coast—sloops and schooners were upon the stocks, various detached settlements were in a course of establishment, and more in project. And all this, with the commerce carried on from Sydney to Parramatta and the villages at the head of the port, and to those on the rivers falling into Broken and Botany Bays, made the fine harbour of Port Jackson a lively scene of business, highly interesting to the contemplator of the rise of nations.

In Sydney and Parramatta, houses of stone or brick were taking place of wood and plaster…a stone bridge over the stream which runs through the town of Sydney was nearly finished, and the whiskey, chariot and heavy-laden wagon were seen moving on commodious roads to different parts of the colony. In the interior the forests were giving way before the axe, and their places becoming every year more extensively occupied by wheat, barley, oats, maize, and the vegetables and fruits of southern Europe; but the following extract from the official returns in 1803, the fifteenth year after the establishment of the colony, will show its progress in a more ostensible manner.

| | |
|---|---|
| Lands employed by government, or granted to individuals — | 125,476 acres. |
| Quantity cleared of wood — | 16,624 |
| Ditto, sown with wheat — | 7118 |
| Last ann. increase | 2165 |
| Ditto, sown with barley, maize, &c.— | 5279 |
| Average produce of wheat lands throughout the colony — | 18 bushels per acre. |

| | | | |
|---|---|---|---|
| No. of horned cattle domesticated— | 2447 | last increase — | 594 |
| Sheep — | 11,232 | " " | 2614 |
| Hogs — | 7890 | " " | 3872 |
| Horses — | 352 | " " | 65 |

The number of wild horned cattle was supposed to exceed that of the tame and to increase faster.

| | |
|---|---|
| Europeans of every description, resident in New South Wales — | 7134 |
| Of which were victualled by government — | 3026 |
| Number of inhabitants at Norfolk Island — | 1200 |

Amongst the obstacles which opposed themselves to the more rapid advancement of the colony, the principal were, the vicious propensities of a large portion of the convicts, a want of more frequent communication with England, and the prohibition to trading with India and the western coasts of South America, in consequence of the East-India-Company's charter. As these difficulties become obviated and capital increases, the progress of the colonists will be more rapid; and if the resources from government be not withdrawn too early, there is little doubt of New South Wales being one day a flourishing country, and of considerable benefit to the commerce and navigation of the parent state.

On 20 July, Lieutenant Fowler quitted the *Investigator*, with the crew selected for him, and took the command of His Majesty's armed vessel *Porpoise*; and on the following day I went on board with the rest of my officers and people, to go with him as passengers. Amongst other preparations for the voyage, a greenhouse was set up on the quarter-deck of that ship; and the plants collected in the *Investigator* from the south, the east, and north coasts of Terra Australis were deposited in it, to be conveyed to His Majesty's botanical garden at Kew; and as we had had the misfortune to lose the gardener of the expedition, and Mr Brown, the naturalist, remained behind, a man from Port Jackson was engaged to take care of the plants during the passage.

The examination of Torres' Strait was one of the most important articles of my instructions which had been executed only in part; and although I could not pretend to make any regular survey in the *Porpoise*, it was yet desirable to pass again through the strait, and lay down as many more of its dangers as circumstances would admit...

In the beginning of August, the *Porpoise* was nearly ready to sail; and two ships then lying in Sydney Cove, bound to Batavia, desired leave to accompany us through the strait. These were the Hon. East-India-Company's extra-ship *Bridgewater*, of about 750 tons, commanded by E. H. Palmer, Esq., and the ship *Cato* of London,

of about 450 tons, commanded by Mr John Park. The company of
these ships gave me pleasure; for if we should be able to make a
safe and expeditious passage through the strait with them, of which
I had but little doubt, it would be a manifest proof of the advantage of the route discovered in the *Investigator*, and tend to bring it
into general use...

The winds were light, and mostly from the eastward during the
first two days of our quitting Port Jackson; and not being able to get
far enough from the land to avoid the southern current, it had
retarded us 35' on the 12th at noon, when the islands of Port
Stephens were in sight. On the following day the wind became more
steady in the south-western quarter, and as our distance from the
land increased, the current abated; and on the 15th, when the latitude was 27° 27', longitude 156° 22', and distance from the coast
about fifty leagues, the set was something in our favour. The wind
was then at south, and our course steered was north for twenty-four
hours, then N by W; and on the 17th at noon we were in latitude
23° 22', longitude 155° 34', and had the wind at SE by S.

Soon after two o'clock, the *Cato* being some distance on our
larboard quarter made the signal for seeing land. This proved to be
a dry sandbank, which bore SSW about three leagues; and the
*Porpoise* sailing faster than the other ships, they were directed to keep
on their course whilst we hauled up to take a nearer view of the
bank. At three o'clock, when it bore S by E five or six miles, we hove
to and sounded, but had no bottom at 80 fathoms. The Cato's
Bank, for so it was named, is small and seemed to be destitute of
vegetation; there was an innumerable quantity of birds hovering
about, and it was surrounded with breakers; but their extent seemed
very little to exceed that of the bank, nor could any other reef near
it be discovered. The situation was ascertained to be nearly 23° 6'
south and 155° 23' east; and then we made sail after the *Bridgewater*
and *Cato*; to take our station ahead of them as before.

Some apprehensions were excited for the following night by
meeting with this bank; but as it was more than two degrees to the

eastward of the great Barrier Reefs, we thought it unconnected
with any other, like the two discovered by Captain Ball and Mr
Bampton, further towards the north end of New Caledonia. I had,
besides, steered for Torres' Strait in the *Investigator*, from reefs
several degrees to the westward, without meeting with any other
danger than what lay near the Barrier or belonged to the strait; and
by the time we had rejoined the ships in the evening, the distance
run from the bank was thirty-five miles, and no other danger had
been descried. It did not therefore seem necessary to lose a good
night's run by heaving to; and I agreed with Lieutenant Fowler, that
it would be sufficient to make the signal for the ships to run under
easy, working sail during the night—to take our usual station
ahead—and to charge one of the *Investigator*'s warrant officers with
the lookout on the forecastle. These precautions being taken, and
the topsails double-reefed, our course was pursued to the N by W,
with a fresh breeze and cloudy weather; and at eight o'clock the
lead was cast, but no bottom found at 85 fathoms. The *Bridgewater*
was then about half a mile on the starboard, and the *Cato* a mile
on the larboard quarter; and their distance seeming to increase at
nine, when our rate of going was eight knots, the fore sail was
hauled up to keep them in sight: wind then at SE by E.

In half an hour, and almost at the same instant by the *Investigator*'s
carpenter on the forecastle and the master who had charge of the
watch on the quarter-deck, breakers were seen ahead. The helm
was immediately put down, with the intention of tacking from
them; but the *Porpoise* having only three double-reefed topsails set,
scarcely came up to the wind. Lieutenant Fowler sprang upon deck
on hearing the noise; but supposing it to be occasioned by carrying
away the tiller rope, a circumstance which had often occurred in the
*Investigator*, and having no orders to give, I remained some minutes
longer, conversing with the gentlemen in the gun room.

On going up I found the sails shaking in the wind, and the ship
in the act of paying off; at the same time there were very high
breakers at not a quarter of a cable's length to leeward. In about

a minute the ship was carried amongst the breakers; and striking upon a coral reef, took a fearful heel over on her larboard beam ends, her head being north-eastward. A gun was attempted to be fired, to warn the other vessels of the danger; but owing to the violent motion and the heavy surfs flying over, this could not be done immediately; and before lights were brought up, the *Bridgewater* and *Cato* had hauled to the wind across each other.

Our fore mast was carried away at the second or third shock; and the bottom was presently reported to be stove in, and the hold full of water. When the surfs permitted us to look to windward, the *Bridgewater* and *Cato* were perceived at not more than a cable's length distance; and approaching each other so closely, that their running aboard seemed to us inevitable. This was an awful moment; the utmost silence prevailed; and when the bows of the two ships went to meet, even respiration seemed to be suspended. The ships advanced, and we expected to hear the dreadful crash; but presently they opened off from each other, having passed side by side without touching; the *Cato* steering to the north-east, and the *Bridgewater* to the southward. Our own safety seemed to have no other dependence than upon the two ships, and the exultation we felt at seeing this most imminent danger passed, was great, but of short duration; the *Cato* struck upon the reef about two cables length from the *Porpoise*, we saw her fall over on her broad side, and the masts almost instantly disappeared; but the darkness of the night did not admit of distinguishing, at that distance, what further might have happened.

Turning our eyes towards the *Bridgewater*, a light was perceived at her masthead, by which we knew she had cleared the reef; and our first sensations were, that the commander would certainly tack and send boats to our assistance; but when a little reflection had enabled us to put ourselves in his place, it became evident that he would not choose to come so near the reef in the night, blowing fresh as it did; and still less to send his boats and people into the breakers to their certain destruction.

The *Porpoise* had very fortunately heeled towards the reef; so that the surfs which struck against her turned-up side, flew over without washing anything off the decks; and the smooth appearance of the water under the lee, afforded a prospect of being able to get the boats out on that side. The experiment was tried with a small four-oared gig, and succeeded; but a six-oared cutter was jerked against the sheet anchor by the violence of the shocks, and being stove, was filled with water.

It was by no means certain how long the ship, being slightly built and not in a sound state, might hold together; it was therefore deemed expedient to lighten her, that she might drive further up the coral bank and lie more easily. On sounding, the depth was found to be 17 fathoms on the windward side, but no more than a few feet on the reef; and Mr Fowler ordered the main and mizen masts, and the starboard anchor to be cut away; but on my suggesting to him the possibility of driving over the reef, with the rise of tide, and sinking in deep water as the *Pandora* had done, the lightening of the ship was not prosecuted further.

Beyond the smooth water close under the lee, there was a line of breakers, and further on the sea appeared to be tranquil; it therefore seemed probable that boats might approach the ship on that side, and if this information could be conveyed to Captain Palmer of the *Bridgewater*, that something might be speedily done towards saving the crew; and as it was likely that my influence with him might be greatest, and being a passenger in the *Porpoise* no charge made my presence on board immediately necessary, I proposed to make the attempt in the gig, to which Mr Fowler assented. The boat being obliged to lie at a little distance from the ship, to prevent being stove, I jumped overboard and swam to her; and we pushed through the breakers to the smooth water, receiving two or three surfs by the way, from which we hardly escaped sinking.

On examining into the condition of the boat, I found nothing to bale out the water, and only two oars which did not belong to it; and instead of the proper crew of four men, there were only three;

but under the thwarts were stowed away three others—the armourer, a cook, and a marine, who did not know how to handle an oar. These last were set to baling with their hats and shoes, and we rowed towards the *Bridgewater*'s light, keeping under the lee of the breakers. That ship was standing from us, and I saw that any attempt to get nearer before she tacked would be fruitless; and even afterwards, it was much to be doubted whether, with two awkward oars and an overloaded boat, we could make any way against the sea on the windward side of the reef. I therefore determined to remain under the lee of the breakers until she should approach, and to lie near the *Porpoise*; that in case of her going to pieces before morning, we might save some of the people. In rowing back we met the cutter, which the men in her, having got the leak partly stopped, had pushed off without an officer, and were going they scarcely knew whither. They furnished us with a third oar, and I desired them to keep close to the gig, near the wreck, until morning. We found the bottom here to be coral rock, and the water so shallow, that a man might stand up in many places without being over head.

I wished to have got on board the ship, to let them know of the boats being safe and what we had discovered of the reef; but the breakers between us, and the darkness of the night cut off all hope of communication before morning. They burned blue lights every half hour, as a guide to the *Bridgewater*; but her light was lost to us in the boats at eleven o'clock, and after two in the morning it was no longer seen from the *Porpoise*. At that time it appeared to be low water, and the ship lay so much more quiet than before, that the apprehension of her going to pieces before daylight had much subsided. To be prepared, however, for the next flood, Mr Fowler employed his people during the night in making a raft of the spare top masts, yards, &c., with short ropes all round it, by which the people might hold on; and a cask of water, with a chest containing some provisions, a sextant, and the *Investigator*'s log books, were secured upon the raft.

*18 August* ~ In the small gig we were quite drenched, the south-east wind blew fresh and cold, and the reflections excited by the great change so suddenly made in our situation, with the uncertainty of what had befallen the *Cato* and even the *Bridgewater*, did not tend to make this long night pass more agreeably. My thoughts were principally occupied in devising plans for saving ourselves, under the apprehension that we might see no more of the *Bridgewater*; but not to discourage the people, I spoke of everybody getting on board that ship in the morning, and of continuing our voyage to England, as not at all doubtful.

Of the poor *Cato*, we could neither see nor hear anything. It appeared that Captain Park, when meeting the *Bridgewater* on opposite tacks, stopped setting his mainsail and bore away to leeward; had he persevered, both ships must have come upon the reef together; but by his presence of mind on this occasion, the *Bridgewater* weathered the breakers and escaped the impending danger. When the *Cato* struck the reef, it was upon the point of a rock, under the larboard chess tree; and she fell over to windward, with her decks exposed to the waves. In a short time the decks and holds were torn up, and everything washed away; and the sole place left, where the unfortunate people could hope to avoid the fury of the sea, was in the larboard fore channel, where they all crowded together, the greater part with no other covering than their shirts. Every time the sea struck the *Cato*, it twisted her about upon the rock with such violent jerks, that they expected the stern, which was down in the water, would part every moment. In this situation, some lashing themselves to the timber heads, others clinging to the chain plates and dead eyes, and to each other, Captain Park and his crew passed the night; their hope being, that the forecastle of the ship might hold upon the rock till morning, and that the *Bridgewater* would then send her boats to save them. From the *Porpoise* they entertained no hope; and until the signal lights were seen, they thought her gone to pieces.

At the first dawning of day, I got on board the *Porpoise* by the help

of the fallen masts. Everybody was in good spirits at seeing the ship
hold together so well, and finding the boats safe; for the gig, with all
in her, had been given up for lost, someone having thought he saw
her sink in the breakers. With the daylight appeared a dry sandbank, not more than half a mile distant, sufficiently large to receive
us all with what provisions might be got out of the ship; and
the satisfaction arising from this discovery was increased by the
*Bridgewater* being perceived under sail, and though distant, that she
was standing towards the reef. On the other side, the appearance of
the poor *Cato*, with the people waving to us from the bowsprit and
forecastle, the only parts above water, was truly distressing.

The reef seemed to be a mile in breadth, and it extended in an
east and west direction to a distance beyond what could be distinguished from the *Porpoise*'s deck; but there were in it several wide,
and apparently deep openings, by which the *Bridgewater* might run
to leeward, and there anchor or lie to, whilst sending her boats to
our assistance. Having made these remarks, I left Mr Fowler and
his people getting up water and provisions; and went to the bank
for the purpose of being ready to go off in the gig so soon as that
ship should be near enough, and pointing out to Captain Palmer
the means by which he might take on board the two crews and
what else might be saved; but he went upon the other tack soon
afterward, and no more was seen of him during the day.

A number of seabirds eggs scattered over the bank, showed that
it was above high-water mark, and I sent the gig back with this
intelligence to Lieutenant Fowler. Seeing that the *Bridgewater* did
not approach, he ordered the boat to lie opposite to the *Cato*; and
Captain Park and his men, throwing themselves into the water with
any pieces of spar or plank they could find, swam to her through
the breakers; and were then taken to the *Porpoise* where they
received food and some clothing. Several were bruised against the
coral rocks, and three young lads were drowned. One of these poor
boys, who, in the three or four voyages he had made to sea, had
been each time shipwrecked, had bewailed himself through the

night as the persecuted Jonas who carried misfortune wherever he
went. He launched himself upon a broken spar with his captain;
but having lost his hold in the breakers, was not seen afterwards.

At low water, which happened about two o'clock, the reef was
dry very near to the *Porpoise*, and both officers and men were assiduously employed in getting upon it provisions and their clothes;
they were brought from thence by the boats, for the depth was
several feet at a distance round the bank. Before dark, five half
hogsheads of water, some flour, salt meat, rice, and spirits were
landed, with such of the pigs and sheep as had escaped drowning;
and every man from both ships had got on shore. Some of the
*Cato*'s sailors appeared in officers uniforms, given to them in the
*Porpoise*; and I was pleased to see that our situation was not thought
so bad by the people, as to hinder all pleasantry upon these promo-
tions. Those who had saved greatcoats or blankets shared with the
less fortunate, and we laid down to sleep on the sand in tolerable
tranquillity, being much oppressed with fatigue; and except from
those of the *Cato*'s men who had been bruised or cut by the rocks,
there was not a complaining voice heard on the bank.

The *Porpoise*'s two cutters and the gig were hauled up to high
water mark; but the latter not having been well secured, and the
night tide rising higher than was expected, it was carried away, to
our great loss.

*19 August* ~ In the morning, we had the satisfaction to see the
ship still entire, and thrown higher up the reef; the *Cato* had gone
to pieces, and all that remained was one of the quarters, which had
floated over the front ledge of the reef, and lodged near our bank.
Of the *Bridgewater* nothing could be seen; and many fears were
entertained for her safety.

For the better preservation of discipline, and of that union
between the crews of the *Porpoise* and *Cato* and passengers of the
*Investigator*, so necessary in our circumstances, it was highly expedient that they should be put on the same footing and united under
one head. The *Porpoise* was lost beyond a possibility of hope, and

the situation of the commander and crew thereby rendered similar to that of their passengers; I therefore considered myself autho- rised and called upon, as the senior officer, to take the command of the whole; and my intention being communicated to Lieutenant Fowler, he assented without hesitation to its expediency and propri- ety, and I owe to Captain Park a similar acknowledgment. The people were then assembled upon the top of the bank; and I informed the seamen of the *Cato*, one or two of whom had shown signs of discontent at being ordered to work, that as they doubtless expected to be fed from our provisions, so they must exert them- selves to save as much as possible; and although they were not in the King's pay, yet as a magistrate acting within the jurisdiction of the Admiralty, I would punish all deviations from obedience and good conduct in them, the same as amongst our own seamen.* I ordered the *Cato*'s men, who had saved nothing, to be quartered in the messes of our people, in the proportion of one to three; and directed Lieutenant Fowler, who had charge of the provisions, to victual all alike. The surgeon of the *Porpoise* was ordered to examine the wounded, and give in a list of those really incapable of duty; and a large party, consisting of as many men as the two cutters could contain went off to the wreck under the command of Mr Fowler, to disembark provisions and stores.

A topsail yard was set up and secured as a flagstaff on the highest part of the bank, and a large blue ensign hoisted to it with the union downward, as a signal to the *Bridgewater*. We expected, if no accident had happened, that she would come to relieve us from our critical situation so soon as the wind should be perfectly moderate; but I judged it most prudent to act as if we had no such resource, and this was justified by the event. Captain Palmer had even then abandoned us to our fate, and was, at the moment,

* When a merchant ship is lost, the seamen not only cease to be in pay, but lose all wages due to them after the last delivery of the cargo; and the sole interest they have to save the stores, even of their own ship, is for the preservation of themselves, or the prospect of being rewarded by the owners or insurers.

steering away for Batavia, without having made any effort to give us assistance. He saw the wrecks, as also the sandbank, on the morning after our disaster, and must have known that the reef was not all connected, since it is spoken of by him as lying in patches; but he did not seek to ascertain whether any of the openings were passable for the *Bridgewater*, and might enable him to take those on board who had escaped drowning. He bore away round all; and whilst the two hapless vessels were still visible from the masthead, passed the leeward extremity of the reef and hove to for the night. The apprehension of danger to himself must then have ceased; but he neither attempted to work up in the smooth water, nor sent any of his boats to see whether some unfortunate individuals were not clinging to the wrecks, whom he might snatch from the sharks or save from a more lingering death. It was safer, in his estimation, to continue on his voyage and publish that we were all lost, as he did not fail to do on his arrival in India.*

---

* Against a British seaman filling a respectable situation, these are heavy charges; but M Palmer is himself the authority. The following extracts from his account are taken from a Calcutta paper, the *Orphan*, 3 Feb. 1804. The *Bridgewater*, he says, 'was just beginning to draw off, when the *Porpoise* was scarcely a ship's length to leeward, settling with her head towards us, and her broadside upon the reef; her foremast was gone and the sea breaking over her. At this moment we perceived the *Cato* within half a cable's, length, standing stem on for us. I hailed to put their helm a-starboard, by which means she just cleared us, and luffed up under our stern; had she fallen on board of us the consequences must have been dreadful indeed'. On the 18th, 'When the day was broke, we had the mortification to perceive the *Cato* had shared the fate of the *Porpoise*; the bow and bowsprit of the latter only at intervals appearing through the surf.' (The *Porpoise* and *Cato* were mistaken for each other.) 'The latter lay with her bottom exposed to the sea, which broke with tremendous fury over her; not a mast standing. Finding we could not weather the reef, and that *it was too late had it been in our power to give any assistance*; and still fearing that we might be embayed or entangled by the supposed chain or patches; all therefore that remained for us to do was either by dint of carrying sail to weather the reef to the southward, or, if failing in that, to push to leeward and endeavour to find a passage through the *patches of reef* to the northward…After passing the reef we lay to for the night; and in the morning we lost sight of it, having drifted to the northward.

The wind blew fresh from the south-eastward on the 18th, and 19th, but on the two following days it was moderate with fine weather; we worked hard on board the *Porpoise*, and by the 22nd had got most of the water and provisions secured in a large tent made with spars and sails; each mess of officers and men had also their private tent; and our manner of living and working had assumed the same regularity as before the shipwreck.

One of the men whose liberty Governor King had granted at my request, being guilty of disorderly conduct, the articles of war were publicly read, and the man punished at the flagstaff. This example served to correct any evil disposition, if such existed; the men worked cordially together, and in all respects we preserved the same discipline and order as on board His Majesty's ships.

Our prospects of receiving succour from the *Bridgewater* having become very feeble, after two days of moderate weather had elapsed, I called a council of all the officers, to deliberate upon the

---

Such is the substantial part of Mr Palmer's account, omitting his own fears and congratulations, and his 'most painful reflexions on the sufferings of the shipwrecked'. Nothing is said of the sandbank; but I have been favoured with a copy of the journal of Mr Williams, third mate of the *Bridgewater*, and the following passages are taken from it. 'At half past seven *a.m.* (Aug. 18.) saw the reef on our weather bow, and from the masthead we saw the two ships, and to leeward of them a sandbank. The weather abated much, we set all our sails, and every man rejoiced that they should have it in their power to assist their unfortunate companions; as there was every probability of our going within two miles of the reef. The morning threatened; but before the wind increased we had time to satisfy ourselves if there were any still in existence; we had nothing to apprehend but what could be seen before we approached so near. The ships were very distinctly to be seen from aloft, and also from the deck; but instead of rendering them any succour, the captain ordered the ship to be put on the other tack, and said it was impossible to render them any relief.

'What must be the sensations of each man at that instant? Instead of proceeding to the support of our unfortunate companions, to leave them to the mercy of the waves, without knowing whether they were in existence, or had perished! From the appearance of the wrecks, there was every probability of their existing; and if any survived at the time we were within sight, what must have been their sensations on seeing all their anxious expectations of relief blasted?

best means of relieving ourselves from the precarious situation in which our misfortune, and Captain Palmer's want of energy and humanity had left us exposed; and it was finally determined, that an officer and crew in the largest of the two six-oared cutters, should endeavour to get to Sandy Cape, sixty-three leagues distant, and from thence along the coast to Port Jackson; and pray His Excellency, the governor, to send vessels to carry us either back to that port or on towards England. But as the safe arrival of the cutter at that season of the year, when strong winds usually prevail from the southward, was a subject of much apprehension; it was resolved that two decked boats, capable of transporting every person remaining on the bank, except one officer and boat's crew, should be immediately laid down by the carpenters, to be built from what was already and might be still further saved from the wreck; and that, if the officer in the cutter did not return with assistance in two months, the boats should then, or as soon after as they could be ready to sail, proceed to Port Jackson.

The first and principal means, however, through which our

---

'Until our arrival at Bombay, nothing particular occurred, except my being sent on shore at Tillicherry with the account of the loss of the *Porpoise* and *Cato*; an account that served for the moment to blind the people. In executing this service, I did, for the first time to my knowledge, neglect my duty, and gave a contrary account; but for this reason—I was convinced that the crews of those ships were on the reefs, and that this was an erroneous account made by Captain Palmer to excuse his own conduct. I left it on shore for the perusal of the inhabitants, after relating the story as contrary as possible. This was the cause of many words; and at length ended with my quitting the ship, and forfeiting my wages and a part of my clothes.'

Such was the conduct of Mr Palmer towards His Majesty's ship *Porpoise*, and towards the *Cato* which had given way in the moment of danger that he might be saved. But the officers and crews of the *Porpoise* and *Cato* reached England in safety; whilst Captain Palmer and the *Bridgewater*, who left Bombay for Europe, have not been heard of, now for many years. How dreadful must have been his reflections at the time his ship was going down! Lieutenant Tucker of the navy, who was first officer of the *Bridgewater*, and several others as well as Mr Williams, had happily quitted the ship in India.

deliverance was to be expected, being the safe arrival of the cutter, the choice of an officer to conduct her was next considered. Lieutenant Fowler proposed, and it seemed to be the general wish, that I should undertake the execution of the task; and being satisfied that the preservation of order on the bank, and the saving of the stores would be left in good hands, the hope of being instrumental to the general safety induced me readily to comply. But to provide against sickness and the various accidents which might arise from the natives of the coast or otherwise, it was necessary that two officers should be in the boat; and Captain Park of the *Cato* being desirous of returning to Port Jackson, to make the necessary statements relative to the loss of his ship, he was appointed my second with the general approbation.

The smaller cutter with an officer, his second, and a boat's crew, I proposed should remain with the stores, and in charge of my charts and books for a few weeks longer than the two months; and then go to Port Jackson also, should no vessel arrive before that time. This precaution was necessary, lest any unforeseen occurrence should delay my return to the bank beyond two months, though not prevent it altogether; that the charts, journals and papers might still be found there, to be taken on to England if wanted. I designed my brother, Lieutenant Flinders, for this service; but Mr Fowler claiming it as the post of honour, I too much respected the principle that influenced him not to accede to his request; and therefore ordered, that the former officer and Mr John Aken, master of the *Investigator*, should take charge of the decked boats, with a master's mate in each capable of conducting them to Port Jackson, should illness or any accident happen to either of the officers.

*23 August* ~ By the evening the *Porpoise* was well-nigh emptied of all the most essential things; and on a survey being made, there was found sufficient water and provisions on the bank to serve ninety-four men, which was our number, for three months, even at full allowance; although many casks were stove in the hold by the bulging of the larboard side, and much dry provisions spoiled by the salt water. The principal contents of the warrant officers store-rooms, as well as the sails, rigging and spars, were also on shore. My books, charts and papers had suffered much damage, from the top of the cabin being displaced when the mizen mast fell; all such papers as chanced to be loose on the night of the shipwreck were then washed away by the surfs, and amongst them a chart of the west side of the Gulf of Carpentaria and part of the north coast, upon which I had been occupied in the afternoon. Part of my small library shared the same fate; but the rest of the charts, with my log and bearing books and astronomical observations were all saved, though some of them in a wet and shattered state. The rare plants collected on different parts of the south, the east, and north coasts of Terra Australis, for His Majesty's botanic garden at Kew, and which were in a flourishing state before the shipwreck, were totally destroyed by the salt water; as were the dried specimens of plants. Fortunately, the naturalist and natural-history painter, who remained at Port Jackson, had put on board only a small part of their collection of specimens; the great mass, with the preserved birds, quadrupeds and insects being kept for a future opportunity. Mr Westall, the landscape painter, had his sketches and drawings wetted and partly destroyed in his cabin; and my little collection in mineralogy and conchology was much defaced, and one-half lost.

The carpenters were employed until the evening of the 25th, in preparing the cutter for her intended expedition; and the rest of the people in adding to the stores on the bank. As the *Porpoise* became lighter, the sea threw her higher up on the reef, and she was much shaken; but we hoped the timbers and beams would hold together at least until the next spring tides, and that everything would be got out. Of the *Cato*, nothing but a few scattered frag-ments had remained for several days before.

Before leaving Wreck Reef, it will be proper to say something of the sandbank to which we were all indebted for our lives; and where the greater part of the officers and people were to remain in expectation of my return from Port Jackson…The length of the bank is about one hundred and fifty fathoms, by fifty in breadth, and the general elevation three or four feet above the common level of high water; it consists of sand and pieces of coral, thrown up by the waves and eddy tides on a patch of reef five or six miles in circuit; and being nearly in the middle of the patch, the sea does no more, even in a gale, than send a light spray over the bank, sufficient, however, to prevent the growth of any other than a few diminutive salt plants. On its north and north-west sides, and at one or two cables length from the reef, there is from 18 to 25 fathoms on a bottom of coral sand; where the *Bridgewater* might have anchored in safety, so long as the wind remained between SW and ESE, and received every person from the wrecks, with provisions for their subsistence...

In searching for something wherewith to make a fire on the first night of our landing, a spar and a piece of timber, worm-eaten and almost rotten, were found and burnt. The timber was seen by the master of the *Porpoise*, who judged it to have been part of the stern post of a ship of about four hundred tons; and I have thought it might, not improbably, have belonged to *La Boussole* or *L'Astrolabe*. Monsieur de La Pérouse, on quitting Botany Bay, intended to visit the south-west coast of New Caledonia; and he might have encountered in the night, as we did, some one of the several reefs which lie scattered in this sea. Less fortunate than we were, he probably had no friendly sandbank near him, upon which his people might be collected together and the means of existence saved out of the ships; or perhaps his two vessels both took the unlucky direction of the *Cato* after striking, and the seas which broke into them carried away all his boats and provisions; nor would La Pérouse, his vessels, or crews be able, in such a case, to resist the impetuosity of the waves more than twenty-four hours. If such were the end of the regretted French navigator, as there is now but too much reason to fear, it is the counterpart of what would have befallen all on board the *Porpoise* and *Cato*, had the former ship, like the *Cato*, fallen over towards the sea instead of heeling to the reef.

An opinion that La Pérouse had been lost in this neighbourhood, induced me when examining the main coast to seek carefully
at every place, amongst the refuse thrown upon the shores, for indications of shipwreck to windward; and could the search have been
then prosecuted to the 15th, or 12th degree of latitude, I am
persuaded it would not have been in vain. Besides the extensive
reefs which skirt the western side of New Caledonia, and the
Barrier Reefs on the opposite coast of New South Wales, we are
now acquainted with the six or eight following distinct banks of
coral in the sea between them, exclusive of Wreck Reef and the
Cato's Bank...

On Friday 26 August, the largest cutter being ready for her
expedition, was launched and named the *Hope*. The morning was
fine, and wind light from the southward; and notwithstanding the
day, which in the seaman's calendar is the most unfortunate of the
whole week to commence a voyage, I embarked for Port Jackson
with the commander of the *Cato*. We had a double set of rowers,
making in all fourteen persons, with three weeks provisions and two
half hogsheads of water; so that the *Hope* was loaded rather too
deeply. At eight in the morning, we pushed off amidst the cheers
and good wishes of those for whom we were going to seek relief;
an ensign with the union downward, had hitherto been kept
hoisted as a signal to Captain Palmer of our distress; but in this
moment of enthusiasm a seaman quitted the crowd, and having
obtained permission, ran to the flagstaff, hauled down the ensign,
and rehoisted it with the union in the upper canton. This symbol-
ical expression of contempt for the *Bridgewater* and of confidence
in the success of our voyage, I did not see without lively emotions.

We made sail to the westward under the lee of the reef and
passed two openings in it of nearly a mile wide. The second league
brought us abreast of a dry sandbank, smaller than that quitted;
and at noon we came to a third, lying ten miles west of Wreck-reef
Bank. Having then lost the breeze, we stopped to cook our dinner
on shore; and in the meantime I shot as many noddies as would

give all the boat's crew a meal. On quitting this third bank, which is near the western extremity of Wreck Reef, we crossed into the open sea, and a breeze springing up at south-east, made sail towards Sandy Cape. Many humpbacked whales were playing about the boat during the whole time we remained under the lee of the reef, but they did not follow us further.

Nothing but clear water was visible at sunset, nevertheless we ran cautiously in the dark, looking out for breakers. The night was fine, and we made good progress by means of the oars, at which the twelve men took watch and watch, as Mr Park and myself did at the helm: it was for this purpose, and to guard against accidents, that I had taken so many men in the boat.

*27 August* ~ At daybreak the wind was ESE, and no land in sight; the boat was going four knots, and at noon our latitude by log was 23° 6' and the distance made from Wreck-reef Bank, ninety miles. The wind freshened in the afternoon, and a cross-sea rose which obliged us to reef the sails, and made the boat very wet. At four we close reefed and hauled to the wind, but this was not enough; the increased hollowness of the waves caused the boat to labour so much, that every plunge raised an apprehension that some of the planks would start from the timbers. Having no other resource, we emptied one of the two casks of water, threw overboard the stones of our fireplace and wood for cooking, as also a bag of peas and whatever else could be best spared; the boat was then somewhat more easy and before dark, the hollow swell had so far subsided that we kept two points from the wind, and again went along in tolerable tranquillity...

*28 August* ~ Our situation being to the south of Sandy Cape, we steered a point more west, in the hope of seeing the land before night; it being my intention to keep near the coast from thence to Port Jackson, that by landing, or running the boat on shore, we might escape foundering at sea should a gale of wind come on...

*29 August* ~ Our favourable breeze died away in the afternoon, and we took to the oars; it however sprung up again from the northward, and brought us within sight of Cape Moreton at sunset. Towards midnight the weather became squally with heavy rain, and gave us all a thorough drenching; but the wind not being very strong in these squalls, our course was still pursued to the southward. After the rain ceased the wind came at SSW; and the weather remaining unsettled, we tacked at daylight to get close in with the land, and at noon anchored under Point Look-out. This was only the fourth day of our departure from Wreck Reef, and I considered the voyage to be half accomplished, since we had got firm hold of the main coast; for the probability of being lost is greater in making three hundred miles in an open boat at sea, than in running even six hundred along shore. It would have added much to our satisfaction, could we have conveyed the intelligence of this fortunate progress to our shipmates on the bank.

The necessity for a supply of fresh water was becoming urgent, for our remaining half-hogshead was much reduced. There were about twenty Indians upon the side of a hill near the shore, who seemed to be peaceably disposed, amusing us with dances in imitation of the kangaroo; we made signs of wanting water, which they understood, and pointed to a small rill falling into the sea. Two of the sailors leaped overboard, with some trifles for the natives and one end of the lead line; with the other end we slung the empty cask, which they hauled on shore and filled without molestation. A shark had followed them to the beach; and fearing they might be attacked in returning, we got up the anchor and went to a place where the surf, though too much to allow of the boat landing, permitted us to lie closer. The cask of water, a bundle of wood, and the two men were received on board without accident; the natives keeping aloof during the whole time, and even retiring when our people approached, though they were without arms and naked. It is probable that the Indians were astonished at the comparison between the moderately white skins of the sailors and their own, and perhaps had heard of my expedition to Glass-house Bay in 1799, in which I had been provoked to make one of them feel the effect of our arms; and had they attempted anything against my two men, we were prepared to have given them a volley from the boat which would probably have been a fearful confirmation of the truth of the report; but happily for both parties, we were not reduced to the necessity.

On rowing to Point Look-out, to continue the voyage, I found the wind so fresh from the southward that the greatest fatigue at the oars could advance us little; we therefore ran to leeward of two rocks, lying a mile and a half north-west from the extremity of the point; and having anchored there, arranged the boat so as that every person might take a better night's rest than we had hitherto been able to enjoy...

On the 4th, we again attempted to beat to the southward; but the wind being light as well as foul, and the sea running high, not much was gained; at noon the weather threatened so much, that it became necessary to look out for a place of shelter, and we steered into a bight with rocks in it, which I judge to have been on the north side of Tacking Point. At the head of the bight is a lagoon; but the entrance proving to be very shallow, and finding no security, we continued on our voyage; trusting that some place of shelter would present itself, if obliged to seek it by necessity. Towards evening the wind and weather became more favourable; in the morning, the Three Brothers were in sight; and at noon I observed the latitude 31° 57', when the middlemost of these hills bore NNW and our distance off shore was two or three leagues.

At this time the wind blew a moderate sea breeze at ESE, Cape Hawke was seen soon afterward, and at eight in the evening we steered between Sugar-loaf Point and the two rocks lying from it three or four miles to the south-east. At four next morning, passed the islands at the entrance of Port Stephens, and at noon the Coal Island in the mouth of Port Hunter bore NW by N; the wind then shifted more to the southward, with squally weather, and both prevented the boat from lying along the coast and made it unsafe to be at sea. After struggling till four in the afternoon, with little advantage, we bore up to look for shelter behind some of the small projecting points; and almost immediately found it in a shallow cove, exposed only to the north-eastward. This was the eleventh day of our departure from Wreck Reef, and the distance of Port Jackson did not now exceed fifty miles.

At this place we slept on shore for the first time; but the weather being squally, rainy, and cold, and the boat's sails our best shelter, it was not with any great share of comfort; a good watch was kept during the night, but no molestation was received from the natives. Notwithstanding our cramped-up position in the boat, and exposure to all kinds of weather, we enjoyed excellent health; one man excepted, upon whom the dysentery, which had made such ravages in the *Investigator*, now returned with some violence.

A cask of water was filled on the morning of the 7th, and our biscuit being all expended or spoiled, some cakes were baked in the ashes for our future subsistence. At eleven o'clock, the rain having cleared away, we stood out to the offing with light baffling winds and towards evening were enabled to lie along the coast; but the breeze at south-east not giving much assistance, we took to the oars and laboured hard all the following night, being animated with the prospect of a speedy termination to our voyage. The north head of Broken Bay was in sight next morning, and at noon the South Head was abreast of the boat; a sea breeze then setting in at ENE, we crowded all sail for Port Jackson, and soon after two o'clock had the happiness to enter between the Heads.

The reader has perhaps never gone 250 leagues at sea in an open boat, or along a strange coast inhabited by savages; but if he recollect the eighty officers and men upon Wreck-reef Bank, and how important was our arrival to their safety, and to the saving of the charts, journals, and papers of the *Investigator's* voyage, he may have some idea of the pleasure we felt, but particularly myself, at entering our destined port.

I proceeded immediately to the town of Sydney, and went with Captain Park to wait upon His Excellency Governor King, whom we found at dinner with his family. A razor had not passed over our faces from the time of the shipwreck, and the surprise of the governor was not little at seeing two persons thus appear whom he supposed to be many hundred leagues on their way to England; but so soon as he was convinced of the truth of the vision before him, and learned the melancholy cause, an involuntary tear started from the eye of friendship and compassion, and we were received in the most affectionate manner.

*8 September* ~ His Excellency lost no time in engaging the ship *Rolla*, then lying in port, bound to China, to go to the rescue of the officers and crews of the *Porpoise* and *Cato*; I accompanied the governor on board the *Rolla* a day or two afterwards, and articles were signed by which the commander, Mr Robert Cumming, engaged to call at Wreck Reef, take every person on board and carry them to Canton, upon terms which showed him to take the interest in our misfortune which might be expected from a British seaman. The governor ordered two colonial schooners to accompany the *Rolla*, to bring back those who preferred returning to Port Jackson, with such stores of the *Porpoise* as could be procured; and everything was done that an anxious desire to forward His Majesty's service and alleviate misfortune could devise; even private individuals put wine, livestock and vegetables, unasked, on board the *Rolla* for the officers upon the reef.

My anxiety to get back to Wreck Reef, and from thence to England with the greatest despatch, induced the governor to offer me one of the schooners to go through Torres' Strait and by the most expeditious passage to Europe; rather than take the long route by China in the *Rolla*. This schooner was something less than a Gravesend passage boat, being only of twenty-nine tons burthen; and therefore it required some consideration before acceding to the proposal. Her small size, when compared with the distance from Port Jackson to England, was not my greatest objection to the little *Cumberland*; it was the quickness of her motion and the want of convenience, which would prevent the charts and journal of my

voyage from being prepared on the passage, and render the whole
so much time lost to this important object. On the other hand, the
advantage of again passing through, and collecting more information of Torres' Strait, and of arriving in England three or four
months sooner to commence the outfit of another ship, were
important considerations; and joined to some ambition of being
the first to undertake so long a voyage in such a small vessel, and a
desire to put an early stop to the account which Captain Palmer
would probably give of our total loss, they proved sufficient inducements to accept the governor's offer, on finding his vessel had the
character of being a strong, good little sea boat.

The *Cumberland* was at that time absent up the river Hawkesbury,
and the *Francis*, the other schooner, was lying on shore and could
not be got off before the following spring tides; on these accounts,
and from the *Rolla* not being quite fitted, it was thirteen days after
my arrival in the boat before the whole could be ready to sail. This
delay caused me much uneasiness, under the apprehension that
we might not arrive before our friends at the reef, despairing of
assistance, should have made some unsuccessful attempt to
save themselves; and this idea pursued me so much, that every
day seemed to be a week until I got out of the harbour with the
three vessels...

The small size of the *Cumberland* made it necessary to stop at
every convenient place on the way to England, for water and
refreshment; and I proposed Coepang Bay in Timor, Mauritius,
the Cape of Good Hope, St Helena, and some one of the Western
Isles; but Governor King objected to Mauritius, from not wishing
to encourage any communication between the French colonies and
Port Jackson; and also because he had understood that hurricanes
often prevailed in the neighbourhood of that island, about the time
of year when I should be passing. He left this matter, however, to
be decided by necessity and my judgment, and gave me two letters
for the Governor of Mauritius, to be forwarded from the Cape, or
by the best opportunity. At those places in the Indian Seas where I

might stop, he requested me to make inquiries into the facility of obtaining cattle for his colony, with the price and the traffic with which they might be best procured; and to send this information by any ship bound to Port Jackson.

*21 September* ~ Everything being prepared for our departure, I sailed out of the harbour in the *Cumberland* at daylight, with the *Rolla* and *Francis* in company. Mr Inman, the astronomer, had taken a passage in the *Rolla* with his instruments; and of the thirteen persons who came with me in the boat, Captain Park and his second mate were on board that ship, and the boatswain of the *Investigator* with the ten seamen composed my crew in the schooner. We had a fresh breeze at south-east and the *Cumberland* appeared to sail as well as could be expected; but the wind becoming stronger towards night, she lay over so much upon the broad side that little sail could be carried; and instead of being tight, as had been represented, her upper works then admitted a great deal of water. Next morning, the wind having rather increased than diminished, I found we should soon be obliged to lie to altogether, and that if we passed Port Stephens there was no place of shelter for a long distance where the schooner could be saved from drifting on shore; the signal was therefore made to tack, and at dusk the *Rolla* and *Francis* ran into Port Stephens. Not being able to reach so far, I anchored in a small bight under Point Stephens, in very bad plight; the pumps proving to be so nearly useless, that we could not prevent the water from half filling the hold; and two hours longer would have reduced us to baling with buckets, and perhaps have been fatal. This essay did not lead me to think favourably of the vessel, in which I had undertaken a voyage half round the globe.

*23 September* ~ Next morning I joined the *Rolla* and *Francis*; and it being then calm, we did not quit Port Stephens until the afternoon. At night the wind again blew strong from the south-east; but the desire to arrive at Wreck Reef overcoming my apprehensions, the schooner was made snug and we persevered. Our inability to carry sail was so much the more provoking, that this wind was as

fair as could be wished; but whilst the *Cumberland* could scarcely
bear a close-reefed mainsail and jib without danger of oversetting,
the *Rolla* went along under double-reefed topsails in great tranquillity; and to avoid parting company was obliged to keep her
courses up, and to back a top sail from time to time...

*7 October* ~ It was six weeks on this day that I had quitted the
reef in the boat, for the purpose of seeking the means to relieve my
officers and people. The bank was first seen from the *Rolla*'s masthead, and soon afterward two boats were perceived under sail; and
advancing nearer, we saw one boat make for the *Rolla* and the other
returning to the bank. The *Porpoise* had not yet gone to pieces; but
was still lying on her beam ends, high up on the reef, a frail but
impressive monument of our misfortune.

In the afternoon I anchored under the lee of the bank, in 18
fathoms coral sand, and a salute of eleven guns from it was immediately fired, the carronades of the *Porpoise* having been transported
from the wreck. On landing, I was greeted with three hearty cheers,
and the utmost joy by my officers and people; and the pleasure
of rejoining my companions so amply provided with the
means of relieving their distress, made this one of the happiest
moments of my life.

The two boats we had seen were the *Porpoise*'s remaining cutter
and a new boat constructed during my absence; it was just
completed, and Lieutenant Fowler had this morning gone out to
try its sailing against the cutter. My safe arrival at Port Jackson
became a subject of much doubt after the first month; and they
had begun to reconcile their minds to making the best use of the
means they possessed to reach some frequented port. The *Rolla*'s
top-gallant sail was first seen in the horizon by a man in the new
boat and was taken for a bird; but regarding it more steadfastly, he
started up and exclaimed, 'D—n my bl—d what's that!' It was soon
recognised to be a sail, and caused a general acclamation of joy,
for they doubted not it was a ship coming to their succour.
Lieutenant Flinders, then commanding officer on the bank, was in

his tent calculating some lunar distances, when one of the young gentlemen ran to him, calling, 'Sir, Sir! A ship and two schooners in sight!' After a little consideration, Mr Flinders said he supposed it was his brother come back, and asked if the vessels were near. He was answered, not yet; upon which he desired to be informed when they should reach the anchorage, and very calmly resumed his calculations: such are the varied effects produced by the same circumstance upon different minds. When the desired report was made, he ordered the salute to be fired, and took part in the general satisfaction...

On the 10th, three days after our arrival, the *Rolla* had received the people destined for her, with part of the provisions and stores; and the *Cumberland* was ready to sail. All those whom I had named, with the exception of my clerk, volunteered to go in the schooner; viz., Mr John Aken, master, and Mr Edward Charrington, boatswain of the *Investigator*, my servant, and seven chosen seamen. A cask containing what had been saved of my specimens of mineralogy and conchology was taken on board, as also the charts, books and papers of every kind, with the instruments received from the Navy Board and the sole time keeper which had not stopped.

Mr Denis Lacy, master's mate of the *Investigator*, desiring to return to Port Jackson, he was charged with my letter to His Excellency Governor King; and I gave him an order to command the new boat. It was about the size of the *Cumberland*, had a deck, and was called the *Resource*; and we manned her with a part of those people whose choice led them back to Port Jackson. I ordered Mr James Aikin, commander of the *Francis*, and Mr Lacy, to take on board for the colony as much of the stores as they should be able; and on their arrival, to make a statement to the governor of the condition in which they might leave the *Porpoise*, and what remained on the bank.

The officers' journals, which were to be sent to the Admiralty at the conclusion of the voyage, had not been demanded at the time of our shipwreck; Lieutenant Fowler was therefore directed

to take all that were saved belonging to the officers embarked with
him in the *Rolla*; and lest any accident should happen to the
*Cumberland*, I committed to his charge a copy of four charts, being
all of the east and north coasts which there had been time to get
ready; with these he took a short letter to the secretary of the
Admiralty, and one to the Victualling Board enclosing such vouch-
ers as had been saved from the wreck. To Mr Inman I gave the
remaining instruments belonging to the Board of Longitude,
reserving only a time keeper and a telescope; the large and most
valuable instruments had very fortunately been delivered to him
before we had sailed from Port Jackson in the *Porpoise*.

These matters being arranged, I pressed Captain Cumming to
depart, fearing that a change of wind might expose the *Rolla* to
danger; but finding him desirous to take off more provisions and
stores, I made sail for a bank or rather islet seven miles distant, at
the eastern extremity of Wreck Reef, for the purpose of collecting
seabirds eggs, and if possible taking a turtle. The *Rolla* joined on
the following day, and I went on board to take leave of Messrs
Fowler and Flinders and the other officers and gentlemen; at
noon we parted company with three cheers, the *Rolla* steering
north-eastward for China, whilst my course was directed for Torres'
Strait...

Oats, maize and pumpkin seeds were planted upon Wreck-reef
Bank, as also upon Bird Islet; and the young plants had come up,
and were in a tolerably flourishing state; some of these may possibly succeed upon the islet, but upon the bank it is scarcely to be
hoped. The cocoa-nut is capable of resisting the light sprays of the
sea which frequently pass over these banks, and it is to be regretted that we had none to plant upon them. A cluster of these
majestic and useful palms would have been an excellent beacon to
warn mariners of their danger; and in the case where darkness
might render them unavailing in this respect, their fruit would at
least afford some salutary nourishment to the shipwrecked seamen.
The navigator who should distribute ten thousand cocoa-nuts

amongst the numerous sandbanks of the Great Ocean and Indian
Sea, would be entitled to the gratitude of all maritime nations, and
of every friend to humanity. I may be thought to attribute too
much importance to this object in saying that such a distribution
ought to be a leading article in the instructions for any succeeding
voyage of discovery or investigation to these parts; but it is from
having suffered ourselves that we learn to appreciate the mis-
fortunes and wants of others, and become doubly interested in
preventing or relieving them...

*20 October* ~ Soon after eight o'clock, breakers came in sight;
and we stood off and on till noon, to fix their latitude and longitude, and ascertain our position with respect to Murray's Islands
before entering the strait...

*22 October* ~ Murray's Islands may be considered as the key to
the best passage yet known through Torres' Strait, and my route to
them in the *Investigator* being circuitous, I wished to ascertain
whether a more direct track might not be found; we therefore
steered to make the north-eastern reefs, and on coming in with the
breakers, ran along their south side at the distance of one or two
miles. At half past seven, the termination of these reefs bore NNW;
but another reef, which extended far to the south, had for some
time been in sight, and a dry sand on its north end now bore SW
by W one mile. In the opening between them was a small patch of
coral, and several green spots in the water round it; but there
appearing to be room for the *Cumberland* to pass on the north side,
I ventured through, sounding in 20 and 23 fathoms without finding
bottom.

This opening is a mile wide, and lies five or six miles, nearly
ENE, from the largest of Murray's Islands; it would consequently
be more direct to pass through it than to follow the *Investigator*'s
track round the north-eastern reefs; but from the narrowness of the
opening and the many green spots where the depth is unknown to
me, I dare not recommend it to a ship, though very practicable for
small vessels in fine weather. The dry bank on the south side of the

opening will probably be covered at three-quarters flood...At four, the coral bottom was seen under the schooner, and the depth was no more than 2 fathoms; we tacked immediately, and in ten minutes were able to weather the end of the reef at the outlet of the middle channel...

Next morning at daylight, Mr Aken went on shore to bring off some shells of the large cockle (*chama gigas*), which the Indians place under the pandanus trees to catch water, and on his return at eight o'clock, we resumed our course to the south-westward, passing between some dry sands before seen in the *Investigator*. I then kept up more southward to fetch the York Isles, and this took us between two other sands surrounded with small reefs. There were many birds, and a pole was standing up on the northern bank; and the wind becoming very light, an anchor was dropped in 14 fathoms under the west side, and I went on shore.

This bank or key was very little above high water; but a young pandanus had been planted on the top and surrounded with a circle of stones, apparently to protect it from the turtle, whose tracks were fresh on the sand. It appeared from thence, that the Indians come here at times; and this tree had been planted with a view, most probably, to obtain fresh water by the same means as at Half-way Island...

*24 October* ~ Booby Isle was in sight from the masthead at one o'clock, bearing nearly WSW; and soon after three we anchored one mile to leeward of it, in 7 fathoms, soft sand. A boat was sent on shore, which presently came back loaded with boobies; and fresh turtle tracks having been perceived, the crew returned to watch, and at midnight we received five turtle. These appeared to be of the species called hawkes-bill; the shells and skins, as also their fat, were of a red tinge, and they had longer necks than the turtle procured at Wellesley's Islands, to which they were much inferior, both in size and quality...

*28 October* ~ At one o'clock the Wessel's Islands came in sight, and I hauled more up, wishing to ascertain their extent to the

northward; but the wind being at ENE, we could not pass to windward before dark, and therefore steered for an opening between
the two outer islands. There were strong ripplings and whirlpools
of tide at the entrance of the opening, with very variable soundings between 5 and 16 fathoms; and finding we could not get
through in time, the sun being then near the horizon, an anchor
was dropped near a small beach on the north side, in 4 fathoms,
out of the set of the tides.

Next morning I landed on the northern island, to take bearings
and search for water, and the boat's crew had axes to cut some firewood. Four or five Indians made their appearance, but as we
advanced they retired; and I therefore left them to themselves,
having usually found that to bring on an interview with the
Australians, it was best to seem careless about it. A Malay prow had
been thrown on the beach, and whilst the boat's crew was busied
in cutting up the wreck for fuel, the Indians approached gradually,
and a friendly intercourse took place; but as no water could be
found, and time was more precious than the company of these
people, they were presented with our axes after the work was done,
and we got under way soon after ten o'clock.

This island appears to be the outermost of the chain called
Wessel's Islands, which extend thirteen leagues in a north-east
direction from the mainland near Point Dale. It seemed to be eight
or nine miles in length, by about five in breadth; the southern part
is sandy and sterile, but some trees are produced; and I saw kangaroos of a small kind, too lean to be worth the pursuit their shyness
required. The natives are of the same colour and appearance as in
other parts of Terra Australis, and go equally naked; their presence
here showed the south end of the island to be not wholly destitute
of fresh water; but in the limited search we had time to make, none
could be found, though traces of torrents denoted the falling of
heavy rains in some part of the year...

*9 November* ~ We carried all sail to gain Samow Strait before
dark; but it was eight o'clock when we hauled round the low

south-west point of Timor, in soundings from 6 to 14 fathoms,
within a quarter of a mile of the reef. There were lights on both
shores, which were useful in directing our course up the strait; but
having unfavourable winds, the northern outlet was not quite
reached at noon next day; and it was near five in the evening before
we anchored abreast of Fort Concordia. This was the thirtieth day
of our departure from Wreck Reef, and two days might be
deducted from them for the deviations and stoppages made for
surveying; the indifferent sailing of the schooner was also against
making a quick passage, for with all the sail we could set, so much
as six knots was not marked on the log board; yet notwithstanding
these hindrances, and the much greater of my six weeks' voyage in
the boat to Port Jackson and twelve days' stay at Wreck Reef, the
*Bridgewater* had arrived at Batavia only four days before we
anchored in Coepang Bay. Had not the unfortunate accident
happened to the *Porpoise*, I have little doubt that we could, with the
superior sailing of that ship, have reached the longitude of Java
Head on the fortieth, perhaps on the thirty-fifth day of our departure from Port Jackson.

Mynheer Geisler, the former governor of Coepang, died a
month before our arrival, and Mr Viertzen at this time
commanded. He supplied us with almost everything our situation
required, and endeavoured to make my time pass as pleasantly as
was in his power, furnishing me with a house near the fort to which
I took the time keeper and instruments to ascertain a new rate and
error; but my anxious desire to reach England, and the apprehension of being met by the north-west monsoon before passing Java,
induced me to leave him as soon as we could be ready to sail, which
was on the fourth day. The schooner had continued to be very
leaky whenever the wind caused her to lie over on the side, and one
of the pumps had nearly become useless. I should have risked
staying two or three days longer, had Coepang furnished the means
of fresh boring and fitting the pumps, or if pitch could have been
procured to pay the seams in the upper works after they were

caulked; but no assistance in this way could be obtained; we however got a leak stopped in the bow, and the vessel was afterwards tight so long as she remained at anchor.

Mr Viertzen informed me that Captain Baudin had arrived at Coepang near a month after I had left it in the *Investigator*, and had sailed early in June for the Gulf of Carpentaria; and I afterwards learned, that being delayed by calms and opposed by south-east winds, he had not reached Cape Arnhem when his people and himself began to be sickly; and fearing that the north-west monsoon might return before his examination was finished, and keep him in the Gulf beyond the extent of his provisions, he abandoned the voyage and steered for Mauritius in his way to Europe...

*17 November* ~ It was my intention on quitting Timor, if the leaky condition of the schooner and the north-west monsoon did not oppose it, to pass southward of all the Sunda Islands and direct for the Cape of Good Hope; but if impeded, to run through some one of the eastern straits, get into the north-east monsoon, and make for Batavia, or any port where the vessel could be repaired. The veering of the wind to the westward of south, accompanied by a swell and the occasional appearance of lightning in the north-western quarter made me apprehensive of being forced to this latter plan; and we prepared a boarding netting to defend us against the Malay pirates, with which the straits between Java and Timor were said to be infested. The wind, however, came back to the eastward, although the south-west swell continued, and we had frequent rain with sometimes thunder and lightning...The schooner was leaky, more so than before, and the pumps were getting worse; but hoping to reach the Cape of Good Hope, I had wholly given up the idea of Batavia as lying too far out of the track; Mauritius besides was in the way, should the vessel become incapable of doubling the cape without repairs. Our course by compass was W by S for three days, and afterwards WSW, with fresh south-eastern breezes and cloudy weather; but in the upper regions of the atmosphere the wind was unsettled, showers of rain were frequent and it appeared that we were only just in time to save our passage.

On 4 December, in 19° 2' south and 83° 50' east, we had a good deal of following sea from the eastward, whilst the ground swell came from the south-west; and the jumble caused by these different movements in the water made the vessel labour exceedingly. I varied the course a point on either side, to keep the wind in the easiest direction; but during this and the following day the leaks augmented so much, that the starboard pump, which was alone effective, was obliged to be worked almost continually, day and night; and had the wind been on the starboard side, it is doubtful whether the schooner could have been kept above water.

This state of things made it necessary to take into serious consideration the propriety of attempting the passage round the Cape of Good Hope, without first having the vessel caulked and the pumps fresh bored and fitted. Should a western wind meet the current settling round the cape, and it was to be expected, there would be much more sea running than we had yet encountered; and with a fresh wind on the starboard side, which might probably occur, the remaining pump would not touch the water until the hold was half full; there was moreover cause to fear, that it also would soon become ineffective from constant use. After turning these circumstances over in my mind for a day or two, and considering what else might be urged both for and against the measure, I determined to put in at Mauritius; and on the 6th in the evening, altered the course half a point for that island, to the satisfaction of the people.

In the orders from Governor King, the ports to be touched at on the way to England were left to my own choice; but when Mauritius had been mentioned amongst others in conversation, the governor had objected to it, both on account of the hurricanes in that neighbourhood, and from not wishing to encourage a communication between a French colony and a settlement composed as is that of Port Jackson. It was these considerations which had made me hesitate to take the step, though the necessity for it was pressing; and as, in the case of accident happening to the schooner, I

might be called to answer before a court martial for going in opposition to the wish of a superior officer, it seemed proper to state in
my journal all the reasons which had any influence on my decision.
This journal is not in my possession; but notes of the statement
were made whilst the recollection of it was strong, and the following was the substance and not far from the words.

1. The necessity of caulking the schooner and refitting the
pumps before attempting to double the cape, were stated nearly
as above; to which was added a hope of obtaining a passage in
a ship where my defaced charts and journals, which remained
untouched from the time of the shipwreck, might be put into a
state to be laid before the Admiralty on arriving in England. In
the case of meeting with such a passage, I intended to let the
*Cumberland* for freight back to Port Jackson, or to sell her, agreeably to the authority given me in Governor King's orders.

2. Considering the proximity of Mauritius to the western coasts
of Terra Australis, which remained to be examined, I was
desirous to see in what state it had been left by the revolution,
and to gain a practical knowledge of the port and periodical
winds; with a view to its being used in the future part of my
voyage as a place of refitting and refreshment, for which Port
Jackson was at an inconvenient distance. It was also desirable to
know how far Mauritius, and its dependencies in Madagascar
which I knew to abound in cattle, could be useful to Port
Jackson in supplying it with breeding stock; an object concerning which the governor had expressed anxiety for information
from any place on the east side of the Cape of Good Hope.

3. The two letters from Governor King to General Magallon,
Governor of Mauritius, instead of being forwarded from the
cape might be delivered in person.

4. I was a stranger to what had passed in Europe for nearly
twelve months, and there was consequently a possibility that war
might again have broken out; my passport from the French
government would be good at Mauritius, but in going to the

cape, it was uncertain what attention the Dutch governor might pay to the orders of the first consul of France; and as promoters and encouragers of science, the character of the nation was not so high as to give me great expectation on that head. Mauritius was therefore much more certain than the cape, since the necessary succour would be there obtained even in case of war; whereas at the cape there might be a risk of losing my charts and journals and of being made a prisoner.

**1788**
**Watkin Tench**
**Edited and introduced by Tim Flannery**

Tench, a humble captain-lieutenant of the marines, arrived
on the First Fleet and, with his characteristic understanding,
humanity and eye for detail, recorded the first four years
of European settlement.

'Not to have read Watkin Tench is not to know early Australia.
An eye that noticed everything, a young man's verve, a sly wit,
an elegant prose style—all brought to bear on an unimagined
place and a very strange micro-society. This is the most readable
classic of early Australian history.'
Robert Hughes

'A thrilling account of the preparations, the voyage, but
especially the first months of settlement in Australia…
Tim Flannery has edited the two texts Tench wrote at the
time into absorbing reads, and added a lip-smacking
introduction. Extraordinary details abound,
especially of contacts between the races.'
Terry Smith, *Sunday Age*

'A remarkably balanced and graphic account…Tench will always
remain the classic contemporary witness of our beginnings.'
Les Murray, *Age*

288pp, paperback, rrp $21.00, ISBN 1 875847 27 8

**LIFE AND ADVENTURES 1776–1801**
**John Nicol**
**Edited and introduced by Tim Flannery**

'A rare treat…Nicol was a cooper by trade and sailed in a great
variety of vessels and capacities. He twice circumnavigated
the globe, saw action in the American War of Independence
and sailed to Port Jackson aboard a convict transport…
The result is a charming account of the world seen through
the eyes of a kindly and thoughtful man with a great
capacity for empathy, a tremendous eye for detail and,
apparently, a spectacular memory.'
*Sunday Age*

'This remarkable little book defies the normal course of
historical writing and gives us a uniquely personal view of the
world as seen from the focsle in the late 18th century…
Tim Flannery is to be congratulated for having the eye to
breathe life back into a person whose story engages readers
today as much as when it was first written.'
*Sydney Morning Herald*

'It's a knockout…Nicol is a sunny, charming, highly observant
guide and a first-rate storyteller.'
*Sun-Herald*

'Spectacularly observant…ranks with many of the better
known classics.'
*Age*

208pp, paperback, rrp $21.00, ISBN 1 875847 41 3

**THE BIRTH OF SYDNEY**
**Edited and introduced by Tim Flannery**

*The Birth of Sydney* tells the story of the founding of one of the
world's great cities. Tim Flannery's brilliant anthology reveals
Sydney's strange and secret life from its unruly beginnings as a
dump for convicts to its arrival as the 'queen of the south'
a century later. In this compelling narrative history we hear
the voices of everyone from Aboriginal women to Russian
sailors, from Elizabeth Macarthur to Charles Darwin and a
host of others.

'Will seduce the most reluctant reader into a passion for
Australian history.' *Australian Financial Review*

'An original book that will become fundamental to the
understanding of this country in the 21st century.' *Age*

'A journey of national self-awareness...entertaining as well
as significant.' *Canberra Times*

'Flannery brings the eye of an expert in natural history and
the passion of a conservationist to his writing as he takes the
reader on geological, geographical, ecological and historical
tours of the Harbour City.'
*Adelaide Advertiser*

368pp, paperback, illus., rrp $23.00, ISBN 1 876485 45 0

## THROWIM WAY LEG: AN ADVENTURE
### Tim Flannery
### WINNER OF SA NON-FICTION AWARD 2000

*Throwim Way Leg* is a book of wonder and excitement, of struggle and sadness, a love letter to an untamed place. Tim Flannery's breathtaking adventures in New Guinea and Irian Jaya ensure you will never think about the bird-shaped island to our north in the same way again.

'Combines an irresistible author with an irresistible subject… a dangerous book that you pick up at your peril, because it is so hard to put down.' Jared Diamond

'Tim Flannery is in the league of the all-time great explorers like Dr David Livingstone.' Sir David Attenborough

'An enthralling introduction to the mountain people of New Guinea—unimaginably remote, charming, cunning, cruel, subtle and appealing—and to their magnificent land.' *New York Times Book Review*

'*Throwim Way Leg* is New Guinea pidgin for "go on a journey". It is a book as fantastic as the wildest science fiction novel, as gripping as the darkest thriller and as moving as a love story…Not even Rider Haggard would have dared to tell a story so surprising.' Matt Ridley, *Daily Telegraph*

352pp, paperback, illus., rrp $23.00, ISBN 1 876485 19 1